The King James Bible and the World It Made

The King James Bible
and the World It Made

David Lyle Jeffrey
editor

BAYLOR UNIVERSITY PRESS

Cover Design by Natalya Balnova
Cover Image: The Holy Bible, containing the Old Testament, and the New. Imprinted at London : By Robert Barker, 1611. Image courtesy of the Rare Book and Manuscript Library, University of Pennsylvania

The Engraving of *Eikon Basilike* in chapter 2 is courtesy of the Beinecke Rare Book and Manuscript Library, Yale University.

Library of Congress Cataloging-in-Publication Data

The King James Bible and the world it made / David Lyle Jeffrey, editor.
211 p. cm.
  Includes bibliographical references.
  ISBN 978-1-60258-416-7 (pbk. : alk. paper)
  1. Bible. English. Authorized--History. 2. Bible. English. Authorized--Influence. I. Jeffrey, David L., 1941-
  BS186.K57 2011
  220.5'20309--dc23

                                    2011017436

BAYLOR
UNIVERSITY

Printed in the United States of America on acid-free paper with a minimum of 30% pcw recycled content.

CONTENTS

INTRODUCTION

David Lyle Jeffrey

T he very notion that words can make a world has its obvious root in the Hebrew of the first book of the Bible. There, however, we are told that the word (*davar*), and the work and works (*davar, davarim*) of which all Scripture is both witness and legacy, are not reducible to social construction. Nor can human kings or moguls of culture claim to have authored the world's best-selling book. Moreover, if a certain translation of the Scriptures in but one of the many later tongues has had an outstanding cultural influence, which here we claim, this is not simply a matter of legacy. Though the authors of this volume show how the influence of the King James Version has been extraordinarily far-reaching and formative, it will be clear that, as with all translations, the one which first appeared on May 5, 1611, was neither entirely original nor actually progenitive of any "world" except analogously; we are obviously using this phrase in a grand metaphorical sense. Yet the very fact that such a metaphor is possible, that its analogy to the divine fiat holds just so far as to illumine and explain a culture far removed and alien from the culture of both Testaments, is remarkable. What the distinguished scholarly authors of this volume are able to show, no less, is that this single, authoritative translation of the Bible became the *authentic* voice of Scripture for English-speaking peoples worldwide for more than three centuries. From Britain to America, Canada, Australia, and even Africa and Southeast Asia, for the sheep of innumerable flocks to hear their shepherd's voice and recognize it trustingly was to hear it in this one English version above all others.

This kind of authority is religious, of course, but precisely because of that quite naturally it grew to be more broadly cultural. From the seventeenth century forward, the KJV became overwhelmingly the Bible of poets, playwrights, and fiction writers, whether Catholic (James Joyce), Jewish (Anthony Hecht, Saul Bellow), or Protestant (from Jonathan Swift to T. S. Eliot, W. H. Auden, Marilynne Robinson, and Richard Wilbur).[1] For similar reasons, the high style of the KJV became the lingua franca of English common law, and not just as we find it in the work of F. W. Maitland, Coke's *Institutes*, or Blackstone's *Commentaries on the Laws of England*.[2] Phrases and cadences from the KJV have echoed in the political rhetoric of many countries; one thinks of Prime Ministers Gladstone and Disraeli in Britain, but also of Abraham Lincoln, Theodore Roosevelt, Woodrow Wilson, Richard Nixon, Ronald Reagan, and Bill Clinton, to name just a few of the American presidents who have crafted their speeches so as to borrow its aura of authority.[3]

The deliberately archaic "voice" of the King James Version was a result of the decision to use certain older forms of formal English in preference to street idiom in the royal translation. This gave, as Laura Knoppers here demonstrates, an effect of "majesty" to its phrasing, a dignity especially apparent in public reading, where the rhetorical character of literally rendered Hebrew made "Hebraisms" in English seem more naturally to express a divine quality in speech. That this effect, howsoever intended by the translators, was even better appreciated by royalists after Cromwell's Puritan Commonwealth was defeated in 1660 was perhaps, she suggests, a consequence of political more than theological aims. Alister McGrath puts it succinctly: the King James translation privileged "the language of the court." But rhetorical "majesty" was not an unwarranted inference from poetic portions of the Old Testament in which it is God who is represented as speaking, as a careful reading aloud of the passages given to God in the "whirlwind" speeches at the end of Job or in his "Comfort ye my people" speech in Isaiah 40 will make clear. That this "high poetry" was almost certainly an intention of the original authors may be confirmed in these and many other passages simply by reading them in Hebrew. The poetry of these speeches *is* "majestic," as we say, and the KJV captures more of it than other translations. G. F. Handel's brilliant musical settings in his *Messiah* seasonally call this to mind even for those readers who turn no more to its "dated" pages.

What has been lost to those who no longer read the King James Version even silently is more than meets the eye. Oddly, part of what gives the KJV both its "high style" and its special theological register is an astonishing literal-mindedness. One example must here stand for many; we may consider a word which in the Hebrew of Exodus is likewise used in speeches ascribed to God, initially when he is indicating to Moses the special quality in Bezalel, son of Uri, to make him a fit workman to craft works of art suitable to adorn the tabernacle. This quality, as Hebrew renders it, is that of being *chokma-lev*, "wise-hearted"; the term usually appears as an adjective, but occasionally as a noun. The translators chose, typically, to render it literally. Thus, *kol chokma-lev*, "all that are wise-hearted" (Exodus 31:6; cf. Exodus 35:25, 36:2) bespeaks qualities in an artist pertinent to the creation of a holy art, a special kind of spiritual wisdom. When the New International Version and New American Standard Bible render this merely as "skill," or the English Standard Version as "ability" (another translation has "expertise"), or *The Message* as "aptitude for crafts," their abstraction levels the higher sense of the Hebrew in a particularly dismal way; if we may shift to Greek to say so, what we have left on the page is only the *techne*, without the *logos*. When we look for other uses of this term in Old Testament Hebrew we find an echo in the very form of wisdom granted by God to Solomon; in response to the young king's wish for the grace of *chokma*, "wisdom," God gives him something more, the qualitatively richer *chokma-lev*, again translated literally in the KJV in such a way as to recall the instances in Exodus. So Solomon is given a *lev chakam*, a "wise heart" (1 Kings 3:12). He too, like Bezalel, will build a sanctuary for the Lord. But there is a further point, albeit made tacitly, and it is that effective leadership is more than a matter of technical competence; essentially, it is an art.

It may well be, as C. L. Wrenn has argued, that

> since the seventeenth century there seems to have been some kind of spiritual contraction which renders the symbolic language properly necessary to religious material no longer receivable: and the loss of older patterns of thought makes a purely synchronic current colloquial language incapable of conveying the thought of the ancient Christian documents.[4]

If Wrenn is right, this diminishment would help to account for the frustrations that, over the last century, have prompted some of the many new translations in English.[5] Market opportunities for publishing companies have also been a factor in the extreme proliferation of translations. Similarly prolific have been the bowdlerized or niche-market editions with commentary attached. The Revolve Bible for teen and "tween" girls, the

Green Bible, prophetic Bibles, the C. S. Lewis Bible, and even a Princess Diana Gay Bible all bear witness to something other than the desire for accurate understanding and holy instruction, however much that claim is featured in the advertising. Translations themselves have become market adapted. Some have a political agenda, such as is instanced notably in the Son and Crescent Bible designed for use among Muslims.[6] Other versions still more overtly expunge and recast original terms to effect a theological program, whether gender-inclusiveness in the case of the New Revised Standard Version, or in the case of an adaptation of the KJV itself by Mormons, Latter-Day Saints contextualization.

The latest edition of the New International Version modifies a controversial revision released in 2005, in which the effort to incorporate gender-neutral language was seen by many in the pew as too extreme; the 2011 revision takes some of that back. The New American Bible recently approved by the U.S. Congregation of Catholic Bishops attempts to reflect current scholarly opinion and research in extensive (and often distracting) footnotes. In the Old Testament it revises also the language of its predecessor accordingly, and occasionally problematically; where the Revised Standard Version followed the KJV in rendering Isaiah 7:14 to say "behold a virgin shall conceive," the new text has, straightforwardly according to the Hebrew (but perhaps now in our loose culture misleadingly), "a young woman shall conceive."[7] Whatever the motivation, it is an awkward fact that we now have such an array of English translations available that the result has been a Babel-like confusion of tongues. A general effect of many such translations has been to level the resonant and poetic language of Scripture in the direction of contemporary vernacular, offering in the place of dignity or "majesty" a flat, accessible but also unchallenging and ever-changing idiom of the marketplace.

That is not the only form of loss: when, for example, a translation chooses "sanctification" (NASB) as a substitute for "holiness" (KJV) for translating *hagiasmon*—as in, "Follow peace with all men, and holiness, without which no man shall see the Lord" (Hebrews 12:14), the substitution of an abstract Latinate word, "sanctification," subtly invokes a particular doctrinal elaboration in place of the simplicity of *quodesh* ("being completely set apart for God"), the OT term reasonably closely translated by *hagiasmon*. Here the doctrinal term more easily confuses than clarifies the biblical author's evident meaning (the whole of the argument in Hebrews is about consecration, "holiness to the Lord," made possible only through the singular holiness of Christ, yet a necessary condition of personal salvation). In the more literal translation of the KJV, a reader's recollection of the pervasive Hebrew concept of holiness as it so centrally appears in Exodus, Leviticus, and the Psalms (e.g., Psalm 15) is almost unavoidable, not least because the Anglo-Saxon word "holiness," which, with its analogues to English "health, wholeness" and German "heil," among other cognates, retains more clearly the original sense of "holy" as "set apart," "purified," and "sacred."

Modern translations, indebted to varying doctrinal preoccupations, can obscure crucial matters in a variety of ways. It is not to our purpose to evaluate such efforts here comparatively (even the better attempts) except to note an irony, namely that the Babel-effect of numerous competing translations replicates in some measure the conditions which prompted the need for the KJV itself in is own day. At a conference in Hampton Court in January, 1604, Dr. John Reynolds, the president of Corpus Christi College, Cambridge, one of only four Puritan leaders in the largely Anglican gathering, argued that dissonance between such as the Bishops' Bible (standard in churches) and the Geneva Bible (most commonly then read in families) was creating theological uncertainties among laypeople, and that this made the development of a common, authoritative translation desirable for the sake of Christian harmony.[8]

One could be forgiven for thinking that a similar case for a common Bible in English is far stronger now than it was then. Yet any such effort will face formidable obstacles. Professor Wrenn, in the mid-1960s, praised Ronald Knox's effort to find a "timeless language" which, in Wrenn's words, "should preserve . . . with minimal change the forms of especially sacred passages which had become hallowed, as it were, by familiar tradition." He meant, of course, the familiar phrasing and terms of the King James Version, to which Knox was considerably indebted. At the same time, Wrenn warned about the temptation to justify new translation as an effort to make the Bible sound considerably more like contemporary discourse: "Of all forms of language the current colloquial at any time, and especially under modern conditions, is the most unstable, trivial, and flat. Translation into it," he warned, "would need to be revised in every generation to remain effective."[9] That linguistic prophecy, so regularly confirmed, has brought more cheer to the book market than to the church.[10]

The achieving of a common translation by the KJV translators was a primary objective, and in part they were striving, as Alister McGrath's essay makes clear, for a reduction in ecclesiastical strife. King James himself had taken exception to the political as well as ecclesiological import of some of the marginal commentary in the Geneva translation. His order that the KJV exclude marginal material other than narrative headings, lexical variants, and identification of New Testament citations of the Old Testament, was to prove of genuine hermeneutical significance. By refusing to represent either historical theological commentary from magisterial tradition (frequently included in medieval Bibles) or any sectarian theological opinion more contemporary, the translators offered up a text less "scholarly" and more open to being construed as perspicuous. What was absent—a marginal witness to theological authorities—was silently and powerfully invested in the magisterial language of the translation itself.

With the smaller-sized editions of 1613–1631, the King James Version became more affordable; a modest householder for the first time in history might own a Bible. Even in families possessing but one book, this was the most common "library." Here too, as in church, it was read aloud. Robert Burns' eulogy for the "big ha'-bible" in "The Cotter's Saturday Night" bears a homely witness to the fact that generations of children learned to read from it. (Its phrases are everywhere in the American primer known as McGuffy's readers, cited there as illustrations for good grammar and eloquent rhetoric.) Moreover, when Bibles first began to be printed in America in the eighteenth century, the KJV "family Bible" put family registers of marriages, births, and deaths between the conclusion of the Old Testament with the words of Malachi—in which God requires the turning of the generations to each other in reconciliation—and the opening genealogy of Jesus in the Gospel of Matthew, which commences the New Testament. American families learned in this way to see themselves as numbered among "the families of the earth" blessed in God's promise to Abraham (Genesis 12:1-3). This gave a forceful and memorable quality to family Bible reading of the King James standard that, as Robert Alter shows, became the warp and woof of American literary language. Mark Noll's essay deepens our understanding of how the rhetorical force built into the KJV for public reading has borne fruit in political rhetoric and aural recognition in America more persistently than in Britain.

Ease of memorization is perhaps one of the most significant cultural as well as ecclesial evidences of the success of the KJV translators in making the language of Holy Writ, even in its admittedly archaic and magisterial phrasing, more natural and more widely efficacious for the preservation of biblical consciousness than any subsequent English translation. Here again the point is weightier than simply a matter of the problems of translation dissonance and linguistic interference; memory of the text is of the essence for a vital biblical culture. What Moses said in Deuteronomy (6:4-9) and what he reiterated memorably in his charge to Joshua, is that for the *sepher Torah*, the book of the law, to have its purpose realized in successive generations, it must be internalized in the hearts of a would-be godly people. Thus, his command: "This book of the law shall not depart out of thy mouth; but thou shalt meditate therein day or night, that thou mayest observe to do according to all that is written therein: for *then* thou shalt make thy way prosperous, and *then* thou shalt have good success" (Joshua 1:8, emphasis added). This injunction, reiterated in Psalm 1:2 as a condition of blessedness, and made graphic in the command to Ezekiel (1:3, 10) and John (Revelation 10:9-11) to "eat this scroll," makes the point about memorization central to any abiding "legacy" or continuing influence of Scripture. When Jesus commands his disciples to "let these sayings sink down into your ears" (Luke 9:44), he is both drawing on and reiterating this condition for faithfulness (cf. John 8:31-32). In this context, the Hebraistic literalism and oratorical phrasing of the KJV translators can be said to have provided for three centuries of English readers of the Bible a better means of effecting memorization than their successors, and in this way too, their provision of a "common Bible" was an achievement of theological as well as cultural value. Memory (and forgetting) constitutes a major theological theme in all of Scripture, and memory is invariably linked there with obedience as the *sine qua non* of faithful reading and cultural fruitfulness.

The story of KJV influence is indebted to this practice of hearing and doing among its implied readers, and has, our writers attest, been most pertinent to the power of the King James Version to have "made the world," notwithstanding occasional infelicities of translation. Further, there are vagaries of transmission aplenty to be found in the story of the KJV, and the reader may ponder these each in his or her own way. Here the essays of David Bebbington and Mark Noll are especially useful in their detailing of many ironies which themselves have contributed to the enduring influence of the KJV. Bebbington notes, for example, that despite its having been crafted to reflect the language of the court, after 1780, when there were questions about the increasingly evident datedness of the translation, it was actually the preference of "the middle and lower ranks" which helped maintain its position as the standard. This did not prevent scholarly pressure for many nineteenth-century modifications, as he shows, and eventually the concerted effort at modernization represented by the Revised Standard Version (1881) was adopted by the Bible Society in 1901. But preference for the older King James Version remained a point of principle among belletrists such as Matthew Arnold, Sir Arthur Quiller-Couch, and T. S. Eliot. As a poet might, Eliot resisted the "decadence" of language in such efforts as the New English Bible. Noll, in detailing reasons for the extra half century of predominance for the KJV in North America (despite a growing chorus of academic criticism concerning inaccuracies made apparent by subsequent scholarship), shows that support from political figures was as important: Theodore Roosevelt and Woodrow Wilson, who saw America's greatness as in part a result of the influence of Scripture in the KJV translation upon the ethical and moral fabric of American life, helped to make it effectively an instrument of civil religion in the United States.

There are, of course, crude instances of bibliolatry associated with any populist fixation on a specific translation. One thinks of the apocryphal story of a mid-twentieth-century preacher saying, "If the King James Bible was good enough for St. Paul, it is good enough for me," and there are to this day small churches named the "King James Bible Church," congregations committed not only to this one translation in opposition to all others, but also to it in a version with guidance to dispensationalist eschatology found in prefaces and notes by C. A. Scofield. Such partiality is not, of course, what the KJV translators had in mind, but it does bear witness to a human tendency to construe authority—and legacy—in a materialist sense. It might be argued, as C. S. Lewis once did, that this impulse should be resisted by turning away even from what he saw as the seductive literary power of the KJV, and (as he perhaps too extremely judged) that this aesthetic predilection might be resisted best by a narrower estimate of the influence and value of King James language.[11] Ironically, it would have been more difficult to make that case in the African American churches, where, among other achievements, normative use of the KJV helped to produce the powerful rhetoric of Martin Luther King.

Another of the remarkable and unintended curiosities of KJV influence is to be found in the enormous role it has had in shaping both the literary language and the spiritual and theological imagination of peoples whose own first language is not English. This is particularly evident in Africa, as Lamin Sanneh has shown. There, though vigorous efforts at translation into indigenous vernaculars proved very fruitful, English remained the language of education and political discourse for many, even after the colonial period had ended. Sanneh demonstrates that in Africa too "the KJV . . . became unintentionally the design and force of narrative life and experience for centuries of English readers, Catholic and Protestant alike." In similar fashion, on the east coast of the Carolinas, where the West African derived language Gullah has long been spoken, even after a translation of the New Testament into Gullah was made for the American Bible Society in 2005, it was printed with the King James Version alongside the Gullah text because, as the translation team notes in their preface, the older English version "was the preference of the Gullah community."[12]

This kind of unexpected reverence for the KJV among those whose maternal language is not English does not necessarily mean that they have used the Bible—or emphasized various parts of it—in the same way as English-speaking readers elsewhere in the world for whom English remains their mother tongue. Here there is material far more complex than our volume can treat adequately. Nevertheless, Philip Jenkins indicates the terrain, pointing out that the dominant preferences of such peoples theologically, manifested in their choice of specific books of the Bible on which to preach and study, are generally inverse to the dominant pattern of their influence in the churches of the Reformation. Luther's ambivalence about such books as Hebrews, James, Jude, 2 Peter, 3 John, and Revelation (Calvin, we may remember, scruples even to comment on Revelation), is not in any way reflected in the teaching emphasis of churches in the global South (including China), many of which find their circumstances to resemble quite closely the situation of the early apostolic church. Thus, the books most neglected by the Reformation are those most preached upon in the world's fastest-growing churches. Whether nominally Protestant or Catholic in orientation, global-South churches tend to read the Bible more with Catholic than Protestant eyes.

There is much to ponder at a moment such as this, as we celebrate four centuries of a great vernacular translation of the Bible—perhaps the greatest since the beginning of modern times. One of the themes which emerges from these essays is that the power of the distinctive voice of the KJV translation turns the reader away from an easy accommodation to what is, after all, a normative, comfortable, and essentially pragmatic medium of communication, lifting the imagination toward something higher and perhaps more true to the revelatory character of theological insight and divine discourse. We are, all of us, of course, prone to want the words of Scripture to seem a little less challenging, to say to us what we want to hear, what we prefer to believe. It is possible that King James himself, despite his own proclivities to self-interest, was apprehending just this tension between reader and text when he wrote in his *Basilikon Doron* these words of caution to those whose habitual reading betrayed more interest in the comfortable familiarities of local culture than in the word itself, "making the Scriptures to be read by their conscience, and not their conscience by the Scripture."[13] Such bias is a peril for translators and scholars as much as anyone. One may, I think, without excessive veneration, credit the translators of the King James Version with having accomplished more than most in keeping to the right side of the trail in this regard. If the KJV has so much "made" the world for so many, surely this is part of the reason for it.

One

THE "OPENING OF WINDOWS"
The King James Bible and Late Tudor Translation Theories

Alister E. McGrath

*T*o its later admirers, the King James Bible was a noble monument of English prose, a classic expression of the beauty of the English language and the religious sentiments and convictions that so often inspired its moments of elegance and passion.[1] Without in any way detracting from its merits as a work of literature, it is important to remember that those charged with its production saw it in a very different manner. It was a *translation*, an attempt to allow English-speaking readers direct access to a life-changing text which otherwise would lie beyond their reach and comprehension. Accessibility and accuracy—not eloquence—were their primary goals. Yet the translation which resulted is now rightly hailed as a literary landmark, even if nearly a century had to pass before its merits were fully recognized.

The decision to execute a new translation of the Bible was announced by James I toward the end of the Hampton Court Conference in January 1604. The conference was convened by James in an attempt to secure some degree of religious consensus toward the beginning of his reign,[2] and at least to allow him to claim that he had heard and addressed the concerns of the Puritan party. We do not entirely understand how the suggestion of a new translation of the Bible came about, nor the reasons which lay behind this suggestion.[3] It was not considered a matter that needed resolution for the religious well-being of England, and does not seem to have been specifically demanded by the Puritan party. The leader of the Puritan delegation—John Reynolds, president of Corpus Christi College, Oxford—urged a change in policy toward authorized biblical translations, arguing that "those which were allowed in the raignes of Henry the eight, and Edward the sixt, were corrupt and not answerable to the Originall."[4] Yet Reynolds' strategy here seems to have been to ask that the Geneva Bible (1560) might be authorized for public use in churches alongside the Bishops' Bible (1568). There was no particular interest in the production of a new translation; the point at issue concerned the authorization of an existing translation. Although the evidence is far from unambiguous, James appears to have introduced the suggestion himself,[5] possibly regarding it as a means of, if not securing religious peace within his troubled nation, at least deferring the outbreak of serious controversy.

Yet it would have been easy for the new Bible to become a focus of debate and division rather than a source of unity. What we know about the context within which the work of translation would take place suggests that the process would be as religiously sensitive as it was religiously important. It is perhaps little wonder that Richard Bancroft (1544–1610)—who became archbishop of Canterbury two months after the Hampton Court Conference—sought to retain as much control over the process as possible, partly through the fifteen "Rules for Translation" which he imposed upon the translators, and partly through dispersing the task in such a way that no individual might exercise undue influence over the procedure.[6] Six independent "Companies of Translators" were assigned to work on specific sections of the Bible, including the Apocrypha.[7]

So how did the king's translators understand their task? What theories of translation, however emergent, informed the work of the six companies who assembled at Oxford, Cambridge, and Westminster as they tried to fulfill James I's vision of a new version of the Bible for his people? This essay explores what is known about the theory and practice of translation in late Tudor England, and reflects on how these informed, stimulated, and—no less importantly—*limited* the evolution of the King James Bible.

The Theory and Practice of Translation in Late Tudor England

The translation of the Bible is a specific case (although one of special significance) of a much more general phenomenon—the rendering of a text originating in a different cultural context into English.[8] In this essay, we shall consider how the translation of this highly influential work was guided by the wisdom of the age, noting its impact on specific passages. I will attempt to contextualize the work of the six companies of translators in the light of what we now know of late Tudor theories of translation, and to establish their role in the shaping of this classic English text.

The work of the King James translators must be set against the resurgence of English national pride in the Elizabethan Age, when the politics of patriotism led to a new sense of confidence in the English language as a means of economic, political, religious, and philosophical discourse.[9] The break with Rome under Henry VIII led to a new concentration on the promotion of English national and cultural identity, focusing on works written in English.[10] In the Middle Ages, English was widely seen as the language of peasants. The nobility spoke French (more accurately, the dialect generally known as "Anglo-Norman"), whereas the academy and church used Latin.[11] The English cultural elite regarded their native language as being incapable of expressing the deepest and most noble thoughts of humanity. While resistance to the translation of the Bible into English during the fourteenth century was largely due to political concerns,[12] a deeper ideological conviction gave it added weight. How could such a primitive language as English capture the theological and spiritual profundities of the Bible?

By the middle of the sixteenth century, such views were in full retreat. A surge in English national pride was mirrored in the growing use of English as a medium of communication at every level. Furthermore, Protestantism's distinctive emphasis upon the religious priority of the vernacular led to the Bible appearing in English—initially against the will of both church and crown, and subsequently with their reluctant support (although in suitably adapted forms).[13] Perhaps no less significantly, a distinct English literary identity began to emerge, marking a growing confidence in English as a medium for the expression of poetic truths.[14] Translation became an integral aspect of this process of linguistic affirmation. The translation of Virgil into English, for example, was seen as both an affirmation of the excellence of English, as well as a means of making Virgil's ideas more widely available.[15] The rendering of Latin and Greek classics into English was seen as culturally enriching, enabling English writers to enter into a more confident and discriminating dialogue with the classical tradition and expanding the language's vocabulary in order to accommodate the growing needs of philosophical, theological, and scientific discourse.

But which type of English are we talking about? Even as late as the 1590s, there was no standard form of English. Translation requires both a source and a target language. Since various English dialects existed in the late 1500s—such as Northern, Midlands, Southern, and Kentish English,[16] none of which had yet achieved cultural dominance—a decision had to be made. Which form of English would be chosen? Each distinct form of English had its own social register and provenance.

While no form of English had achieved outright dominance of the nation, there was no doubt about which was in the political ascendancy by 1600. The southern forms of English dominant in London, and particularly the court of St. James, had by then emerged as the regnant orthopraxy.[17] Richard Carew is a rare example of a contemporary writer who takes pleasure in the diversity of English, and protests at any attempt to force translation into a single sociological niche.[18] The King James Bible would reinforce this trend toward uniformity, privileging the language of the court. Virtually all of its translators were from the southeast of England.

The 1590s could be singled out as marking the onset of a decades-long period of particular linguistic malleability, in which new trends developed and were consolidated.[19] The two literary sources which are generally recognized as having exercised the greatest influence over the shaping of the English language during this period were the works of William Shakespeare on the one hand, and the new Bible of 1611 on the other. Both would contribute significantly to the shaping of modern English, not least by introducing phrases which were picked up and developed, both in literary culture and everyday language.

Yet this process was not quite as straightforward as might be thought. Part of the pressure leading to linguistic development around this time was the realization that English simply did not have a sufficiently capacious vocabulary to deal with the growth of both the arts and the sciences. New terms needed to be introduced, partly to cope with technological and theoretical advances. The "inkhorn" controversy of the late sixteenth century focused on how such new terms were to be developed. Were they to be crafted from Anglo-Saxon roots? Or could they be forged from Latin and Greek roots? Or should they be avoided altogether? Sir Thomas Elyot (1490–1546) was an enthusiastic minter of new words, and is widely credited with the introduction of neologisms such as "persist" and "participate." Yet others frowned on such a practice, which they held to lead to contamination of an essentially pure language.

Roger Ascham (c. 1515–1568), John Cheke (1514–1557), and Thomas Wilson (1524–1581)—humanist scholars based at St John's College,

Cambridge—sought to cultivate a restrained and rhetorically informed approach to linguistic development, urging that the cultivation of elegance should be seen as integral to the process.[20] They were critical of the use of inkhorn words, which they regarded as little more than mangled verbal bastardizations derived from questionable foreign sources. Cheke set out his concerns about such terms in a letter written to his friend Sir Thomas Hoby:

> I am of this opinion that our own tongue should be written clean and pure, unmixt and unmangeled with borrowing of other tongues; wherein if we take not heed by time, ever borrowing and never paying, she shall be fain to keep her house as bankrupt. For then doth our tongue naturally and praisably utter her meaning when she borroweth no counterfeitness of other tongues to attire herself withall, but useth plainly her own.[21]

Examples of Cheke's ultimately abortive attempts to eliminate inkhorn religious terms from biblical translation by using new words coined from Anglo-Saxon roots include "onwriting" (for "inscription"); "hundreder" (for "centurion"); "moond" (for "lunatic"); and "byword" (for "parable").

Yet by the time that King James had commissioned his new translation of the Bible, this controversy lay largely in the past. Certain basic principles came to be accepted as normative, even if their application proved problematic and contentious. While rejecting the idea of coining neologisms for their own sake, or cultivating verbal pretentiousness, most writers came to the view that the borrowing of terms from classical antiquity could be justified on both utilitarian and rhetorical grounds.

Something of the motivation of the translators can be gleaned from the preface "The Translators to the Reader," written on their behalf by Myles Smith, defending both the necessity of translation of the Bible, and the particular approach which they adopted to this mammoth task. Smith uses a series of images to emphasize the importance of accessibility to the sacred text: translation is like opening a window, so that light may enter; it is like rolling away the stone from a well, so that all may drink; it is like drawing aside a curtain, so that we may see into most sacred of places.[22]

The images so carefully assembled by Myles Smith emphasize the central theme of allowing access to a life-giving and life-changing resource. Without translation, ordinary people cannot draw cool and refreshing water from Jacob's well. The task of the translator is thus to remove barriers so that the people of God can gain access directly to the riches of the biblical text. The translators must therefore be invisible and the translation must therefore be transparent, not getting in the way of readers, but connecting them directly with the original texts.[23]

As Theo Hermans has pointed out, the images used by Renaissance translators to refer to their task "appear to be highly functional" and "form an integral and essential part of the Renaissance theory of transla-tion."[24] Yet the images here used by Smith are not those used by Tudor translation theorists[25]—such as the "re-dressing" of original texts—but are heavily influenced by aspects of biblical narratives, tending to focus on the spiritual benefits accruing from translation rather than on the translation process itself. They may not unreasonably be seen as theo-logical counterparts to more secular images of translation, emphasising the spiritual rather than the cultural improvements that such translation was held to convey.

Smith, of course, was alert to the theological dimensions of reading Scripture. No matter how good the translation, the grace of God was required if the text was to be properly understood and appropriated in the life of faith.

> [God] removeth the scales from our eyes, the veil from our hearts, opening our wits that we may understand his word, enlarging our hearts, yea correcting our affections.[26]

Yet the healing capacities of God's grace in applying the word to the inter-nal world of the believer negates neither the necessity nor the importance of translation. Erasmus' point was well taken:[27] good biblical transla-tion preempts bad biblical exegesis. God's spirit may continue to apply spiritual realities to the believer's heart, as in the apostolic age; yet he no longer personally translates those words so that we may each hear the word of God directly "in our own tongue" (Acts 2:8). An intermedi-ary is required, whose linguistic footprint is vanishingly small, to render Hebrew and Greek in good English. We may not be reading Scripture as it was originally written, yet the wisdom of the age was that the hallmark of a good translation was the invisibility of the translator, thus creating the impression of a direct engagement with the original text on the part of the English reader.

Translation might be recognized as important; yet this was not matched by any agreement about how it might be best undertaken. The growing Tudor interest in making the political, literary, philosophical, and religious treasures of the classical age available to English culture at large was not stimulated or informed by any kind of consensus about the translation process itself. Indeed, the translation projects of the age were often governed by a theoretical vacuum. One of the few works by an Englishman dealing with this subject to be published around this time was Laurence Humphrey's Latin treatise *Interpretatio linguarum* (1559), which appears to have attracted little attention—possibly because it required translation itself.[28] Translation into English during the Elizabethan Age appears to have been conducted without the benefit of an informing theory. Individual translators may have known what they were doing; there was, however, no general agreement on what determined best practice in the field.[29]

The Political Dimensions of Translation

A further complication was that translation—like most literary undertakings—took place against a politicized context.[30] The political instability of England throughout much of the later Tudor period caused nervousness on the part of translators, who often adapted the text of classic works to resonate with values that were deemed prudential in the political context of the day.[31] Anything that hinted at the merits of political subversion, or which might be held to encourage social instability, was regarded as unacceptable.

The translation of classic works was occasionally made politically sensitive by external concerns. For example, Thomas Wilson's translation of Demosthenes' *Olynthiacs* and *Philippics* appeared in 1570, during a period of considerable tension in Anglo-Spanish relations. By a none too subtle use of marginal notes and judicious liberty in translation, Wilson turned Demosthenes' treatise into a hard-hitting piece of anti-Spanish propaganda and a trenchant critique of Elizabethan foreign policy toward the Spanish Netherlands.[32] In the hands of a politically savvy translator, a past classic became a weapon in contemporary political debate. The translators of the Geneva Bible of 1560 had earlier shown how marginal notes could be used to encourage a certain interpretation of the translated text;[33] Wilson deployed precisely the same technique for political ends.

Yet it was more often domestic agendas and concerns that intruded on the translation process. An excellent illustration of the political motivations and accommodations of translators can be seen in Thomas Paynell's 1557 revisions of Alexander Barklaye's translation of Sallust's *Bellum Iugurthinum*.[34] Paynell may have possessed a questionable degree of skill as a translator; he was, however, acutely alert to the realities of the political context. Late in Mary Tudor's reign, the threat of open violent revolt against an unpopular monarch from a religiously and socially alienated English population could not be ignored.[35] Paynell therefore offered a "perused and corrected" revision of Barklaye's work, in which Sallust is made to affirm the importance of obedience to the monarch, and emphasizes the utter futility of rebellion.[36]

The close connection of church and state throughout the Tudor and Jacobean periods was such that this politicization of the translation process extended to religious issues—especially when these had institutional implications. The use of certain English terms to refer to ecclesiastical realities—such as "church" or "bishop"—was heavily freighted with significance. The marginal notes of the Geneva Bible (1560) caused disquiet in English religious circles throughout the Elizabethan period on account of their obvious antimonarchical sympathies.

The third rule that Richard Bancroft would impose on the six companies of translators reflects this acute sensitivity: "The old ecclesiastical words to be kept, namely, as the word *church* not to be translated *congregation &c.*" Verbal alterations to the text of Scripture, as Bancroft wisely realized, could become the prelude to structural alterations to the established forms of church life. Retention of traditional ecclesiastical language came to be seen as a bulwark against the agenda of more radical reformers—such as the increasingly influential Puritan wing of the established church.

Yet one further point must be made. The translators appointed by King James did not start their translations from ground zero, with complete freedom to render passages as they saw best. They were compelled to base themselves on earlier English translations, which they might improve where necessary, but could not disregard. Myles Smith ingeniously presents this limitation, imposed upon the translators by the ever-cautious Richard Bancroft, as a virtue.

> Truly (good Christian reader) we never thought from the beginning that we should need to make a new translation, nor yet to make of a bad one a good one . . . but to make a good one better, or out or many good ones one principal good one.[37]

As we shall see, this privileging of past readings at times caused the new translation to be trapped in the language of the past. Yet it also forestalled any suspicion of radical innovation or whimsical changes on the part of the translators. The handsome tribute of the translators to their predecessors made it clear that they were standing on the shoulders of giants,[38] seeing further on account of the excellence of those who had gone before them.

Translation, then, was a complex matter for the Tudor age. It was not simply a question of what was to be understood by the translation process itself; it was about coping with the potential political implications of its outcomes, which could easily lead to unintended and unwelcome social consequences. The translation of the Bible was thus fraught with dangers, not least because of its potential to catalyze religious discontent and polarization in a religiously divided nation. The death of Elizabeth I in 1603 exposed the religious fault lines in English society.[39] What might be done to prevent religious tensions from exploding into civil war?

One way of doing this was to construct a "narrative of history" which positioned individuals and organizations in such a way as to emphasize both their historical significance and their social, religious, and political virtues. The construction of such narratives is now known to have been a major feature of the late Elizabethan and Jacobean ages.[40] One such narrative—the "Gloriana Cult"—emphasized Elizabeth I's glorious reign and its positive impact on English national identity and global significance.[41] Bancroft's directions to the translators both presupposes and reinforces a narrative of religious continuity within England, positioning both the new translation and the Church of England as creating religious harmony and preserving religious and social continuity. This theme, echoed in Smith's preface, helps us understand both Bancroft's analysis of the contemporary religious situation and the means by which he might engage it.

As James VI of Scotland journeyed to London in 1603 to become James I of England, he was made acutely aware of the religious tensions within his new realm.[42] Did he propose a new translation of the Bible as a means of fostering a new sense of religious identity in this fractured nation? Did he see himself as an icon of religious peace and unity, with his new Bible as the foundation of a stable social and religious order? Sadly, we have virtually no means of knowing. What we can do, however, is consider the translation itself, and reflect on the issues that the translators had to face.

The King James Translation: Some Reflections

Despite being constrained in their freedom, the King James translators must be judged to have produced a piece of English prose with their own distinct imprint and tone. Though forced to incorporate much from earlier translations, they appear to have been able to navigate their way to a remarkably eloquent and accurate translation. In the final part of this essay, we shall consider some distinct features of the resulting translation and consider their implications for its reception.

Yet any translation from a Hebrew or Greek original requires a defense of the specific textual form on which it is based. The King James Bible was based on the best text of its day. Although the term *textus receptus* is thought to date from 1633, this version of the New Testament text existed long before the invention of this specific term to designate it. Erasmus of Rotterdam had edited what he considered to be the best version of this text in 1516.[43] Yet Erasmus' editorial work was controversial at many points. For example, Erasmus added what is now Acts 8:37 to his Greek text, despite the virtual absence of any textual support in the Greek manuscript tradition. He seems to have believed that the occurrence of the verse in the Vulgate constituted adequate grounds for its inclusion. Similarly, Acts 9:6 was interpolated from the Vulgate, despite its absence from the Greek originals. Erasmus relocated the doxology of Paul's letter to the Romans, which the Byzantine text places at the end of the fourteenth chapter, to the end of the sixteenth, following the Vulgate. Yet Erasmus initially chose to omit the "Johannine Comma" (1 John 5:7-8) because there was no support for the text in the Greek manuscripts at his disposal.[44] Following protests from churchmen throughout Europe, this "Comma" was retained, and is included in the King James Bible.[45]

Subsequent developments in biblical scholarship have forced revisions to the text on which the King James Bible was based.[46] Yet these seem minor compared with the revisions generally agreed to be necessary on account of the significant changes in the English language since 1611. English is a living—and hence a *changing*—language, which undergoes change as a result of its development. In what follows, we shall consider some aspects of the King James translation and reflect on their significance and their often unintended outcomes.

The Tendency toward Literal Translation

Late Tudor translation theories recognized both the merits and the limitations of a literal translation of the original text.[47] A wooden literal adherence to the original text might give rise to accuracy but not necessarily to elegance, nor to a right understanding.[48] Creativity on the part of the translator might indeed yield an elegant and attractive text yet fail to convey the original text's proper meaning.[49] It is a matter of empirical observation that the King James translators chose to stay as close to the verbal structure of the original biblical text as possible, while allowing themselves the freedom to depart from it as they judged fit,[50] even if the reasons for this approach are not entirely clear. An obvious explanation may lie to hand in Erasmus' well-known comment that certain terms or phrases require multiple renderings if their full sense is to be grasped: *quo major est varietas, hoc plus est fructus*.[51]

The King James translators thus tend to offer a literal translation of the original biblical text, even when this seems strange to English ears. For example, consider the following familiar text concerning the reaction of the wise men to seeing the star of Bethlehem: "They rejoiced with exceeding great joy" (Matthew 2:10). The English is curious, and reads less satisfactorily than Tyndale's more natural translation of 1525: "They were marvelously glad." Yet the Second Oxford Company of translators chose to render each element of the original Greek precisely as they found it.

In his 1813 essay "On the Different Methods of Translating," F. D. E. Schleiermacher argued that there were only two real strategies open to translators. "Either the translator (i) leaves the author in peace as much as possible and moves the reader toward him; or (ii) he leaves the reader in peace as much as possible and moves the writer toward him."[52] The King James translators tended to favor the former approach, retaining the original word order and structure, even where an adjustment of the text toward the lexical patterns already familiar to the reader would have seemed entirely appropriate.

This specific approach to translation can be argued to give rise to two important features of the King James Bible. Perhaps the more obvious is easily noted by anyone who has looked at printed editions of this Bible—namely, that words added by the translators to bring out the meaning of the text, but which are not themselves present in the original, are typeset in such a way that they are distinguished from the remainder of the text.[53] The translators felt it right to make an absolute distinction between the biblical text itself and those slight additions they felt obligated to make to bring out its true meaning, even if the interposed words were generally uncontroversial.

Second, and perhaps more interestingly, the King James translators tended to retain lexical characteristics of the original texts, even where these were generally better and more accurately expressed in English through minor alterations. For example, the historical present tense is often used by the gospel writers to add emphasis to important past actions. While it would be more natural to use the English simple past tense to translate such passages, the King James Bible tends to use the present tense to describe such past actions: "Then cometh Jesus from Galilee to Jordan unto John" (Matthew 3:13).[54] The lexical structures of the original are thus transferred to the original, arguably leading to loss of linguistic transparency at this point.

More interestingly, a number of phrases were translated directly from the original Hebrew or Greek, without any attempt to adapt them to the normal patterns of spoken English.[55] Familiar examples from the Hebrew include: "to lick the dust" (Psalm 72:9; Isaiah 49:23; Micah 7:17); "to fall flat on his face" (Numbers 22:31); "a man after his own heart" (1 Samuel 13:14); "to pour out one's heart" (Psalm 62:8; Lamentations 2:19); and "the land of the living" (Job 28:13; Psalm 27:13; Psalm 52:5). From the Greek, we might note "the powers that be" (Romans 13:1) and "a thorn in the flesh" (2 Corinthians 12:7).

The impact of such literal translation of Hebrew and Greek phrases was thus cause English to adapt in order to accommodate them. Despite their initial strangeness, such terms became accepted through increased familiarization and use, becoming naturalized in the English language and enriching its voice.[56] This was clearly an unintended consequence of the translation process, which is known to have raised concerns at the time. Yet the growing familiarity of the King James Bible led to its more memorable phrases being picked up and incorporated, particularly at the literary level.[57] Later generations generally had no idea that standard set English phrases such as "the apple of my eye," a "den of thieves," or "led like a lamb to the slaughter" reflected fundamentally Hebraic modes of speech.

The Perpetuation of Older Versions of English

The English spoken by William Tyndale in the 1520s differed significantly from that spoken in London in the 1610s.[58] The passage of time across these two generations brought about significant changes in written and spoken English.[59] In certain respects, Tyndale's English would have sounded more than a little archaic at the court of St. James in 1611. Yet Bancroft's translation rules had the (presumably) unintended effect of locking the six companies of translators into many of the verbal habits of earlier generations. As a result, Tyndale's English remained a presence in every subsequent English translation of the Bible.[60] A set of rules designed to ensure ecclesial conservatism appears to have had the accidental consequence of maintaining linguistic conservatism as well.

Personal pronouns are a case in point.[61] Since the thirteenth century, the terms "thou," "thee," "ye," and "you" had come to denote not merely the singular and plural second person, but complex socially constructed degrees of familiarity and distance. Middle English adopted to some extent the French distinction between "tu" and "vous," in which the singular form "tu" is used by those of higher social status to address those of lower social status, and the plural form "vous" is employed in formal address or by those of lower social status to address those of higher social status. Although this convention is not used entirely consistently in Middle English texts, it indicates the complex interaction of linguistic and social factors in the shaping of English at this period.

By the end of the sixteenth century, however, the forms "thou," "thee," and "thy" were in decline. In Shakespeare's *Richard III* (1591), the singular or plural form "you" is used 379 times in conversations which cross social and class boundaries between commoners, nobility, and royalty. The older forms were nevertheless retained in the King James Version, despite clear shifts in the patterns of written and spoken English. Even by the standards of 1610, the continued use of such forms would have been seen as slightly archaic.

A similar issue emerges in relation to verbs, most notably the third person singular form of the present tense. Although early Tudor spoken English used forms such as "he saith" or "she goeth," by 1610 these were being replaced with "he says" and "she goes."[62] There is evidence that, even where the older orthography was used in the Jacobean age, it was pronounced as if it were the new form. In other words, the phrase written as "he saith" might be pronounced as "he says." Once more, the King James Bible chose to retain the older forms, despite the clear indications of future trends.

Finally, the difficulties associated with expressing the genitive form of the neuter impersonal pronoun needs to be noted.[63] The term "its" is used only once in the King James Bible (Leviticus 25:5). The older Middle English form of the neuter possessive—"his"—is retained at several points, such as the following: "Ye are the salt of the earth: but if the salt have lost his savour, wherewith shall it be salted?" (Matthew 5:13). "Salt" is not being treated here as a masculine noun; the older neuter possessive form "his" is retained, despite increasingly being replaced with "its" in written and spoken English. Occasionally, this leads to cumbersome translations, which could easily have been rendered much more eloquently by using the word "its."

Examples of this awkwardness lies to hand particularly in the work of the First Westminster Company of translators, which avoided the term "its" by using the somewhat clumsy term "thereof": "But flesh with the life thereof, *which is* the blood thereof, shall ye not eat" (Genesis 9:4). Tyndale's translation of the same passage shows how easily such stilted translations might be avoided: "Only the flesh with his life which is his bloud se that ye eate not." Though retaining the Middle English form of the neuter possessive ("his"), Tyndale's translation of 1530 still flows more easily and naturally than that of 1611.

What we know of the political dimensions of translation in the late Tudor era highlights the potential threat this was seen as posing to the *status quo*. Bancroft's translation rules were clearly designed to minimize any possible challenge to the existing ecclesial situation. Yet his proposals were freighted with linguistic implications. These rules may thus have caused the King James Bible to seem unnecessarily archaic in its language from the outset, serving to hasten the emergence of the early twentieth-century perception that it was outdated. When a translation itself requires translation, it is clearly time to move on.[64]

There is no indication that the translators regarded the issue of long-term linguistic changes as being of importance to their work, nor do we find any reflections on their possible implications for the durability of the new translation. Perhaps the translators felt that, like the many English translations that preceded them,[65] their work might be read for little more than a generation before it was displaced by another. After all, their own work could be seen as displacing the Bishops' Bible of 1568, published a generation earlier. For all they knew, another new translation might be commissioned a generation later in 1650, allowing their successors to make appropriate adaptations to altered patterns of speech and writing. As recent scholarship has made abundantly clear, there was no expectation on the part of the translators or sponsors that the King James Bible would achieve either classic status or extended chronological acceptance. They wrote for the exigencies of their present situation, not for an unknown future posterity.

Verbal Discretion and the Failure to Discern the Synoptic Problem

As the preface "The Translators to the Reader" makes clear, the translators did not see themselves as being under an obligation to use precisely the same English translation of Hebrew or Greek terms in each and every case. Rather, they allowed themselves a flexible creativity in rendering the text which did not bind them absolutely to a fixed convention of rendering words and phrases. An example will make this point clear. According to the King James Bible, Paul and his colleagues took delight in their calling: "[We] *rejoice* in hope of the glory of God . . . we *glory* in tribulations . . . we also *joy* in God." The same Greek verb—which would normally be translated as "rejoice"—is in fact being translated in different ways (here italicized) at each of its three occurrences. There can be no doubt that this flexibility allowed the translators to achieve a judicious verbal balance which enhanced the attractiveness of the resulting work. Yet inevitably, a price was paid for this in terms of the accuracy which some had hoped for, in that important verbal resonances or identities were sometimes airbrushed out of the text to achieve elegance. Might this have led to a delay in English New Testament readers recognizing the scholarly issue now referred to as the "Synoptic Problem"?

In 1764 the Welsh theologian Henry Owen (1716–1795) suggested that some form of literary dependence could be discerned within the first three gospels.[66] Luke, in his view, appeared to use material originally found in Mark and Matthew. This early version of the "Two-Document Hypothesis," more usually associated with the German scholar Johann Jakob Griesbach (1745–1812), depends upon the identification of verbal similarities between the first three gospels as the basis of a theory of their textual interconnectedness.

Yet most English writers of the late sixteenth and early seventeenth century had no reason to develop or explore such theories, as the vernacular translations available to them—above all, that of the King James Bible—did not bring out the phenomenon of synoptic parallelism. The textual clues were obscured by translation protocols that allowed them to be weakened, if not altogether erased. Failing to appreciate the possible theoretical importance of such verbal identities, the Second Oxford Company of translators, who were responsible for translating the Gospels, did not offer identical English translations of identical Greek originals. For example, compare the King James rendering of two passages, which are identical in the original Greek:

> Watch and pray, that ye enter not into temptation: the spirit indeed is willing, but the flesh is weak. (Matthew 26:41)

> Watch ye and pray, lest ye enter into temptation. The spirit truly is ready, but the flesh is weak. (Mark 14:38)

The translation and orthography are quite different in each case noted above, masking the fact that these passages are identical in the original Greek. The reader limited to a knowledge of this text only in English would easily miss the textual resemblances which later led Owen to propose his documentary hypothesis.

It is important not to be unfair to the King James translators at this point. Even Tyndale's translation of 1525 fails to disclose the verbal identity of the two passages, even if he brings it out much more clearly than the Second Oxford Company of translators.[67] The flexible translation policy set out by Myles Smith can allow readers to miss important similarities between original texts, or prevent recognition of intratextual allusion where it occurs.

There are many other aspects of the King James translation that merit further discussion—such as the final stages of the revision in Stationers' Hall, London, at which the text was read aloud, partly for convenience, but partly to allow the oral transparency of the translation to be confirmed. If this text was to be read aloud in churches, audiences needed to be able to understand it immediately. Others in this collection will deal with some of these themes. For our purposes in this essay, however, the important point is simply to note the significant impact of this translation upon the shaping of the English language, and the particular difficulties that arose when it achieved the status of a classic two generations after its appearance.

Conclusion

This essay has focused on the intellectual and political context within which the King James translators worked, with a view to understanding both how they understood their task and how these constraints affected its outcomes. I see no reason to suppose that the King James translators believed or hoped that they were producing a religious and literary classic. They had a job to do, and they wanted to get it done well. They may have been working to other people's rules and agendas. Yet most would have understood perfectly well that translation was a politically and religiously accommodated craft. For example, Sir Henry Savile (the only layman, incidentally, among the translators), a member of the Second Oxford Company of translators, showed himself to be a master of the politics of translation in his 1591 translation of Tacitus.[68] There is no reason to suppose he was exceptional among the translators in possessing such discernment, which was required of anyone hoping to cope with the political realities of that age.

At point after point, the King James Bible shows itself to be a text shaped by the intellectual, political, and linguistic realities of its day. There seems to have been no thought or hope of writing for the future. Yet though so clearly written for its own day, this Bible curiously failed to gain popular or even official support on its publication in 1611.[69] Even in the early years of the reign of Charles I, the Geneva Bible of 1560 was clearly the preferred translation of most English readers.[70] The King James Bible only really began to win popular and official support after the restoration of the monarchy in 1660, probably because its royal associations were welcomed as a stabilizing influence after the political and social chaos of the final years of the Puritan Commonwealth.[71]

Thereafter, its rise to classical status seemed unstoppable. The "Augustan Age" following the Glorious Revolution of 1688 and ending with the death of Alexander Pope in 1744 claimed it as a literary and religious masterpiece, welcoming its judicious statements as antidotes to the religious extremism and instability that had plagued England in the seventeenth century. George Frederick Handel's oratorio *Messiah* (1741) showcased the King James Bible,[72] marking its coming of age as an English cultural icon. Few, it seemed, were aware of how deeply it had been shaped by regnant theories of translation in the late Tudor era. Perhaps even fewer were interested in the technicalities of textual reception and translation. It was the final literary outcome, not the process by which this was achieved, that now commanded such respect and assent.[73]

Today's reader may wonder what might have happened if history had taken a different course. What if the translators had embraced the English of their own age, rather than that of two generations earlier? Might the King James translation have achieved an even greater acceptance over time? We shall never know. What we can say—and what needs to be said—is that the translators, while aiming at accuracy, achieved an eloquence that has resonated throughout the English language world, shaping both the form of the English language itself and our expectations of the voice and tone that are appropriate for speaking about God. In reading the King James Bible, we are not simply hearing the lost voices of the Tudor and Jacobean ages. We can still hear the "still, small voice" (1 Kings 19:12) of a God who spoke to an earlier generation, and speaks still to its successors.

Two

TRANSLATING MAJESTY
The King James Bible, John Milton, and the English Revolution

Laura L. Knoppers

*O*n the chilly afternoon of January 31, 1649, King Charles I stood on a recently erected scaffold outside the Banqueting House at Whitehall awaiting execution. The public beheading was a crucial step in a struggle that had begun with paper bullets in parliamentary pamphlets and newsbooks, moved through civil war and parliamentary victory to the king's trial and condemnation, and would continue even after the king's death.[1] At each stage, Parliament strove to strip away from Charles Stuart both the tangible and ineffable attributes of majesty: crown, kingdom, power over the militia, and the link between earthly monarch and divine.

Yet the scene on the scaffold gave evidence not only of Parliament's victory and its control of the judiciary and military, but also of beliefs that would be more difficult to eradicate. Charles I, having earlier taken communion and said his final prayers with his chaplain, Bishop Juxon, carried out his final act with dignity and determination. He wore extra clothing against the cold, not for comfort but to prevent shivering that might be misconstrued as fear. Having avowed his innocence, the king affirmed his commitment to the established church and to the rights and liberty of the people. And he prepared to die: "I have a good Cause, and a gracious God on my side. . . . I goe from a corruptible, to an incorruptible Crown: where no disturbance can be, no disturbance in the world."[2] Stooping down and laying his neck on the block in preparation for the blow of the axe that would separate head from body, Charles cautioned the disguised executioner to "stay for the sign" (indicating his readiness). The reply of the executioner, presumably the most hardened of characters, was striking, indeed under the circumstances remarkable: "Yes I will: and it please your Majesty."[3] If the elaborate apparatus of public trial, sentencing, and punishment was meant to transform Charles Stuart into a criminal—a traitor and tyrant—the axe-wielding executioner instinctively and readily acknowledged the king's majesty.

Such majesty was a prominent feature of the Authorized Version of the Bible that had been commissioned by Charles' father, King James I, and published thirty-eight years earlier.[4] In translating the Hebrew, Aramaic, and Greek texts into English, drawing upon and emending earlier English Bibles as well as having at hand such resources as the Greek Septuagint and the Latin Vulgate, the King James translators highlighted majesty.[5] In so doing, they created a text that not only shaped religious faith and practice, but would prove crucial to monarchy in a time of crisis. Before and after the English civil wars, regicide, and the short-lived republic, Charles I and his supporters drew upon the King James Bible to stress the majesty—power, splendor, greatness, and divine right—of monarchy. While considerable scholarly attention has been given to radical uses of the Bible in the English Revolution, this essay considers less well-examined royal and royalist uses, as well as the shifting responses by polemicist and poet, John Milton.[6] The majesty of kings and of the divine in the 1611 Bible became crucial not despite but because of the mid-seventeenth-century revolution.

The Hampton Court Conference and the Work of Translation

While in some ways his personality and uncouth habits might make King James I of England (and VI of Scotland) seem an incongruous figure to oversee a translation of sacred Scripture, James delighted in theological debate, had translated the Psalms, and had written on the divine right of kings.[7] Convening the Hampton Court Conference in January 1604, "like a good Physition, to examine & trie the complaints [regarding the church], and fully to remove the occasions thereof . . . or to cure them,"[8] King James did more than "pepper" the hapless Puritan divines, outnumbered and outmaneuvered by a phalanx of bishops, clergymen, and professors.[9] When Puritan scholar John Reynolds "moved his Majestie, that there might bee a newe *translation* of the *Bible,* because, those which were allowed in the raignes of *Henrie* the eight, and *Edward* the sixt, were corrupt and not aunswerable to the truth of the Originall,"[10] James embraced the idea, but turned it against the translation favored by the godly. The king averred that he

wished, that some especiall paines should be taken in that behalfe
for one uniforme translation (professing that hee could never, yet,
see a Bible well translated in English; but the worst of all, his Majestie thought the *Geneva* to bee) and this to bee done by the best
learned in both the Universities, after them to bee reviewed by the
Bishops, and the chiefe learned of the Church; from them to bee
presented to the *Privie-Councell*; and lastly to bee ratified by his *Royall authoritie*, and so this whole Church to be bound unto it, and
none other.[11]

From university scholars, to bishops, to the church, privy council, and
king: hierarchy and order were to be observed and confirmed even by the
process of the new biblical translation.

Attentive to the Greek Septuagint, the Latin Vulgate, and earlier
English translations, including the Bishops' Bible, which they were specifically instructed to follow, the translators set out not so much to produce a wholly new work as to amend and polish what was amiss.[12] A
Translators' Preface included in the 1611 edition presented the work in
terms that notably downplayed the impact of translation on the meaning of the text. Likening their endeavors to opening or uncovering, the
translators minimized any actual construction of meaning: "Translation
it is that openeth the window, to let in the light; that breaketh the shell,
that we may eat the kernel; that putteth aside the curtaine, that we may
looke into the most Holy place; that remooveth the cover of the well, that
wee may come by the water, even as *Jacob* rolled away the stone from the
mouth of the well, by which meanes the flockes of *Laban* were watered."[13]

Other metaphors in the preface similarly depict the translation from
one language to another not as the creation of meaning or the construction of a conceptual world, but as polishing an already formed object:
"For by this meanes it commeth to passe, that whatsoever is sound
alreadie . . . will shine as gold more brightly, being rubbed and polished;
also, if any thing be halting, or superfluous, or not so agreeable to the
originall, the same may bee corrected, and the trueth set in place. And
what can the King command to bee done, that will bring him more true
honour then this?"[14] Yet this final question reveals that the process of
translation would not be a simple opening up or disclosing, a burnishing
or polishing. Rather, in translating the King James Bible, the Jacobean
scholars not only changed the text from one language into another, they
also adapted ancient polity to early modern England.[15] This Bible, in a
process initiated and overseen by a king who believed firmly in divine
right, evinces language that will bring that king "true honour."

Nonetheless, the Translators' Preface goes on to insist that words themselves have a kind of neutrality, that "wee have not tyed our selves to an uniformitie of phrasing, or to an identitie of words," and that a wide vocabulary will be employed. The translators observe that "nicenesse in wordes was alwayes counted the next step to trifling," and that "we cannot follow a better patterne for elocution then God himselfe; therefore hee using divers words, in his holy writ, and indifferently for one thing in nature: we . . . may use the same libertie in our English versions out of *Hebrew & Greeke,* for that copie or store that he hath given us."[16]

Usages of Majesty in the King James Bible

In this context, then, reiterated words in the King James Bible take on even more significance. And one important reiterated term, I would argue, is *majesty.* The word itself derives from the classical Latin *majestas,* base of *major,* comparative of *magnus,* great (der, Lat. *majestas;* cf. *major, magnus*). Core meanings in English are dignity of a god or exalted personage, or of an office; majesty, grandeur (in a thing, or its appearance, or in language); or majesty of the people or state (the harming of which is seen as a crime).[17] In seventeenth-century England, majesty was most often used in reference to the greatness and glory of God, as well as to the dignity or greatness of the monarch. Indeed, by the end of the century, majesty had almost wholly superseded other customary forms of address to the sovereign in England.[18] Yet with political tensions and the outbreak of civil war, other uses of majesty, with reference to the law and justice, came increasingly to the fore. As we shall see, John Milton's emphasis on majesty as the power and dignity of the people, drawn from the history of the Roman Republic, challenged and sat uneasily alongside both royal majesty and its biblical analogue in the King James Bible.

The word majesty (spelled either "maiestie" or "maiesty") appears seventy-two times in the text, headings, and notes of the King James translation, as well as an additional eighteen times in the opening dedication to King James and the Translators' Preface.[19] The proportion is heavily weighted toward the Old Testament and apocryphal books, in which the word appears sixty-two times, versus only six instances in the New Testament. As we shall see, some usages are unique to the King James Version; others are unusual but not unique, while others reaffirm the usage of earlier English Bibles. By examining the nature and significance of the uses of majesty in the King James translation compared with such earlier English versions as the Miles Coverdale (1535), Great Bible

(1540), Thomas Matthew (1549 ed.), Bishops' Bible (1568 ed.), Geneva (1587), and Rheims-Douai (1582–1610),[20] we will see a striking enhancement of certain kinds of majesty, particularly with respect to powerful monarchical figures linked with attributes of the divine. Overall, in the context of the dedication and Translators Preface, the uses of majesty in the King James Bible helped to enhance an image of earthly monarchy closely linked with the divine. But we shall also see that such language of majesty came particularly to the fore not in the calm of Jacobean compromise but in the turmoil and upheaval of the foreshortened reign of James' son, Charles I.

The framework of the King James Bible would have impressed upon its readers the idea of majesty, and in particular the majesty of the king. The opening dedication to King James is not only in larger typeface than the rest of the Bible, but it uses the term "majesty" eleven times. The dedication highlights the king's sovereignty, power, and relation to the divine. From its laudatory opening line—"Great and manifold were the blessings (most dread Soveraigne) which Almighty God, the Father of all mercies, bestowed upon us the people of England, when first he sent your Majesties Royall person to rule and raign over us"—to references to "the appearance of your Majestie, as the Sunne in his strength" and to "the zeale of your Majestie towards the house of God," majesty is the title of choice for the monarch.[21] And such majesty links the earthly monarch with God himself. Having completed their work, the translators profess to "hold it our duety to offer it to your Majestie, not onely as to our King and Soveraigne, but as to the principal moover and Author of the Worke."[22] As king and sovereign, mover and author, James I resembles and embodies attributes most often seen in God himself.

Given the translators' preference for a varied vocabulary, recurring words in the King James Bible warrant particular attention. It is striking that a variety of Hebrew, Aramaic, and Greek terms are rendered in the King James translation as "majestie." The translators render as "maiestie" or "maiesty" five different Hebrew words, including: 1) *gā'ôn* (height, pride, presumption, eminence);[23] 2) *hādār* (adornment, splendor, splendor and majesty);[24] 3) *hôd* (majesty);[25] 4) *gē'ût* (rise, illustriousness, presumption);[26] and 5) *g^edûlâ* (greatness).[27] The King James Version also translates the Aramaic words *r^ebû* (greatness)[28] and *hădar* (majesty)[29] as "majesty." In the Apocrypha, a variety of Greek words are translated as "majesty" in reference to the deity, to Jeremiah in his preternatural or angelic state, or to Mesopotamian kings such as the great Persian monarch Artaxerxes.[30]

The King James translation of the New Testament also renders the Greek terms *megalosynē* (greatness) and *megaleiotēs* (grandeur, splendor, majesty) as "majesty."[31]

Where and in what contexts does the term "majesty" appear in the King James Bible? What is perhaps most striking from a birds-eye view is that majesty most often applies to the deity. Many of its usages refer to Yahweh as supreme covenantal God and king of Israel, from pre-monarchic to post-exilic times. Some of these instances of majesty are added headings, while others translate the Hebrew or Aramaic. The King James translation frames Yahweh's giving of the law to Moses on Mount Sinai, recounted in Deuteronomy, with the heading "the Majestie of God." With the unification of the tribes of Israel and centralization of power, the majesty of Yahweh also becomes embodied in the dynastic kingship of the house of David.[32] Tellingly, the King James Bible uses the term "majestie" to describe David and Solomon as they take on increased power and prestige, develop a centralized administration, and implement a dynastic succession. First Chronicles in the King James Bible, for example, uniquely uses the term "majestie" when Solomon succeeds David to the kingship of a united Israel, stressing the majesty of divine and earthly kings.

In the 1 Chronicles account, David names Solomon as his heir and the people bring sacrifice to the Lord. David's prayer attributes majesty to the divine: "Blessed bee thou, Lord God of Israel our father, for ever and ever. Thine, O Lord, is the greatnes, and the power, and the glory, & the victorie, and the majestie: for all that is in the heaven & in the earth, is thine" (1 Chronicles 29:10-11). While the Hebrew original, *hôd*, easily allows the translation of "majesty" (as well as "power" and "splendor"), earlier English Bibles use such terms as "thanks" or "praise."[33] As Solomon, anointed by the priest Zadok, ascends to the throne, the King James Version depicts him receiving majesty from the Lord: "And the Lord magnified Solomon exceedingly in the sight of all Israel, and bestowed upon him such royal majestie [*hôd*], as had not been on any king before him in Israel" (1 Chronicles 29:25). Again, earlier English Bibles had rendered the Hebrew original with variations on "so glorious a kingdom."[34] The wealth, power, and prestige of Solomon, whose empire stretched from the Mediterranean to the Euphrates, made him an appealing model for the ambitious King James (who in fact recurrently compared himself to Solomon), and the distinctive use of the language of majesty here is striking.

The King James translation of the book of Psalms also offers important instances of the conflation of human and divine majesty. The Davidic thanksgiving for victory in Psalm 21 attributes majesty both to God and to the king. Hence, this Psalm moves from "The king shall joy in thy strength, O Lord, and in thy salvation how greatly shall he rejoyce" (21:1) to "His glory is great in thy salvation; honour and Majestie hast thou layde upon him" (21:5). Notably, earlier English translations do not take the Hebrew term, *hādār*, to mean "majesty," but rather "honor" or "great worship."[35] Similarly, Psalm 29:4 in the King James Version stresses the majesty of the divine voice: "The voice of the Lord is powerfull: the voyce of the Lord is full of Majestie." While the King James translation renders the Hebrew original, *hādār*, as "majesty," earlier English translations use other terms such as "glorious," "with honor," or "in magnificence."[36] Psalm 45:2-4 again conflates human and divine majesty in its praise of King David: "Thou art fairer then the children of men; grace is powred in thy lips: therfore God hath blessed thee for ever. Gird thy sword upon thy thigh, O most mightie: with thy glory and thy majestie [*hādār*]. And in thy majestie [*hādār*], ride prosperously . . . and thy right hand shall teach thee terrible things." Here not only majesty, but the powerful right hand and terrible deeds distinctive of Yahweh become attributes of the earthly king, David. Of earlier English translations, only the Bishops' Bible uses majesty here.[37]

Later Psalmic praise in the King James Version continues to employ the language of majesty. Psalm 96:5-6 lauds divine creation: "For all the gods of the nations are idoles: but the Lord made the heavens. Honour and majestie [*hādār*] are before him: strength and beauty are in his sanctuary." Again, most earlier English Bibles had chosen other terminology: glory, worship, magnificence.[38] The King James translators likewise rendered David's praise of the divine in Psalm 104.1b-2 as "thou art clothed with honour and majestie (*hādār*). Who coverest thy selfe with light as with a garment: who stretchest out the heavens like a curtaine."[39] Further, Psalm 145:5-6 in the King James uses language to describe God that is strikingly similar to earlier praise of the king: "I will speake of the glorious honour of thy majestie [*hôd*]: and of thy wonderous workes. And men shall speake of the might of thy terrible acts: and I wil declare thy greatnesse." Here the usage is not unique, but reaffirms a select number of the earlier English translations, including the Bishops' Bible.[40]

The King James Old Testament also applies "majestie" to Mesopotamian kings, some of whom usurp the attributes of the divine. The book of

Daniel offers two ominous instances of such false assumption of majesty. Nebuchadnezzar, the great king of Babylon, proclaims his own majesty just as he is about to be struck down with madness for his failure to acknowledge the supremacy of the Israelite God. Hence, Daniel 4:30: "The King spake, and said, Is not this great Babylon, that I have built for the house of the kingdome, by the might of my power, and for the honour of my majestie?" Here the Aramaic *hădar* is rendered "majesty" in most earlier English Bibles.[41] But Nebuchadnezzar's restoration after seven years of madness more distinctively uses the language of majesty: "At the same time my reason returned unto me . . . I was established in my kingdome . . . and excellent Majestie was added unto me" (Daniel 4:36). Here, while the King James renders the Aramaic *rᵉbû* (greatness) as "majesty," earlier English Bibles use "worship," "glory," or "magnificence."[42]

The story of Belshazzar in the book of Daniel also foregrounds divine punishment for usurped majesty. Responding to the Babylonian King Belshazzar's plea to interpret the handwriting on the wall that has ominously disrupted his great feast, Daniel reiterates the lesson of Nebuchadnezzar which Belshazzar has failed to learn: "O thou king, the most high God gave Nebuchadnezzar thy father a kingdome, and majestie, and glory, and honour. And for the majestie that hee gave him all people, nations, and languages trembled and feared before him. But when his heart was lifted up, and his minde hardened in pride: he was deposed from his kingly throne" (Daniel 5:18-20).[43] The King James translation turns the Aramaic *rᵉbû* into "majesty," confirming a select number of earlier usages.[44] Having failed to learn from Nebuchadnezzar's notorious disregard for divine majesty, Belshazzar meets a swift and sudden doom.

Similarly, the majesty attributed to the great Persian King Artaxerxes (Ahasuerus), who takes the Jewish Esther as his wife, indirectly attests to the power of Yahweh both in the book of Esther and in the apocryphal Rest of the Book of Esther in the King James Bible. In the Rest of the Book of Esther, after Aman (Haman) conspires against Mardocheus (Mordechai) and the Jews, Esther (who has not yet revealed her Jewish identity to the king) mourns in sackcloth and ashes, then puts on glorious apparel and—uninvited and hence risking death—approaches the king, who "sate upon his royall throne, and was clothed with all his robes of majestie all glittering with golde and precious stones, and he was very dreadfull" (Rest of Esther 15:6). Here the "majestie" of the king's clothing has been derived from Greek *stolēn tēs epiphaneias* (literally "robes of manifestation"), translated in earlier English Bibles as "goodly array."[45] The King James Version also uses majesty to describe the king's own face: "Then lifting up his countenance that shone with majestie, he looked very fiercely upon her: and the Queene fell downe and was pale, and fainted" (Rest of Esther, 15:7). The "majestie" of the king (*pepyrōmenon doxē*, literally "flashed with glory"), elsewhere translated as "clearness,"[46] here underscores King Artaxerxes' power and the terrible risk that Esther takes. When the king embraces and revives her, Esther attributes her fainting not to his anger but to "feare of thy majestie" (*apo phobou tēs doxēs*, "for fear of your glory"; Rest of Esther 15:13), a translation that confirms earlier usage.[47] That a king of such majesty changes his order against the Jews, responding to Esther's appeals, enhances the power of the Jewish God to save his people and punish his enemies.

The King James Old Testament also depicts majesty as part of divine judgment on Judah and on other nations. Isaiah, an eighth-century prophet in Judah, asserts divine majesty in envisioning a coming kingdom and the destruction of Judah's enemies. Under the heading of "Wickednesse is the cause of Gods forsaking. Hee exhorteth to feare, because of the powerfull effects of Gods Majestie," Isaiah 2:10 reads: "Enter into the rocke, and hide thee in the dust, for feare of the Lord, and for the glory of his Majestie [*gᵉdûlâ*]." The chapter ends with a vision of men fleeing into the clefts of the rocks and into caves "for feare of the Lord, and for the glory of his Majestie [*gᵉdûlâ*]; when hee ariseth to shake terribly the earth" (Isaiah 2:19, 21). In both instances here, the King James Version reaffirms the usage of majesty in the vision of divine power and judgment in other English translations.[48]

Finally, the exilic prophet Ezekiel evokes divine majesty in his oracles of judgment against Judah and Jerusalem, including his vision of the destruction of the temple in Jerusalem because of their cultic sins: "As for the beautie of his ornament, he set it in majestie [*gᵉdûlâ*]: but they made the images of their abominations, and of their detestable things therein: therefore have I set it farre from them. And I will give it into the hands of the strangers for a pray, and to the wicked of the earth for a spoile, and they shall pollute it" (Ezekiel 7:20-21). Again, the King James Bible consolidates earlier uses of majesty here.[49]

In highlighting majesty both through the translation of varied original Hebrew, Aramaic, and Greek words, in chapter and page headings, and in an opening dedication to the king, the 1611 Bible built upon and employed ancient traditions of majesty linked with monarchs such as Solomon, David, and even the Babylonian rulers Nebuchadnezzar and

Belshazzar and the Persian king Artaxerxes. King James may well have envisioned the new translation as enhancing monarchical power, as ridding England of the popular Geneva translation with its subversive marginal notes, and bolstering himself as the divinely anointed and divinely appointed head of the established church and state. Pragmatic, canny, even cunning, and willing to compromise when necessary, James managed to hold together divergent forces in the Church of England. The king could not have foreseen that one of the most important roles this new Bible would play would be as a resource for the monarchy in crisis and defeat.

The King James Bible, Charles I, and Civil Wars

Like his father James I, Charles I embraced biblical language to enhance monarchical authority. But, unlike his father, Charles was thin-skinned and imperious in manner, not prone to consultation or compromise.[50] Charles' concern with order and hierarchy in church and state was implemented by loyal High Church prelates and bishops such as William Laud, bishop of London and eventual archbishop of Canterbury. As tensions heated up in the late 1630s and early 1640s, the King James Bible inspired both reverence and revolution. Much attention has been given to the saturation of biblical language in the manifestoes and sermons of the godly, including Oliver Cromwell, parliamentarian and country gentleman who rose through the ranks to lead the Parliamentary Army and eventually take power as lord protector.[51] But the Bible was a contested authority, equally accessible to roundhead and royalist. For King Charles, the biblical language of majesty proved crucial in life—and in death. For John Milton, removing majesty from Charles I meant rewriting not only royal propaganda but also the King James Bible.

Tensions over the king's High Church policies, fiscal innovations, and rule without Parliament, followed by an ill-judged attempt to impose the English Book of Common Prayer on Presbyterian Scotland and the resultant Bishops' War, brought England into full-fledged civil conflict by 1642. In December 1648, Parliamentarians still wanting to negotiate with the defeated king were purged by force by Colonel Thomas Pride and his soldiers. The remnant of Parliament, or, more properly of the House of Commons, set up a special tribunal, the High Court of Justice, to charge and try the king. The court had only the thinnest veneer of legality, and the king refused to recognize its legitimacy. Only when the perhaps foregone guilty verdict was handed out did Charles try to defend himself, and then he was quickly silenced.[52] Following the public execution, Charles I was buried without ceremony in the chapel at Windsor Castle. As Bishop Juxon was not given permission to use the outlawed Book of Common Prayer for the burial, this too was in silence.

Yet if the king had no funeral liturgy or even a tombstone, a different kind of monument was constructed in print by loyal supporters whom the new regime struggled to contain. Most important among the elegies, sermons, and remembrances flooding a shocked nation was *Eikon Basilike: The Portraiture of His Sacred Majesty in His Solitudes and Sufferings*.[53] Available soon after the January 1649 execution, and going through thirty-five English editions in the first year alone, *Eikon Basilike* was likely compiled by clergyman John Gauden from papers written by the king himself while imprisoned; the text was presented as the king's own prayers and meditations.[54] Through twenty-eight meditations on events of the civil war, each concluding with a prayer, Charles I examined his conscience before God, prayed for his people, and considered his own death. Scholars have noted how the poignant first-person account found an immediate and wide audience, an audience that could identify with the king as a Christian, husband, and father.[55] But the book's power also came, I would argue, from its dual depiction of Charles as Christian and king, as everyman and divinely anointed sovereign, whose majesty was inherent and ineradicable. The psalmic depiction of kingly majesty violated and betrayed by enemies appealed to divine majesty for redress, justice, and punishment.

The title of *Eikon Basilike* (literally, "the royal image") indicates that it is a paradoxical portrait, of sacred majesty alone and suffering. The book opens with a frontispiece by William Marshall of the king at prayer (figure 1). The image makes apparent the doubled nature of the text. Charles gives up his earthly crown for a Christlike crown of thorns; he tramples earthly glory beneath his feet. Yet, he remains a king, clothed in regal ermine. The viewer is reminded at once of the king's humility, his role as an exemplary Christian searching his conscience and preparing to meet his maker, and the unique majesty that the royal robes signify. Majesty inheres in the king and links him to divine majesty. The language of the King James Bible helped to enhance this majesty, challenging and reinterpreting the parliamentary display of justice and punishment.

The frontispiece of *Eikon Basilike* (figure 1) links Charles with both the biblical David and with Christ himself, in the garden of Gethsemane. As the king meditates on and prays over the various events of civil

FIGURE 1: The frontispiece of *Eikon Basilike* by William Marshall.

war, searching his conscience and ending every chapter with a prayer, he speaks in the language of the Psalms and the Gospels, figuring his own agony, his desire to forgive as both David and Christ forgave. *Eikon Basilike* brings the ancient biblical texts to bear on immediate political circumstances in mid-seventeenth-century England. Reinforcing the "sacred majesty" of the title page, nine of the twenty-eight chapters in *Eikon Basilike* contain the appellation "majesty." Such chapter titles range from "Upon His Majesty's calling this last Parliament" and "Upon His Majesty's going to the House of Commons," to "Upon His Majesty's retirement from Westminster," "Upon His Majesty's Letters, taken, and divulged," and "Upon their denying His Majesty the Attendance of His

Chaplains," to "Meditations upon Death . . . and His Majesty's closer Imprisonment in Carisbrooke-Castle."

In discussing politics and civil war events, Charles defends his majesty in part on legal and political grounds. Insisting on his own freedom to govern by the law as he sees fit, Charles denies that "the Majesty of the Crown of *England* [is] bound by a Coronation Oath, in a blind and brutish formality, to consent to what ever its subjects in Parliament shall require."[56] Responding to Nineteen Propositions that would have curtailed royal prerogative, Charles refuses "to betray the Sovereignty of Reason in my Soul, and the Majesty of my own Crown to any of my Subjects." But the text also widely uses Christian sentiments and the biblical language of majesty. Charles professes to forgive those subjects who have turned against him: "And indeed, I desire always more to remember I am a Christian, than a King; for what the Majesty of one might justly abhor, the Charity of the other is willing to bear."[57]

Eikon Basilike links an attack on kingly majesty with attack on the divine (evoking conflation of kingly and divine majesty such as we saw earlier in Psalm 45:2-4). Charles prays *"that I may have those to forgive, who bear most proportion in their offences to those trespasses against thy majesty, which I hope thy mercy hath forgiven me."*[58] Drawing upon the conflation of divine and human majesty in the Old Testament, the king writes that " 'tis no wonder if men not fearing GOD, should not Honour their KING. They will easily contemn such shadows of God, who reverence not that Supreme, and adorable Majesty, in comparison of whom all the glory of Men and Angels is but obscurity." Charles goes on to align himself with the figure of Moses and the majesty of God that we saw uniquely rendered in the King James translation of Deuteronomy: "Nor shall their black veils be able to hide the shining of My face, while God gives Me a heart frequently and humbly to converse with him, from whom alone are all the traditions of true glory and majesty."[59]

Above all, Charles embraces the persona of King David, using the psalmic language of majesty. Having depicted himself as, like David, surrounded by enemies who seek to *"slander the footsteps of thine Anointed,"* the king prays: *"Thou, O Lord, art the fountain of goodness, and honour; thou art clothed with excellent Majesty; make me to partake of thy excellency for wisdom, justice, and mercy, and I shall not want that degree of Honour, and Majesty, which becomes the Place in which thou hast set Me."*[60] Here, Charles evokes the distinctive language of majesty that we saw earlier in the King James translations of Psalm 21:5, "Honour and Majestie hast thou layde upon him"; Psalm 96:6, "The Lord made the heavens. Honour and majestie are before him"; and Psalm 104:1, "Thou art clothed with honour and majestie." Divine majesty guarantees the king's own. The psalmic language and prayers of *Eikon Basilike* "translate," or move, divine and kingly majesty from ancient Israel to the immediate circumstances of the English Revolution. Despite the king's insistence that he forgives his enemies, the language of divine majesty implies that those enemies will be avenged by a higher hand.

Eikon Basilike was perhaps the best seller of the seventeenth century, appearing in multiple editions from tiny duodecimos, small enough to hide in a pocket, to large octavos. Considerable evidence attests to the book's being widely and carefully read. Early readers affirmed the role of majesty in the king's book, and in the portrait itself. One early owner pasted silk and ermine on the frontispiece, while another colored in the image with ink. Early readers inscribed not only their ownership signatures, but their family histories, births, baptisms, weddings, and deaths.[61] Indeed, the usage of the king's book most closely resembles the treatment of family Bibles. But not all readers were similarly persuaded.

Defending the Revolution: John Milton's Polemical Prose

Early readers responded to and battled over *Eikon Basilike* in print. The now best known of these responses was that of poet and polemicist John Milton, who supported the regicide and had been hired by the new Council of State to compose and translate diplomatic correspondence. Among Milton's new duties was to prepare a rebuttal to *Eikon Basilike.* In the preface to his *Eikonoklastes in Answer to a Book Intitl'd the Portrature of his Sacred Majesty in his Solitudes and Sufferings* (1649), Milton disclaims any desire to combat the dead, and especially dead kings, who most often prove "but weak and puny Adversaries." Yet Milton explicitly sets out to strip away the ethos of kingly majesty: "Nevertheless for their sakes who through custom, simplicitie, or want of better teaching, have not more seriously considerd Kings, then in the gaudy name of Majesty, and admire them and thir doings, as if they breath'd not the same breath with other mortal men, I shall make no scruple . . . to take up this Gauntlet, though a Kings, in the behalf of Libertie, and the Common-wealth" (*CW* 5:63).[62]

Part of Milton's strategy is simply to leave out "majesty" from chapter titles as he quotes and rebuts the king's arguments in polemical, sometimes scathing language. Hence, the chapters of *Eikonoklastes* become "Upon his going to the House of Commons," "Upon his Retirement from

Westminster," "Upon his Letters tak'n and divulg'd," "Upon his going to the Scots," and so on, with "majesty" from the original titles silently elided. Another part of Milton's strategy is to mock the king's professed concern for his majesty. To the king's defense of his bringing armed "gentlemen" into Parliament, Milton jeers: "Gentlemen indeed; the ragged Infantrie of Stewes and Brothels; the spawn and shiprack of Taverns and Dicing Houses," adding, "An illustrious Majestie no doubt, so attended: a becoming safety for the King of *England*, plac'd in the fidelity of such Guards and Champions" (*CW* 5:102). To Charles' resistance to seeing the "majesty" of his crown as bound by his coronation oath, Milton replies testily: "What Tyrant could presume to say more, when he meant to kick down all Law, Government, and bond of Oath?" (*CW* 5:133).

Milton also challenges the king's appropriation of psalmic language and the persona of David: "He borrows *Davids* Psalmes," but "had he borrow'd *Davids* heart, it had bin much the holier theft" (*CW* 5:258). Elsewhere Milton adds scornfully that "it is not hard for any man, who hath a Bible in his hands, to borrow good words and holy sayings in abundance; but to make them his own, is a work of grace onely from above" (*CW* 5:264). While Charles "borrows heer many pentitential Verses out of *Davids* Psalmes," so did "many among those Israelites, who had revolted from the true worship of God" (*CW* 5:264).

Yet while chastising the king for his illicit use of biblical language and precedent, Milton's endeavor to strip majesty from the king moves away from biblical authority. Milton emphasizes legality, that majesty originates with the people: "And what were all his most rightful honours, but the peoples gift, and the investment of that lustre, Majesty, and honour, which for the public good & no otherwise, redounds from a whole Nation into one person?" (*CW* 5:237–38). Far from majesty being a God-given, sacred, and ineradicable quality of the monarch, it is the conditional gift of the people. When the king fights the Parliament and the people, Milton argues, he "fights against his own Majesty and Kingship, and then indeed sets the first hand to his own deposing" (*CW* 5:238). On the subject of majesty, Milton finds legal language more amenable to his argument than the biblical texts he has attempted to wrest away from the king.

Asked again to defend the fledgling English republic, this time to a European audience, Milton once more takes up, among other topics, the question of majesty. In *Pro Populo Anglicano Defensio* (1651), Milton continues to attempt to strip majesty away from kingship. But in doing so, he not only rewrites *Eikon Basilike*, but the King James Bible as well. Moving away from the biblical presentation of majesty as a divine attribute sometimes given to earthly kings, Milton "translates"—in this case, firmly moves—majesty into a secular and political context, asking "What king's majesty [*majestas*] high enthroned ever shone so bright as did the people's majesty of England?" (*CW* 7:5). Milton turns to Roman history and the majesty of the Roman people. From Cicero, he concludes that "in our reading we find majesty [*majestatem*] in those days more frequently ascribed to the Roman people than to kings" (*CW* 7:183). Against the European scholar Claudius Salmasius, who had castigated the English regicide, Milton argues: "As you have endeavored to take all power out of the people's hands, and vest it in the king, so you would all majesty [*majestatem*] too: a delegated transferred majesty if you will, but surely not their original primary majesty, any more than their original primary power" (*CW* 7:387–89). Milton moves on to the question of treason, or *lese-majesty*: " 'A king,' you say, 'cannot commit treason [*crimen majestatis*] against his people, but a people can against their king.' And yet a king is what he is for the people only, not the people for him" (*CW* 7:389). Later Milton responds to Salmasius' claim that no legal basis exists for charging the king with treason or lese-majesty by applying the same defense to Parliament: "Nor, say I, do they [the laws] declare that Parliament can be guilty of lese-majesty [*læsæ Majestatis*] . . . in deposing a bad king . . . but our laws do plainly declare that a king may indeed hurt his own majesty [*suam majestatem lædere*], and diminish it, yes and wholly lose it" (*CW* 7:527). Milton firmly lodges majesty in the people and the Parliament, rather than the king. In so doing, he rewrites the nature and significance of majesty as found not only in *Eikon Basilike* and other royalist defenses, but also in the King James Bible.

Paradise Lost and "Majestie Divine"

And yet Milton continued to develop a concept of majesty that could incorporate the Bible and divine majesty without attributing that majesty to human kings. *Paradise Lost*, on one level, continues the redefining and dispersal of majesty with which we see Milton grappling in his regicidal prose.[63] The poem, however, takes up in the form of narrative and theme the challenge of how to strip majesty away from earthly kings without stripping it from the divine.

Paradise Lost depicts divine majesty largely in reflected, mediated, and parodied forms. In his theological treatise *De Doctrina Christiana*,

Milton considers the majesty of God under the rubric of the language of accommodation, asking how the language in which the Bible describes God conveys divine truth without derogating from divine majesty (*CW* 14:31–37). *Paradise Lost* takes up in its narrative related questions: How is the majesty of God reflected in his creation, both in proper and improper forms? How does kingship usurp divine majesty? How does divine majesty reassert itself through punishment and mercy? In his great epic retelling of the fall and redemption of mankind, ranging in space from hell to heaven to earth and in time from the exaltation of the Son to the Last Judgment, Milton points to the splendor and power of divine majesty and the dangers of false usurpation.

Paradise Lost opens with the fallen angels in hell. We see and hear nothing of divine majesty until the war council, when the fallen angel and soon-to-be-devil Mammon proposes that they build an infernal kingdom of their own, imitating the majesty of heaven through the material riches of the kingdom of hell:

> This deep world
> Of darkness do we dread? How oft amidst
> Thick clouds and dark doth Heav'ns all-ruling Sire
> Choose to reside, his Glory unobscur'd,
> And with the Majesty of darkness round
> Covers his Throne; from whence deep thunders roar
> Must'ring thir rage, and Heav'n resembles Hell?
> As he our darkness, cannot we his Light
> Imitate when we please? (*PL* 2.262–70)[64]

Mammon points the fallen angels, gathered in consult in their newly built palace of Pandemonium (all-demons), toward the "Desart soile" of hell, rich with "Gemms and Gold" (*PL* 2.270–71). But, as the wary reader recognizes, the war council debate on how to defeat God by force or deceive God by fraud is doomed. Blinded by avarice, wrath, sloth, and ambition, the angels misread, although the reader should not, their remnants of heavenly glory as evidence that they can rise and regain their lost power. When Satan's right-hand spokesman, Beelzebub, "Majestic though in ruin" (*PL* 2.305), rises to cut off the debate and proposes the Satanically inspired "easier enterprize" (*PL* 2.345) of seducing man to sin, the reader sees the debasement of the remaining vestiges of divine majesty.

Paradise Lost dramatizes the dangers of taking on attributes of God by depicting Satanic rebellion as, in part, a false usurpation of divine majesty. Satan is a false ruler, a false king. As book 2 opens, Satan appears

"High on a Throne of Royal State" (*PL* 2.1), presiding over the infernal council. Later, the reader sees a similarly false Satanic exaltation in the war in heaven:

> High in the midst exalted as a God
> Th' Apostate in his Sun-bright Chariot sate
> Idol of Majesty Divine, enclos'd
> With Flaming Cherubim, and golden Shields;
> Then lighted from his gorgeous Throne. (*PL* 6.99–103)

Satan, like the biblical Nebuchadnezzar, displays false majesty precisely at the moment he is about to be overthrown. Both idol-maker and idol, Satan will be driven out as terribly as the fleeing subjects in the visions of Isaiah and Ezekiel. Indeed, it is Ezekiel's chariot in which the Son of God rides in Milton's epic account, driving the rebel angels before him out of heaven and into the gulf of chaos and hell.

Thus such usurpation only enhances the power of divine majesty, shown in punishment and in mercy. Countering Satanic destruction and war with goodness and creation, Milton's Son of God, "with Radiance crown'd / Of Majestie Divine" (*PL* 7.194–95), enters a second time into a chariot to create new worlds. Though Milton's prose attacks on Stuart majesty move away from biblical sources, in his great epic poem Milton reclaims the biblical story. *Paradise Lost* depicts the primeval moment of angelic rebellion as a false and doomed kingly usurpation of divine majesty: majesty, in Milton's poem, is fully evinced only in divine action and, in turn, is at last reflected in new divine creation of earth and humankind.

Hence, in the innocence of Eden and in nakedness rather than splendor and wealth, Milton's Adam and Eve reflect the majesty of God:

> Two of far nobler shape erect and tall,
> Godlike erect, with native Honour clad
> In naked Majestie seemd Lords of all,
> And worthie seemd, for in thir looks Divine
> The image of thir glorious Maker shon,
> Truth, wisdome, Sanctitude severe and pure,
> Severe but in true filial freedom plac't. (*PL* 4.288–94)

The poem's first description of Adam and Eve overturns all preconceptions of earthly majesty and strikingly contrasts with royalist uses of Adam as father-king. Stripped away from association with material wealth, with power over nations, with Solomonic riches and empire, majesty is relocated in the Edenic couple and in the virtues of honor, truth, wisdom, and sanctitude.

And indeed majesty characterizes Milton's Eve more than his Adam. Majesty is an attribute not so much of Adam, who acts as head and guide in Milton's Pauline gender hierarchy, as of the graceful but subordinate Eve. The epic narrator describes how Eve, perceiving that Adam is about to begin an abstruse dialogue with the visiting angel, "With lowliness Majestic . . . / And Grace" (*PL* 8.42–43), rises from her seat to work in the garden, "among her Fruits and Flours, / To visit how they prosper'd" (*PL* 8.44–45). Adam recounts to the angel how a newly created Eve assents to their marriage: "seeing me, she turn'd; / I follow'd her, she what was Honour knew, / And with obsequious Majestie approv'd / My pleaded reason" (*PL* 8.507–10). Engaged in debate with Adam on the morning of the fall, Eve is described in terms of "Virgin Majestie" (*PL* 9.270).

Milton returns to his biblical base with the language of majesty in *Paradise Lost*. Divine majesty, falsely appropriated by Satan and the rebel angels, although appropriately evinced in the earthly creation, cannot legitimize earthly monarchy. Eve, more than Adam, receives the language of majesty. The poem both reasserts the majesty of the divine and defines that majesty in such a way as to hinder any kind of identification with earthly kings. As such, Milton's great poem recuperates the biblical language of divine majesty—of power, might, and mercy—that is absent from Milton's polemical prose but that is so strikingly depicted in the King James Bible.

But if *Paradise Lost* powerfully employs biblical language and descriptions of majesty in terms apart from earthly monarchs, the poem appeared in a changed political world. Begun in the late 1650s, by the time the epic poem was published in 1667, the dissociation of majesty and monarchy could only be made in the literary realm. For Stuart monarchy was back, and the people to whom Milton had ascribed majesty had bitterly disappointed him. In *The Readie and Easie Way to Establish a Free Commonwealth* (1660), a tract desperately attempting to stave off kingship even as the king's return became a near surety, Milton castigated a nation that followed in the steps of both backsliding Israel and the corrupt Roman Republic: "How they can change thir noble words and actions, heretofore so becoming the majesty of a free people, into the base necessitie of court flatteries and prostrations, is not only strange and admirable, but lamentable to think on" (*CW* 6:123). In March 1660, Parliament invited Charles II, son of the executed Charles I and grandson of James I, to return from more than a decade of exile and resume the English crown. Charles returned in May 1660 to wildly enthusiastic crowds. A lavish coronation and resumption of the full accoutrements of kingly majesty would follow.

With the return of monarchy, the established Church of England was restored. And a revised 1662 Book of Common Prayer included a new liturgy for commemoration of Charles I as royal saint and martyr, a commemoration that would remain in the prayer book until 1859. As the martyred King Charles I gained a new afterlife as an Anglican saint, his son gained the crown imagined in *Eikon Basilike,* and at least some of his unlucky enemies received harsh punishments of hanging and quartering. And, beginning in 1662, the King James Bible replaced the Great Bible as the official version used in church liturgy. It was perhaps not the story that James I had envisioned when he endorsed a new translation of the Bible. But majesty had at last returned to the Stuart dynasty, on earth and in heaven.

Three

THE KING JAMES BIBLE IN BRITAIN
FROM THE LATE EIGHTEENTH CENTURY

David W. Bebbington

*T*he King James Bible was in a strong sense a product of the eighteenth rather than the seventeenth century. Variant texts had circulated since 1611, and the established version was not defined until two
scholars made corrections in the middle years of the eighteenth century.
F. S. Parris, Fellow of Sidney Sussex College, Cambridge, and Benjamin
Blayney, Fellow of Hertford College, Oxford, produced modified texts
for their respective university presses, two of the three permitted Bible
publishers, in 1743 and 1769. The version edited by Blayney, which incorporated Parris' modifications, soon became the universally accepted text
which has hardly altered since. It differed from the Bible as published in
1611 in no fewer than 24,000 places. Many of the changes were to tidy up
accumulated printers' mistakes, but some were by no means trivial.[1] That
modifications of this degree were possible without any outcry points to
a significant feature of the King James Bible for much of the eighteenth
century. Although it was the version used by nearly every Protestant in
the land, it was not yet a sacrosanct cultural icon. Certainly the translation commanded by James I was not venerated as "the Authorized Version," a term that, as we shall see, was to become its standard title in
Britain but which still had not been coined in the eighteenth century. The
people of England heard a different version, essentially the sixteenth-
century translation by Miles Coverdale, whenever they went to a parish
church and heard the Psalms recited. Dissenters from the Church of England and Presbyterians in Scotland sang metrical Psalms, which, though
no more than paraphrases, nevertheless represented the inspired text in

another distinct form. The eighteenth century saw no fewer than sixteen other English translations of the whole Bible and twenty-eight of the New Testament.[2] Although there was in some quarters a belief that the King James Bible, clustered about as it was with many spiritual associations, ought not to be tampered with, its text was not regarded, especially in educated circles, as a pillar of British civilization.

That view is confirmed by a sampling of contemporary opinion. A history of Bible translations, which first appeared in 1731 and reached its third edition in 1818, included in its chapter on the King James Version a large number of critical observations and only a single favorable estimate.[3] Matthew Pilkington, a clergyman who had risen to be a prebendary of Lichfield, wrote in 1759 with some distaste of the "uncouth and obsolete words and expressions" of the King James Bible.[4] One of the eighteenth-century translators of the Bible, a Quaker named Anthony Purver, rejected the notion that "the last Translation in King James's Reign must not be altered" since "the Pedantry of that Reign is become a Ridicule, and the Style intolerable."[5] In a century that prided itself on its good taste, its classical learning, and increasingly on its improvements over the past, the King James Bible seemed a relic of barbarism. Edward Harwood, a Presbyterian minister in Bristol, took it upon himself in 1758 to publish *A Liberal Translation of the New Testament* in accordance with the standards of the age. The verse at the opening of the Lord's Prayer had been rendered in the 1611 version as: "After this manner therefore pray ye: Our Father which art in heaven, Hallowed be thy name" (Matthew 6:9). Harwood translated these words of Jesus as follows:

> In order to guard you from mistakes in this important concern I will propose the following as the model for your devotions—O Thou great governour and parent of universal nature—who manifestest thy glory to the blessed inhabitants of heaven—may all thy rational creatures in all the parts of thy boundles dominion be happy in the knowledge of thy existence and providence, and celebrate thy perfections in a manner most worthy thy nature and perfective of their own![6]

Those who sympathized with such refined amplification were not going to idolize its King James predecessor.

The prevailing estimate of the translation of 1611 was transformed in the half-century beginning around 1780. A number of factors were responsible for a marked increase in the appreciation of the King James Bible. In the first place, the classical taste that had dismissed the writings of the seventeenth century as unsophisticated began to give way to a delight in past works for their own sake. While still conscious of the literary standards of the day, a contributor to the *Critical Review* wrote in 1787 that the idioms of the old translation were not at fault: "Nor would we lose the noble simplicity, and energetic bravery, for all the idiomatic elegance which a polished age can bestow." The King James Bible was a "venerable relic."[7] At a time when monastic ruins were coming into favor, relics were approved. The rise of what is sometimes called "historicism" meant that the old was now presumed to be freighted with wisdom rather than deficient in quality. Again, the devotion to the Scriptures current among the rank and file of the people was becoming a mark in favor of the version they read. Whereas the attitudes of the common people were often held in disdain by the intellectuals of the eighteenth century, toward its end the view that the masses were a reservoir of good sense began to advance. In 1778 Vicesimus Knox, headmaster of Tonbridge School in Kent, urged that the "prejudice" of the middle and lower ranks in favor of the present translation ought to be respected.[8] The greater esteem for the old and for the common people constituted dimensions of the Romantic revolution rolling over Europe. By the 1820s, the language of the early seventeenth century had become so much in vogue that the most popular preacher in London, Edward Irving, deliberately adopted its archaic idiom. "The whole Philosophy of Europe serveth infidelity," as Irving once declared, sounded more powerful than if he had used the current form of the verb, "serves."[9] The characteristic of the times was not to modernize the English Bible but to imitate its accepted translation.

A second reason for the higher valuation of the King James Bible was its growing association with national feeling. The French Revolution of 1789 ushered in an era when Britain faced a succession of acute dangers—from the republican regimes that waged war against the country, then from the even more formidable threat of Napoleon, and, after the defeat of the emperor, from the peril of revolution at home. Patriotism climbed fresh heights, and, as Linda Colley has argued, its most powerful motor had long been anti-Catholicism.[10] Militant Protestantism was a stout ideological weapon against the Catholicism of France. The open Bible was a symbol of what differentiated the peoples because, even when the revolutionaries threw off the Catholic yoke, they were still perceived as the victims of their want of scriptural training. The King James Bible was distinctly Protestant. Catholics denounced it and used instead their own Douai-Rheims editions. Thus, when biblical extracts were produced for schools in Ireland, where Catholicism was dominant, the passages were provided in the Douai-Rheims version as well as in the King James Version.[11] The accepted version of the Bible, furthermore, seemed a bastion of the existing order in Britain. High Churchmen who specially valued the bond of church and state became strongly attached to the King James Version. It might contain some minor errors, Bishop John Jebb of Limerick admitted to a correspondent in 1829, but it ought not to be revised because "in the present days of unsettlement and appetency after change, the only safety lies in keeping things as they are."[12] Other High Churchmen took a similar line. H. J. Todd, a royal chaplain as well as rector of Settrington in Yorkshire, published *A Vindication of our Authorized Translation and Translators of the Bible* in 1819, and in the following year the Regius Professor of Hebrew at Oxford, Richard Laurence, issued a learned treatise on the impossibility of improving the original text on which the King James Bible was based.[13] There was a rallying to the cause of the translation of 1611 because it undergirded the fabric of social order in the country.

The King James Bible gained in standing, in the third place, because of the foundation of the British and Foreign Bible Society in 1804. The society was one of the innumerable agencies created in the wake of the Evangelical Revival of the previous century. As the number of evangelicals grew, they required a larger number of Bibles for use and distribution. The society exploited modern methods such as stereotyping to reduce expenses and set up auxiliaries throughout the land to promote the cause. Members of auxiliaries were entitled to obtain Bibles at cost price up to the amount of half their subscription, hugely increasing the circulation of the Scriptures.[14] By 1824, only twenty years after the foundation of the society, there were as many as 859 auxiliaries with 500 supporting ladies' organizations. By 1832 there were over 100,000 subscribers.[15] Crucially for our purposes, the society distributed at home nothing but editions of the Bible of 1611. It even exalted the text by issuing it without annotation. Some of the most popular editions of the Scriptures in the eighteenth century had been printed with copious notes. Philip Doddridge, the Independent divine of Northampton, and Thomas Scott, an Anglican clergyman of strong evangelical convictions, had produced Bibles in which their commentary often occupied three-quarters or more of the page.[16] The inclusion of notes remained the policy of two High Churchmen, George D'Oyly and Richard Mant, in an edition of 1817 that was designed to inculcate sound Anglican principles.[17] But the Bible Society committed itself from its foundation to print the Bible "without note or comment" so that the text of the King James Bible was implicitly deemed to be self-interpreting. The rule did not mean a prohibition of alternative readings and cross-references in the margins, which were included in many of the society's editions from 1810.[18] The society's policy, however, also bore testimony to their respect for the current version, since, at least since Blayney's revision, that was the customary way of issuing it. It is perhaps not surprising that the society was charged with allowing its translations into foreign languages to be taken from the established English version rather than from the original languages.[19] The British and Foreign Bible Society institutionalized the growing esteem for the King James Version.

A fourth explanation of the rising tide of admiration for the translation of 1611 was its redefinition as "the Authorized Version." The title emerged for the first time in a debate provoked by the creation of the Bible Society. Whereas the society's evangelical supporters considered the new agency a bulwark of the existing social order, the High Church party thought it a sinister development. It threatened the work of the Society for Promoting Christian Knowledge, the established Anglican organization for circulating the Scriptures. Furthermore, the timing was unfortunate. During 1804, the year of the society's foundation, Napoleon's forces were poised to invade the country, and in the heightened alarm, the equal presence of Dissenters alongside Churchmen on the society's committee seemed potentially subversive. Had not Dissenters once killed an English king, Charles I? Thomas Sikes, the High Church vicar of Guilsborough, Northamptonshire, warned that, when the production of the sacred text was being entrusted to "sectaries," nobody could be confident that they would not tamper with the translations. In order to calm such fears, John Owen, one of the society's secretaries, replied that the organization was limited to producing versions *"printed by authority."* When an opponent pointed out that this restriction had not been stated formally, the society hastened in May 1805 to revise its constitution so as to read, "The only copies in the languages of the United Kingdom to be circulated by the Society, shall be the authorised version, without note or comment."[20] Thus the phrase "the authorized version" was launched on the world as an apologetic device for the Bible Society. By 1819 the phrase had been heard so often that it crept for the first time into the *Times* newspaper, though still with a lowercase "a," showing that it was not yet a title.[21] The steady growth of the usage is documented in the number of times in each subsequent decade the phrase occurred in the *Times*: 1820s, 7; 1830s, 41; 1840s, 61; 1850s, 91.[22] By the last of these decades, the expression was starting to be capitalized, demonstrating that it had emerged as a title.[23] Thereafter "the Authorized Version" became the standard term for the 1611 Bible in Britain, where the phrase "King James Bible" was hardly ever used. The new title surrounded this particular text, as it was originally intended to do, with an aura of unique legitimacy. It helped forward the process by which the version became embedded more deeply in the national culture.

There was nevertheless criticism of the received version. In 1809 John Pye Smith, principal of the Independents' Homerton College and probably the most scholarly Dissenter of his generation, declared that it was a disgrace that nothing had been done to remove the blemishes that disfigured the Bible of 1611. "We do not wish," he went on, "to see our common version, now become venerable by age and prescription, superseded by another entirely *new*; every desirable purpose would be satisfactorily attained by a *faithful* and *well-conducted* revision."[24] In the following year, Herbert Marsh, the Lady Margaret Professor of Divinity at Cambridge, likewise declared in favor of revising the Bible of 1611. Intermittently the same call was heard, as by James Scholefield, the Regius Professor of Greek at Cambridge and an evangelical, in a book of 1832.[25] The essential problem for these critics was the inaccuracy of the rendering of the original. Sometimes the objection extended to the alterations made during the transmission of the text of 1611, essentially the changes made by Parris and Blayney. A Baptist schoolmaster and publisher, Thomas Curtis, wrote in 1832 to the Cambridge University Press to complain about its "grossly inaccurate copies, if copies they may be called, of the Authorized Version."[26] Curtis, who was the spokesman for a committee of Dissenters who wished to break the monopoly of the ancient universities, together with the King's Printer, over Bible production, managed to provoke Oxford University Press into issuing a facsimile of the 1611 Bible in order to demonstrate, at least to its own satisfaction, that subsequent changes were insubstantial.

The most outspoken and sustained campaign against the King James Bible, however, was mounted by the Unitarians. The Unitarian Society for Promoting Christian Knowledge commissioned Thomas Belsham, minister of Essex Street Unitarian Chapel, London, to publish a revised New Testament based on a corrected Greek text in 1808.[27] Unitarians in general found the translation of 1611 tendentious. Instead of the pure word of Scripture, complained John R. Beard in 1857, "we have Scripture perverted and coloured by kingcraft and priestcraft."[28] In the previous year, a Unitarian in the House of Commons, James Heywood, had proposed a motion calling on the government to take the initiative in revising the Bible.[29] Although Heywood was brushed aside, he had made his mark as a representative of the religious community that consistently showed the most dissatisfaction with the existing Bible.

The demand for revision could succeed only if opinion within the Church of England veered in its favor. By the 1850s, with greater prosperity in the nation generating enhanced social harmony, the fabric of the state seemed less likely to shatter if the Bible were altered. With the restoration of convocation, the ancient parliament of the church, in 1854, there was an arena where such issues could be broached. Two years later, William Selwyn, Lady Margaret Professor at Cambridge, proposed in convocation that there should be an inquiry into the need for revision.[30] Opinion began to shift. By 1860 it was estimated that opponents of revision still greatly outnumbered supporters, but only a decade later the convocation of Canterbury actually appointed a committee to prepare what became the Revised Version.[31] The arguments that swayed the decision are plain. By far the most important was the case that the Authorized Version, as it was now called, contained false renderings. It was a powerful contention that early manuscripts of the New Testament not available to the translators of 1611 required that a more accurate Greek text should now be the basis for translation. There was also a consideration that weighed heavily with Anglican clergymen brought up on the classics. It is revealing that J. B. Lightfoot, Hulsean Professor of Divinity at Cambridge and one of the leading members of the revision team, charged the translators of the King James Bible with "an imperfect knowledge of Greek grammar."[32] The men of 1611, Lightfoot and his colleagues believed, had deliberately introduced different renderings of the same Greek word, creating artificial distinctions, and had committed the opposite error of making the same rendering of different words, obliterating distinctions in the original. The King James Version must be modified, classical scholars now held, so as to vindicate a more precise way of construing the Greek text. The argument that the language of the King James Bible could seem obscure was distinctly subordinate. Usually this point was limited to the claim that there were a few archaisms that needed attention. The obscurity seemed more of a problem to the Baptist preacher C. H. Spurgeon, by no means a classicist, who in 1859 endorsed revision with the remark that, "I love God's Word better than I love King James's pedantic wisdom."[33] Classicists, however, who were used to translating, did not see a dated form of language as a major difficulty. Nevertheless, it became the established view in educated circles that there was sufficient reason to revise the Authorized Version. The result was the first official effort to produce a new version of the Scriptures since 1611.

It might be supposed that the revisers, fired by scholarly zeal, would perform drastic surgery, but that was by no means the case. The principles for the operation laid down by convocation are revealing. The first was: "To introduce as few alterations as possible into the Text of the Authorised Version consistently with faithfulness." Only the requirement of improved accuracy, that is to say, should justify tampering with the existing English Bible. The second principle showed even more conservatism: "To limit, as far as possible, the expression of such alterations to the language of the Authorised and earlier English Versions."[34] That rule dictated that the archaic quality of the Bible should be retained. Hence, for example, the revisers added "haply" to "lest," an obsolete usage by the nineteenth century, in seventeen cases where the King James Bible did not.[35] Lightfoot, who was one of the members of the New Testament revision committee most eager for modification of the text, nevertheless showed no inclination to alter the character of the translation. "The stately rhythm and the archaic colouring," he wrote, "are alike sacred in the eyes of all English-speaking peoples."[36] To the predominantly Anglican revisers even the book titles of the Authorized Version, which they heard read aloud in public worship, seemed untouchable. Thus, although in the early manuscripts the first gospel was headed simply "According to Matthew," the revisers still called it "The Gospel according to Saint Matthew." A parallel revision committee in America, by contrast, followed the early manuscripts.[37] When changes in the text were under discussion on the English committee, two-thirds of the revisers had to vote for an alteration. Hence many readings preferred by a plain majority were relegated to the margin.[38] The practice of revision, far from showing any detachment from allegiance to the Authorized Version, revealed an extreme loyalty to it. C. J. Ellicott, the chairman of the New Testament committee, avowed "the great reverence that we have ever felt for that venerable version."[39] The whole exercise was a respectful revision, not a fresh translation.

The Revised Version of the New Testament appeared in 1881, and the Old Testament followed four years later. The public response was, in general, mildly favorable, but the attachment to the older version was usually evident. A Wesleyan Methodist reviewer in the *Expositor* approved the retention of "the archaic tone of the Authorised Version."[40] A Baptist rejoiced in the denominational magazine that the new Bible had not lost the "music and rhythm" of the old.[41] One reviewer in the *Church Quarterly Review*, representing mainstream Anglican opinion, pronounced the Revised Version to be valuable for study, but to be only a supplement to the Authorized Version, which he still regarded as "the perennial fount from which thought and imagination as well as piety and prayer will continue to be unconsciously supplied."[42] Others were more critical. John Clifford, the leading minister of the General Baptists, thought the new version was "too conservative of the *Old*."[43] More contemporaries, however, considered it too radical because it broke with the familiar text. One voice denounced the Revised Version unsparingly. J. W. Burgon, the redoubtable High Church Dean of Chichester, believed the manuscripts on which the older Bible was based were superior to those adopted by the revisers and so dismissed their efforts as sacrilegious destruction of "a noble Version."[44] Burgon's condemnation helped inhibit the acceptance of the newer Bible. Prebendary H. W. Webb-Peploe, a prominent evangelical Anglican who was strongly attached to the King James rendering, successfully resisted the circulation of the Revised Version by the Bible Society until 1901.[45] Only in a few places did the Revised Version become normal. It was used, for example, in the chapel of Ridley Hall, Cambridge, a broader-minded evangelical Anglican institution. In 1940 two Cambridge dons toured the places of worship in the town in the manner of iconoclastic Puritans of the seventeenth century and observed satirically that they took away from the chapel a "superstitiouse booke called ye *Revised Version* & did put ye Bible in place thereof."[46] The Authorized Version remained "the Bible" even after the publication of its intended improvement.

There was a chorus of praise for the Bible of 1611 in the later nineteenth century. It became fashionable to concentrate on the book's nonreligious qualities. "As a mere literary monument," wrote the historian J. R. Green in 1874, "the English version of the Bible remains the noblest example of the English tongue, while its perpetual use made it, from the instant of its appearance, the standard of our language."[47] This type of exaggeration was commonplace. Only one English book attained Homer's level of sublimity, claimed the literary critic Matthew Arnold in 1861, and that was the Bible, for it combined "perfect plainness of speech" with "perfect nobleness."[48] Even unlikely figures bore testimony to the appeal of the Authorized Version. F. W. Faber, a man with all the zeal of a convert to the Roman Catholic Church, commented that the "uncommon beauty and marvellous English of the Protestant Bible" was "like a music which can never be forgotten."[49] Charles Bradlaugh, the chief English freethinker, habitually referred to "our version" even when pointing out alleged errors in the text.[50] When an ancient Egyptian obelisk, Cleopatra's Needle, was erected in 1878 on the new Victoria Embankment along the River Thames in central London, several copies of the English Bible were deposited in a cavity in its pedestal among "memorials of Great Britain in the nineteenth century."[51] The Authorized Version was a national treasure. In the Darwinian race against extinction, as an Edwardian commentator put it, "the intrinsic superiority of this Jacobean revision enabled it to outdistance all competitors, and to come down to our own day with universal acceptance as the fittest which had alone survived." It could "no more become obsolete than Shakespeare himself."[52] The King James Bible had become a symbol of the national culture.

The climax of the adulation of the Authorized Version came at its tercentenary in 1911. It was the year when the prospect of the coronation of King George V put the country into a posture of celebration. There was royal patronage for the Bible commemorations. The king sent a message of congratulations to the National Bible Society of Scotland; he took the queen to a Bible Exhibition at the British Museum; and he received a bound Bible from a deputation including the Archbishop of Canterbury, the president of the National Council of the Evangelical Free Churches, the speaker of the House of Commons, and assorted other dignitaries.[53] Bible Sunday was observed with special services in many congregations on March 12 in Scotland and on March 26 in England and Wales.[54] The culmination came on March 29 with a grand national thanksgiving in the Albert Hall in London. The event was marred by a group of women demanding the right to vote who unrolled a banner just as the Prime Minister, Herbert Asquith, was beginning his speech. Paradoxically, however, their protest was further evidence of the place of the King James Bible in the national consciousness. The banner not only proclaimed "Votes for women" but also went on to say, "To loose the bands of wickedness, to undo the heavy burdens, and to let the oppressed go free."[55] It was quoting Isaiah 58:6 from the Authorized Version. Two features of the celebrations were especially noteworthy. One was that the occasions gathered the Protestant churches together in ecumenical concord. Thus, at a thanksgiving service in Bishop Auckland, County Durham, the Bishop of Durham preached the sermon, but the lessons were read by Primitive Methodist and Congregational ministers. The event was seen as "a distinct advance towards religious unity."[56] The other striking feature was the extent to which the language of celebration was expressed in Romantic terms. The Bible of 1611, according to a leading article in the representative Free Church newspaper *British Weekly*, was stamped in an atmosphere of "heroism" with "the temper of poetry and enthusiasm."[57] The Authorized Version, declared an editorial in *Life & Work*, the magazine of the Church of Scotland, was "like some fine ancient Gothic cathedral in the midst of the jerry-built streets of a modern town."[58] The same magazine carried an article entitled "The Romance of the English Bible."[59] The Romantic sensibility that had raised the status of the King James Version in the nineteenth century continued to sustain it in the twentieth.

The ecumenical endorsement and the Romantic language were alike associated with another factor that buoyed up the reputation of the Authorized Version, its identification with the nation. Church and chapel, the two great streams of national life, were united in praise for the English Bible; and Romantic feeling provided fuel for nationalism. "The Authorized Version cannot dispute with the Revised the palm of accuracy," admitted the guidebook to the 1911 British Museum Bible Exhibition; "yet it is entwined with the heart of the nation."[60] The Bible of 1611 was credited with extraordinary historical agency. "It raised the nation at one bound," wrote William Muir in one of the many books published at the tercentenary, "to the foremost among the nations of Europe, and more than aught else has kept it there ever since."[61] A whole genre of histories of the Bible published between the mid-nineteenth and mid-twentieth centuries argued that the scriptures in the vernacular were the secret of Britain's greatness.[62] The English Bible, according to one history that appeared in 1914, had nurtured the national traits of "hatred of falsehood, respect for law and order, love of fair play, reasonableness, and a singular freedom from the passionate outbreaks that have marked so much of the history of other nations."[63] Sometimes authors recognized, especially in the twentieth century, that the Bible of 1611 was shared property. It unites us, wrote a historian of the Bible in 1901, with "the whole English-speaking race."[64] That was why the American ambassador received the loudest ovation at the Albert Hall celebration in 1911.[65] As the discourse of race reached its peak in the 1920s, a United Free Church of Scotland minister, James Baikie, voiced his astonishment that a Jewish book expressing the ideals of "a race not only alien from, but singularly antipathetic to the average Anglo-Saxon" when translated into English had formed "the racial conscience."[66] More often, however, the Authorized Version was treated as a common possession of all the lands of the British empire, binding them together. The Bible, declared Muir, is "the true strength and inspiration of an imperial people."[67] At a time when empire was a foundation of national identity, the link reinforced the location of the King James Bible near the core of Britishness.

Yet there were limits to the popularity of the Authorized Version. To purist scholars there was the insurmountable barrier of its inaccuracy. A Methodist New Testament specialist complained in 1911 that the very familiarity of the Bible in regular use obscured the true meaning of the text.[68] In 1940 Cecil Cadoux, the church historian at the Congregationalists' Mansfield College, Oxford, trenchantly evaluated the attractions of the Authorized against the Revised Version. "Give what weight you please to the arguments about rhythm, music, dignity, and the devotional value arising from long familiarity and sacred associations; these surely ought not, in the judgement of any educated and responsible Christian, to outweigh questions of truth and falsehood."[69] Cadoux was claiming that the popular preference for the King James Bible was misplaced. Then there was the continuing Roman Catholic rejection of the Authorized Version, which was seen as a "Protestant Bible," in favor of renderings of the Vulgate. Hugh Pope, a scholarly Dominican, charged that the men responsible for the 1611 Bible had sometimes acted as interpreters rather than as translators.[70] When new Roman Catholic versions of the Scriptures appeared—that by Ronald Knox in 1945/1949 and the Jerusalem Bible in 1966—they showed scant regard for the idiom of the Authorized Version. Knox saw no reason why the Bible should be archaic.[71] And a third limitation on the veneration for the King James Bible arose from a widespread sense that William Tyndale, the first man to publish the English New Testament in the sixteenth century, was worthier of praise than the translators of 1611. Part of Tyndale's appeal lay in his adventurous life and martyr's death. Baikie's 1928 account of the evolution of the English Bible, like many others, lingered over Tyndale's story, allocating him three chapters and the Authorized Version only one more.[72] The dependence of the men of 1611 on Tyndale's phraseology also meant that commentators often transferred much of the glory for the translation to the solitary pioneer. "The ease and freshness and limpid purity which they enviously admired in the Bible," according to Professor Curtis of Aberdeen in 1911, "were mainly due to him."[73] When in 1994 Tyndale's quincentenary was celebrated, there still was a distinct tendency, as in his biography by David Daniell, to lower the estimate of the King James Bible in order to exalt the standing of the earlier translator.[74] So "AVolatry," as it has been called, was not absolutely universal.[75]

The reverence for the King James Bible, furthermore, was sometimes restricted in scope even among those who professed it. A growing number of intellectuals began to value the Bible not for its religious power but for its literary quality. The process was begun by James Frazer, a fellow of Trinity College, Cambridge, and the author of *The Golden Bough* (1890). As the leading social anthropologist of his generation, Frazer was fascinated by religion but saw it as a passing phase of human experience destined to be superseded by science. In 1895 Frazer published *Passages of the Bible Chosen for their Literary Beauty and Interest*.[76] Although he used the Revised Version to ascertain the correct meaning, the extracts were all taken from the Authorized Version. During the years down to the Second World War there were at least four publications with the title *The Bible as Literature*.[77] A rift had opened, as Gordon Campbell has put it, between two ways of treating the King James Version—as a literary artifact or as a sacred text.[78] Already in 1911 the perceptive Scottish theologian James Denney issued a protest against seeing the Bible as literature. The Bible belonged to the church, literature to the world. Literature was a form of free art, but the Bible was purposeful, practical, with an end beyond itself. The two were in different spheres.[79] Similarly, in 1935 the poet T. S. Eliot warned against regarding the Bible solely as a literary work. Admirers of the Bible as a monument of English prose were "merely admiring it as a monument over the grave of Christianity."[80] After the Second World War, the literary scholar C. S. Lewis developed a related case further. In a lecture delivered in 1950, Lewis contended that the literary impact of the Authorized Version had been minimal. It had exerted an influence over English vocabulary, though Tyndale deserved the credit for that, and over imagery, though the phenomenon was difficult to identify, but little over style and none at all over rhythm. In any case, most of the qualities of the Authorized Version were owed to the original languages.[81] Lewis' eloquent assault on the orthodox magnification of the Bible's sway over literature was motivated partly by the academic impulse to puncture received opinion, but it was also a result of his fear as a Christian that the Bible was not being treated as divine revelation. The vogue for admiring the qualities of the King James Version was obstructing appreciation of the Bible's ultimate purpose.

That apprehension led to a succession of twentieth-century translations of the Bible. The work of Adolf Deissman of Heidelberg and then Berlin around the opening of the century led to a recognition that the New Testament was originally composed not in a vocabulary reserved for sacred use but in the language of everyday speech. Scholars such as J. H. Moulton began to argue that "blind admiration for the *ipsissima verba* of the Authorised Version" must not prevent efforts to make the words "live anew after three centuries."[82] The shift of opinion is evident in two renderings of the New Testament by James Moffatt of Mansfield College, Oxford, and later of the United Free College, Glasgow. In 1901 he published a version that preserved the archaic language of the Authorized Version; but in 1913 he issued a translation in modern speech.[83] His Old Testament of 1924 showed how up-to-date his idiom had become. At Song of Songs 1:3, the Authorized Version's "Therefore do the virgins love thee" became "The girls are all in love with you."[84] Occasional progressive ministers such as John Clifford had already adopted the modern version issued in 1903 by R. F. Weymouth,[85] but the spate of translations in contemporary language came only after the Second World War. J. B. Phillips, dismayed as a young clergyman by the biblical ignorance of the young people of his London parish, published his *Letters to Young Churches* in 1947.[86] After three hundred and fifty years of the Authorized Version, he believed, "many exciting and challenging truths have been rendered impotent by the sheer beauty of language as well as by familiarity of repetition."[87] That was one of the reasons why the Revised Standard Version, published in the United States in 1952, was widely accepted in Britain; but another was that its continuing echoes of the Authorized Version made it suitable for public reading.[88] The time seemed to have come, however, for an entirely new translation sponsored by all the main British denominations. The result was the New English Bible (New Testament, 1961; Old Testament, 1970). It, too, aimed for a dignified style and so sometimes followed the text of the King James Bible closely. At other times it lapsed into academic abstraction, as when Psalm 94:20 was rendered "Shall sanctimonious calumny call thee partner?"[89] Many deemed it little more intelligible to the general public than the Authorized Version. Although the Revised Standard Version and the New English Bible were both approved for use in the Anglican communion service in 1965, the Authorized Version was still thought to be on almost every lectern ten years later.[90] In 1984 a careful survey of Scottish churches showed that 40 percent of them remained attached to the King James Bible.[91] The later twentieth century saw an onslaught on the previous dominance of the King James Version, but not its immediate collapse.

The delay in capitulation to modern versions was a consequence of resistance by two distinct parties. One consisted of members of the cultural elite, engaging in defense of the national way of life against what they saw as vandalism. T. S. Eliot, who had declined to act as a literary adviser to the translators of the New English Bible, set the tone for these people when, in reviewing its New Testament in 1961, he dismissed the work as "an active agent of decadence." The latest translation, he insisted, lacked the "verbal beauty" of the Authorized Version, which was "a masterpiece of literature."[92] Those who thought like Eliot watched with dismay as the Church of England engaged in liturgical experiments over the next two decades. The Prayer Book, they believed, was being supplanted by modern vulgarity. The result of this process, *The Alternative Service Book* of 1980, actually showed many signs of the continuing influence of the King James Bible. It included words such as "beseech" and "evermore," which had long dropped out of regular usage.[93] Yet many traditionalists considered the novel liturgies as inferior to the Prayer Book of 1662, just as they considered the New English Bible inferior to the Authorized Version. Accordingly, just before the *Alternative Service Book* was to be launched, there was a concerted effort to preserve both Prayer Book and Authorized Version in the worship of the Church of England. A widely signed petition in favor of both was submitted to its General Synod in November 1979. The petition was followed up by a letter to the *Times*, which its authors, all senior members of the University of Oxford, saw as a more influential medium. Their motivation was plain, for they were a coalition of believers and unbelievers. They were concerned not for the communication of the faith but for the transmission of "our common culture." "The Authorized Version of the Bible," they wrote, "the idioms of which have passed into common speech, unless it is read as scripture in our churches, will become inaccessible."[94] Others concurred, the Bishop of Peterborough claiming that some of the statements in favor of change in the General Synod were so bent on destruction that they might have come from "the lost and unspeakable speeches of Attila the Hun."[95] About thirty Conservative Members of Parliament put down a

supportive motion in the House of Commons, and six months later a
Gallup Poll showed that a majority of those consulted who called themselves "Church of England" preferred the older forms.[96] Although these
measures only slowed the inexorable advance of newer liturgies, Prayer
Book services containing lessons from the Authorized Version continued
to be offered in certain parishes for the dwindling band of traditionalists
down into the twenty-first century. For them, the King James Bible was
still a cultural icon.

The other party of defenders of the Bible of 1611 consisted of those
who saw it as a bastion of the truth. Many evangelicals were suspicious
of new translations because of their apparent doctrinal unsoundness.
Thus the Revised Standard Version gave comfort to deniers of the virgin
birth by rendering Isaiah 7:14 not "a virgin shall conceive" but "a young
woman shall conceive," and the New English Bible dropped the concept
of propitiation from the New Testament.[97] The Good News Bible of 1976
might still attract mistrust because of its very free translation, but the
New International Version of two years later provided a text with which
evangelicals could hardly cavil. Yet some continued to prefer the King
James Bible. Organizations such as the Bible League and the Trinitarian
Bible Society promoted the Authorized Version alone. In 1984, 92 percent of congregations of the Free Church of Scotland and the Free Presbyterian Church adhered to this policy.[98] In England there were small
groupings such as the Free Church of England (Continuing), a secession
from the Church of England following its ordination of women in 1993,
which were committed to the same course.[99] The rationale was given by
John Thackway, editor of the *Bible League Quarterly*, in 1997. "The AV," he
wrote, "is the Bible turned as exactly as possible into a pure Anglo-Saxon
that expresses the original Hebrew and Greek. It is not Elizabethan English but *biblical* English, and therefore enduring English."[100] The Authorized Version, according to a prominent member of the Trinitarian Bible
Society, was based on manuscripts which, as Dean Burgon had contended
against the Revised Version, were superior to those used by subsequent
translators.[101] There was a significant doctrinal implication. Thackway
and his circle believed that the King James Version, and not just the original manuscripts of the Bible, was a faithful medium of revelation. God's
word had been not just inspired at its composition but also preserved over
subsequent history. The idea of inerrancy was unsatisfactory because it
confined the attribute to the originals. Thackway therefore urged that
"the Bible we hold in our hands today" should be described as infallible

rather than as inerrant.[102] To demur at inerrancy in this way was to take issue with a conventional position upheld by those on the conservative wing of Evangelicalism. Here was a group of evangelicals whose commitment to the King James Version molded their whole theology.

As the quatercentenary of the King James Bible approached, there were still congregations stoutly maintaining their allegiance to it. The Riverside Baptist Church in Exeter, for example, described itself on its notice board in 2010 as "A fundamental, Bible believing Evangelical church (AV 1611)."[103] But that position was in decline. In evangelical circles, a persisting user of the 1611 Bible complained, "It is almost fashionable . . . to begin conference addresses by holding up . . . the Authorized Version to ridicule."[104] Yet in British society at large there was a continuing attachment to the version. In the autobiography of Tony Blair, the former Labour Prime Minister, published in 2010, there were several echoes of the text of 1611: "graven image," "fought the good fight," and even a whole verse: "Which of you, intending to build a tower, sitteth not down first, and counteth the cost, whether he have sufficient to finish it" (Luke 14:28).[105] In preparation for the quatercentenary, a King James Bible Trust was set up under Frank Field, an energetic Anglican and Labour Member of Parliament. The trust achieved remarkable success in putting across its case that there was something the nation needed to celebrate. The queen's message delivered to the nation on Christmas Day 2010 drew attention to the occasion; starting on the following January 3, a series of three programs on the main BBC radio channel by James Naughtie, a leading political commentator, told the story of the King James Bible on consecutive days; and on Sunday, January 9, the day's radio broadcasting was interrupted by seven readings of selected passages by distinguished figures from the arts world.[106] At a Whitehall reception, the historian Niall Fergusson, himself an unbeliever, spoke of the influence of the King James Version over the whole world; and the militant atheist Richard Dawkins made the memorable comment on YouTube that "It's important that religion should not be allowed to hijack this cultural resource."[107] "Will the Authorised Version still be reigning in 2011?" a commentator had asked a century before.[108] The answer was a definite no. Yet there can be little doubt that the Authorized Version was now more warmly appreciated by public intellectuals than by most Christians in the pews.

Over the previous two and a half centuries, the King James Bible had passed through a striking trajectory. In the middle years of the eighteenth century, the version was generally used but not especially respected. Its status rose from the last years of the century onwards as a taste for the past developed, the translation became identified with national feeling, the British and Foreign Bible Society circulated it, and the title the "Authorized Version" emerged. Criticism of the defects of the translation nevertheless created a demand for revision, but both the practice of the revisers and the reaction of the public confirmed the high esteem enjoyed by the King James Version. Appreciation by a wide cross section of the population culminated in the celebrations of 1911, when it was hailed as a marvel of religion and literature alike. The English Bible, it was generally held around that date, was the foundation of national greatness. Dissenting voices came from critical scholars, Roman Catholics, devotees of Tyndale, and increasingly from those within the churches who thought the cult of the Bible as literature was obscuring its spiritual value. The result was the plethora of new translations which gradually eclipsed the Authorized Version during the later twentieth century. The rearguard defense of the older Bible was mounted by intellectuals concerned for its cultural role and conservative evangelicals bolstering their doctrinal position. The former were rather more salient than the latter by 2011. The changing estimate of the King James Bible was clearly bound up with the whole history of Britain during the period, political as well as ecclesiastical, social as well as intellectual, but the key explanation for the trajectory was identified by both C. S. Lewis and Ronald Knox. The two men pointed out that the enthusiasm for the translation of 1611 rose and fell with the growth and decay of Romantic sensibility.[109] A "taste for the primitive and the passionate," as Lewis called it, flourished in Britain during the nineteenth and much of the twentieth centuries, but was superseded in the later twentieth century by other attitudes that have been variously labelled "expressivist," "postmodernist," or simply "anti-Romantic." The Authorized Version, fortified by the preferences of the times, could withstand the call for greater accuracy in the nineteenth century but not the challenge of more intelligible versions in the twentieth. This cultural factor, more than any other, explains the altering fortunes of the translation of 1611. The reputation of the King James Bible in Britain was hugely but temporarily enhanced by Romantic feeling.

Bibliography

Ballard, Frank. *Which Bible to Read—Revised or "Authorised"?* 2nd ed. London: H. R. Allenson, 1898.

Beard, John R. *A Revised English Bible the Want of the Church and the Demand of the Age.* London: E. T. Whitfield, 1857.

Beet, Joseph Agar. "The Revised Version of the New Testament." *Expositor*, August 1881, 92–110.

Blaikie, James. *The English Bible & Its Story: Its Growth, Its Translators & Their Associations.* London: Seeley, Service, 1928.

Blair, Tony. *A Journey.* London: Hutchinson, 2010.

Blunt, David. *Which Bible Version: Does It Really Matter?* London: Trinitarian Bible Society, 2007.

Bradlaugh, Charles. *The Bible: What Is It?* London: Austin, 1870.

British Museum Bible Exhibition 1911: Guide to the Manuscripts and Printed Books Exhibited in Celebration of the Tercentenary of the Authorised Version. London: British Museum, 1911.

Bruce, F. F. *The English Bible: A History of Translations.* London: Lutterworth, 1961.

Burgon, John W. *The Revision Revised.* London: John Murray, 1883.

Cadoux, C. J. "The Revised Version and After." In *The Bible in Its Ancient and English Versions*, edited by Henry Wheeler Robinson, 236–66. Oxford: Clarendon, 1940.

Campbell, Gordon. *Bible: The Story of the King James Bible, 1611–2011.* New York: Oxford University Press, 2010.

Canton, William. *The Bible and the Anglo-Saxon People.* London: J. M. Dent & Sons, 1914.

———. *A History of the British and Foreign Bible Society.* 5 vols. London: John Murray, 1904.

Carpenter, J. Estlin. *The Bible in the Nineteenth Century.* London: Longmans, Green, 1903.

Coleman, Roger. *New Light and Truth: The Making of the Revised English Bible.* Oxford: Oxford University Press, 1989.

Colley, Linda. *Britons: Forging the Nation, 1707–1837.* New Haven, Conn.: Yale University Press, 1992.

Craik, Henry. *Hints and Suggestions on the Proposed Revision of our English Bible.* London: Bagster and Sons, 1860.

Daniell, David. *The Bible in English: Its History and Influence.* New Haven, Conn.: Yale University Press, 2003.

————. *William Tyndale: A Biography.* New Haven, Conn.: Yale University Press, 1994.

Doddridge, Philip. *The Family Expositor.* 6 vols. London: John Wilson, 1739–1756.

Drane, John. "Bible Use in the Scottish Churches." In *Prospects for Scotland: Report of the 1984 Census of the Churches,* by Peter Brierley and Fergus Macdonald, 26–29. Bromley, Kent: MarcEurope, 1985.

Ellicott, C. J. "The Revision of the New Testament: Its Origins, Method and Characteristics." *Baptist Magazine,* July 1881, 298–308.

Faber, Frederick W. *The Life of S. Francis of Assisi.* London, 1853.

Frazer, James G. *Passages of the Bible Chosen for their Literary Beauty and Interest.* London: Adam and Charles Black, 1895.

Hemphill, Samuel. *A History of the Revised Version of the New Testament.* London: Elliot Stock, 1906.

Herbert, A. S. *Historical Catalogue of Printed Editions of the English Bible, 1525–1961.* London: British and Foreign Bible Society, 1968.

Hoare, Henry W. *The Evolution of the English Bible.* London: John Murray, 1901.

The Holy Bible, containing the Old and New Testaments, with Original Notes... by the Rev. Thomas Scott. 4 vols. London: Bellamy and Robarts, 1788–1792.

The Holy Bible Two-Version Edition. Oxford: Oxford University Press, 1899.

Howsam, Leslie. *Cheap Bibles: Nineteenth-Century Publishing and the British and Foreign Bible Society.* Cambridge: Cambridge University Press, 1991.

Irving, Edward. *Babylon and Infidelity Foredoomed of God: A Discourse on the Prophecies of Daniel and the Apocalypse which Relate to these Latter Times, and until the Second Advent.* 2 vols. Glasgow: for Chalmers and Collins, 1826.

Knox, Ronald A. *On Englishing the Bible.* London: Burns Oates, 1949.

[Laurence, Richard]. *Remarks upon the Critical Principles and the Practical Application of those Principles adopted by Writers who have at Various Periods recommended a New Translation of the Bible as Expedient and Necessary.* Oxford: by W. Baxter for J. Parker, 1820.

Lewis, C. S. *The Literary Impact of the Authorized Version.* London: Athlone, 1950.

Lewis, John. *A Complete History of the Several Translations of the Holy Bible and New Testament into English both in Manuscript and in Print.* First printed 1731. 3rd ed. London: W. Baynes, 1818.

Lightfoot, J. B. *On a Fresh Revision of the English New Testament*. London: Macmillan, 1871.

Martin, Roger H. *Evangelicals United: Ecumenical Stirrings in Pre-Victorian Britain, 1795–1830*. Metuchen, N.J.: Scarecrow, 1983.

Moulton, W. F. *The History of the English Bible*. 5th ed. London: Charles H. Kelly, 1911.

Muir, William. *Our Grand Old Bible*. London: Morgan and Scott, 1911.

Newth, Samuel. *Lectures on Bible Revision*. London: Hodder & Stoughton, 1881.

Nineham, Dennis, ed. *The New English Bible Reviewed*. London: Epworth, 1965.

Norton, David. *A History of the English Bible as Literature*. Cambridge: Cambridge University Press, 2000.

Pope, Hugh. *English Versions of the Bible*. St. Louis, Mo.: B. Herder, 1952.

"The Revised English New Testament." *Church Quarterly Review*, July 1881, 522–39.

Spurgeon, Charles Haddon. Preface to *The English Bible: History of the Translation of the Holy Scriptures into the English Tongue with Specimens of the Old English Versions*, by Hannah C. Conant, xi–xv. London: Arthur Hall, Virtue, 1859.

Stuart, James. "The Revised Bible." *Baptist Magazine*, July 1885, 316–23.

Thuesen, Peter J. *In Discordance with the Scriptures: American Protestant Battles over Translating the Bible*. New York: Oxford University Press, 1999.

Todd, Henry. *A Vindication of our Authorised Translation and Translators of the Bible*. London: F. and J. Rivington, 1819.

Weigle, Luther A., and C. F. D. Moule. "English Versions since 1611." In *The Cambridge History of the Bible: The West from the Reformation to the Present Day*, edited by S. L. Greenslade, 361–82. Cambridge: Cambridge University Press, 1963.

Wilson, Derek. *The People and the Book: The Revolutionary Impact of the English Bible, 1380–1611*. London: Barrie & Jenkins, 1976.

Four

THE KING JAMES VERSION AT 300 IN AMERICA
"The Most Democratic Book in the World"

Mark Noll

*I*n 1911 the collective leadership of the English-speaking world stood at attention to salute the King James Version of the Bible (KJV). The president, the king, the prime minister, and other statesmen of the first rank led a great chorus of praise for the literary, political, ethical, and religious virtues of what their contemporaries were hailing as "the greatest book in the English language";[1] the most vital book in the world";[2] and "the chief classic of our English language and literature."[3]

This year, in 2011, we are witnessing well-publicized events and the publication of numerous books about the origins and long-term influence of the KJV, but not the same concentrated attention from the same lofty summits of culture and society. Queen Elizabeth did devote part of her 2010 Christmas broadcast to praising the KJV as "a masterpiece of English prose" and as providing "the most widely recognised and beautiful description of the birth of Jesus Christ."[4] Early in January an op-ed piece in the *New York Times* also commended the KJV for how "it captures and preserves the unavoidable rhythms of good English" and how its enduring popularity as a classic of the language falsifies what T. S. Eliot and C. S. Lewis asserted about the KJV's influence resting on its religious rather than its aesthetic character.[5] Yet for the most part, celebrations of the King James Version in 2011 seem to have been left to academics and aficionados. It was far otherwise a century ago.

This chapter begins with a brief attempt to situate the 1911 celebrations of the KJV in the general history of Scripture in broader American history. It then canvasses the main points that were emphasized in the many speeches and publications that commemorated the tercentenary. It pauses for more extensive examination of the major speeches on the KJV that were delivered by Theodore Roosevelt, Woodrow Wilson, and William Jennings Bryan in the spring of 1911. The chapter ends by examining the relatively few commentators who directly addressed the relationship of the KJV as a cultural artifact to its character as a Christian book. My own reflections probe connections between the prevalence of the KJV and the problems of biblical civil religion, manic biblical politics, and populist anti-intellectual biblicism. The overall purpose of the chapter is to discern how the prominence of the King James Version in American history, as illustrated at the 300th anniversary, both advanced and retarded the cause of Christianity.

The Bible in American History

By the first decade of the twentieth century, the Bible occupied a prominent but rapidly shifting place in American society and culture. On the one hand, it remained an indispensable reference point for the nation's churches and a much-noted factor in a national culture that still reflected the strong imprint of its dissenting Protestant foundations. On the other hand, it was well on the way to losing the preeminent place that for the first two-thirds of the nineteenth century it had enjoyed in the nation's law, public policy, scholarship, and even theology. A comparison with the era of the Civil War illustrates the indecisive role that Scripture had come to play by early in the twentieth century.

At the close of the Civil War in 1865, American civilization to a striking degree was a Bible civilization.[6] Nowhere in the world did such an extensive presence of the Christian Scriptures exert such a broad impact on such a substantial portion of a national population as in the United States. A sharp difference of opinion over whether Scripture permitted the institution of slavery had contributed substantially to the antagonism that brought on the conflict; a more general confidence of righteous biblical standing, in both the North and the South, justified all-out commitment to the war effort. In particular, the belief among Confederates that the Bible, rightly interpreted, sanctioned their cause may have extended the war a year or more past the time when rational assessment revealed the futility of fighting on. The climactic public statement about the meaning of the war was delivered on March 4, 1865, when in his Second Inaugural Address Abraham Lincoln, who was not even the member of a church, quoted the King James Version four strategic times in that very short speech. Biblical allusions or quotations had informed many of the era's landmark expressions, like Lincoln's own early declaration in 1858 (quoting Matthew 12) that a "house divided" could not remain intact, or Julia Ward Howe's "Mine Eyes Have Seen the Glory of the Coming of the Lord," the lines of which contained an average of more than one biblical allusion each. For combatants, the American Bible Society and kindred Northern philanthropies provided 5 million copies of the Bible or New Testament, or more than one copy each, to Federal military personnel. The South, despite its few printing presses and the boycott on trade enforced by the North, still managed to secure hundreds of thousands of Bibles for its armies, where the Scriptures had a measurably stronger impact than among their better-supplied Northern counterparts.

The character of the nation's Bible civilization in 1865 must be stated precisely. It was not that all Americans were regular Bible readers or that even a majority of citizens accorded serious attention to Scripture. The crucial point is that in a society with a very thin federal government, except for war mobilization itself, with neither mass communication nor mass entertainment nor mass national merchandising, no serious intellectual or institutional competition to the Christian churches, and no national organizations that matched the reach of religious voluntary societies—in such a setting, Bible-dependent ideologies, Bible-referenced language, Bible-derived moral categories, and Bible-exalting institutions were, compared to all other centers of value, demonstrably ascendant.

Yet this situation changed rapidly after the end of the war. Developments in many spheres undermined the once universal preeminence of Scripture and hence of the KJV. Over the course of the nineteenth century, state courts had chipped away at the notion that Scripture contributed foundationally to the common law. Not only had efforts at national legislation failed to enshrine daily Bible readings in tax-supported schools, but Catholics, Jews, and secularists were making steady progress at ending the practice in a growing number of localities. The role of Scripture in the nation's intellectual life was being complicated by intensifying debates over biblical higher criticism and heightened self-confidence in the superiority of scientific knowledge over scriptural knowledge. Major national developments like the end of Reconstruction, the so-called "redemption" of the white South, and the burgeoning of industry took place with little of the scriptural assessment that had attended parallel developments in the antebellum era. Biblical usage among Catholics who had never patronized the KJV was becoming ever more prominent.

In the early twentieth century, uneasiness about the future of the King James Version added to the more general uncertainty about the place of the Bible. The introduction of well-publicized revisions of the KJV suggested that perhaps the reign of this once hegemonic translation was coming to an end. To be sure, the five new editions (not reprintings) of the Bible published in 1911 were all either the KJV or the KJV with other versions in parallel format. But for the years 1908 to 1914, the publishing record revealed more pluralism in favored texts than had formerly been the norm. In that seven-year period, twenty-two of the thirty-nine new Bible editions were the KJV, but eight were the American Standard Version of 1901, one was this version with its British cousin the English Revised Version, and seven others included Catholic, Jewish, and alternative Protestant translations.[7] For its part, the American Bible Society continued its prodigious output of Bibles and New Testaments, with a total of almost 7 million for the two years from mid-1910 to mid-1912, or one for every thirteen Americans.[8] But since some of that total was made up of American Standard Versions, it was not certain that even the Bible Society would continue its historical commitment to the KJV.

The rapidly changing place of Scripture was reflected strongly among the nation's Protestants, whose patronage had made this translation a cornerstone of American civilization. American Protestants had always been fractious and contentious, but in the early years of the century internal fault lines were becoming permanent fissures. Examples from 1911 are telling. In that year, Oxford University Press released a special tercentenary edition of the Scofield Reference Bible that had appeared for the first time only two years before. Also in 1911, Francis Grimké, a prominent African American Presbyterian minister in Washington, D.C., continued his ministry that combined theological conservatism with advanced views on race. His speaking in 1911 included a memorable address entitled "The Paramount Importance of Character," almost half of which quoted Scripture to define "the true standard by which to estimate individuals and races."[9] Walter Rauschenbusch in 1911 was struggling to find time to complete a book that would be published the following year as *Christianizing the Social Order*. His time was constrained because of demands resulting from the 1907 publication of *Christianity and the Social Crisis*. In both books extensive quotation from especially the Old Testament provided Rauschenbusch with the substance of his appeal for a social gospel.[10] Also in 1911 the pamphlet series entitled *The Fundamentals: A Testimony to the Truth* entered its second year. Of the twenty-five articles that made up the first four numbers of this series, fifteen were devoted to defending traditional Protestant attitudes toward Scripture.[11]

In 1911 the Bible, in other words, remained prominently central for Protestants; for each of these examples, most of the citations, quotations, and allusions were to the King James Version. But the rough Protestant consensus that had once prevailed about the general message of Scripture was no more. The Scofield Bible promoted a conservative biblicism and engagement with the eschatological future. Francis Grimké also promoted a conservative biblicism but with intense social engagement in the here and now. Walter Rauschenbusch practiced a modern biblicism with intense social engagement. And *The Fundamentals* advocated a conservative biblicism with no social engagement required.

The overall picture in 1911, therefore, was of a national landscape where Scripture, still most often in the shape of the KJV, remained very much alive. Yet it was also a landscape in which common Protestant attachment to the KJV hid gaping fissures within the Protestant world, and where the Protestant world was rapidly losing the authority it had once enjoyed in directing the life of the nation. Against this backdrop took place an extraordinary range of enthusiastic celebrations of the KJV that were as fervent in their adulation of this ancient text as they were oblivious to the parlous character of Scripture in American life of the era.

Celebrating the King James Version

In 1911 the three main celebrations of the King James Version took place in London, New York, and Chicago, but they were joined by a host of less elaborate observances and a flurry of publications from both religious and secular sources.[12] The first event, which was extensively covered in the American press, took place in London, at the Royal Albert Hall on Wednesday, March 29.[13] It featured representatives from many churches, public addresses by the British prime minister Herbert Asquith and the American ambassador Whitelaw Reid, and also a public reading of letters from President William Howard Taft and King George V. The one discordant note on this grand occasion was an intervention by suffragettes who unfurled a banner urging "Justice for Women" when the prime minister arose to speak.[14] But the rest of the ceremony rode a high wave of exaltation, as illustrated by Ambassador Reid's contention that the Bible "has furnished, and furnishes, the strongest and most indestructible bond for the present practical unity in aims and aspirations of the great English-speaking family of nations which, as has been so often said, occupies over one-fourth of the inhabitable surface of the globe, and governs nearly one-third of its inhabitants. (Cheers)."[15]

The exultant mood was sustained at a mass meeting in New York's Carnegie Hall on Tuesday, April 25. This gathering included the singing of "How Firm a Foundation"; a reading from a 1611 edition of the King James Version owned by the American Bible Society; participation by leaders of Episcopal, Dutch Reformed, and Quaker churches; a presentation by Secretary of State John W. Foster, who read the same letter from President Taft that was presented in London; and a speech by British Ambassador James Bryce, who read King George's earlier response to President Taft's letter and then spoke himself about the cultural bonds between the United States and Britain that had been sustained by common use of the KJV.[16]

The next week in Chicago, five days of celebration began on Sunday, April 30, when more than one thousand churches held individual or union services; they concluded with a mass rally at Orchestra Hall on Thursday, May 4. The Sunday gatherings were addressed by luminaries, including the Oak Park Congregationalist minister W. E. Barton, who would later write a much-read book on the religion of Abraham Lincoln, and the University of Chicago theologian Shailer Mathews, who was renowned as one of the nation's leading modernist theologians. Elsewhere in Chicago tributes rained down, including one from the rabbi of Chicago's Israel Temple.[17] The Thursday climax of Chicago-area celebrations featured choruses from Haydn's "Creation," Mendelssohn's "Elijah," and Handel's "Messiah"; a reading from a 1611 KJV normally held "under lock and key" at the Newberry Library; and a series of speeches ending with an address by William Jennings Bryan.[18]

Themes that would be developed extensively in the American celebrations were adumbrated first in early March by the formal letters from President William Howard Taft and King George V. Taft declared that the King James Version was "the Bible of our American forefathers. Its classic English has given shape to American literature. Its spirit has influenced American ideals in life and laws and government." The same sentiment moved King George V, who in his joint statement with President Taft observed that "the version which bears King James's name is so clearly interwoven in the history of British and American life that it is right we should thank God for it together."[19] The day after these statements were read at the Carnegie Hall celebration, the *New York Times* commented editorially that, while it probably was time to move on to newer, more reliable translations of Scripture, nonetheless, the then-300-year-old version still deserved to be considered "the bud of the herb of civilization, the spring of a new day, the trumpet of a prophecy."[20]

Encomia that echoed the president and the king came from near and far. They sounded a great deal like much commentary of our own day that praises the literary excellence of the KJV, notes its stimulus for literature, and heralds its broad cultural impact. A typical report called the KJV "the foundation of our civilisation and our religion" and claimed that "if we were to take the Bible out of the world we would destroy music, art, and literature."[21]

As has been the case since the early nineteenth century, much tercentenary comment also hymned the King James Version for its beneficent effects on the English language and English literature. The catalogue of authors, scientists, politicians, and religious figures specified as decisively influenced by this Bible was very extensive, including as only a partial list John Bunyan, Thomas Carlyle, James Clark-Maxwell, Samuel Taylor Coleridge, Charles Dickens, Michael Faraday, W. E. Gladstone, Thomas Ken, Abraham Lincoln, John Locke, Thomas Babington Macaulay, the geologist Hugh Miller, John Milton, Isaac Newton, John Ruskin, Walter Scott, the Earl of Shaftesbury, Alfred Lord Tennyson, Walt Whitman, and William Wilberforce.[22] Then, as now, pundits emptied the treasure chest of their own vocabularies to praise the KJV for its contribution to the language: it was "the great clearing-house of idea and phrase, of story and figure, of thought literal and symbolic, the comrade of all ranks of mind from humblest to highest";[23] "the noblest monument of the English language in the time of its greatest perfection and vigor";[24] "the chief classic of our English language and literature";[25] and "the most noble, beautiful, and wonderful book which the world holds to-day."[26] Others praised "the simplicity, vigor, clarity and beauty of its style . . . its unequalled perfection merely as a literary product,"[27] "its vast simplicity and moving eloquence,"[28] and concluded that "the Bible has . . . been an untold formative power to mold the English language itself into that 'incommunicable simplicity' which is its strength and beauty."[29] In short, when considering the language and literature, "There is but one sun in the firmament, though there may be a moon (or moons) and galaxies of stars."[30]

Occasionally authors paused in this floodtide of praise for nuance. One commentator gave William Tyndale credit for "the peculiar genius . . . the mingled tenderness and majesty, the Saxon simplicity—the preternatural grandeur" of the King James Version.[31] Another pointed out the curious fact, which few others addressed, that "the language of the Authorized Version was more often used in the common writing and speaking of the nineteenth century than in either the seventeenth or eighteenth centuries."[32] But mostly the accolades for the KJV were an unending recital of literary and linguistic virtues.

Many of those who spoke in 1911 followed Ambassador Bryce in heralding the KJV for preserving the cultural unity of Britain and America. One account conceded that King James' insistence on a version without marginal notes came "from a selfish purpose," but also averred that the result was "a Bible for all classes, binding the whole Protestant world together by a tie which has withstood the political and religious wars and strifes throughout the generations that have followed."[33] Not surprisingly, some of the commentary got carried away, as when one report on the Albert Hall celebration stated that separate languages would certainly have developed on the two sides of the Atlantic were it not for "the fact that until within recent years during all those three centuries every child in England and America heard the King James translation of the Bible read aloud daily."[34]

Description of the King James Version's role in uniting the English-speaking people flowed naturally into describing the translation's role in promoting political ideals. This theme, which Woodrow Wilson would stress in his May speech, appeared in many accounts, with a Methodist providing one of the clearest: "For the English-speaking peoples [the KJV] is the fountainhead and perpetual spring of our common laws and free institutions. Tyranny, oppression and class privilege cannot survive where the principles of the Bible are imbibed; and not a little of the history of liberty among English-speaking peoples is directly due to the fact that the inspiring sentences of this book have been familiar to the ears and understanding of the common people."[35] An author in Canada contended that the history of the KJV was so "interwoven with the national history of freedom and independence and personal religion" that "it is to us of the English race not only the Word of God, but also and essentially our National Book."[36] To the south of Canada, the Bible more directly was "the most precious possession brought to the New World by the English settlers who laid the foundation of the American commonwealth."[37] Several commentators made special reference to Abraham Lincoln's adept use of the KJV, with one even applying to him the epithet of John Wesley, that Lincoln "was essentially a man of one book—the Bible."[38]

To sharpen this account of the King James Version's place in general political history, several spoke also of the particular bond that the translation had created between the United States and Britain. Prime Minister Asquith in his London address was most direct. He proclaimed that a "solemn pact" to forever outlaw war between the two nations would be especially fitting in the tercentennial year. His reasoning skipped over the events of 1776 and 1812, as well as the hostilities that nearly broke out in 1862 after the United States navy took two Confederate diplomats off the British packet ship *Trent*. But it was a passionate statement nonetheless: "War between English speaking people would not only be a crime against civilization but an unforgivable breach of those new commandments which are enshrined and consecrated in the New Testament upon which both nations have been bred."[39]

With such a chorus of praise for the KJV, but with also the awareness that the celebrations were in honor of a text now three hundred years old, it is not surprising that some observers reflected on the possibility of a newer version. A particularly interesting article by Edgar J. Goodspeed, who later produced a memorable translation of the New Testament, noted the King James Version's inferior Greek text, its difficulties in rendering tenses and proper names, and some outright errors. Yet Goodspeed was also highly appreciative of the translation: "Not only is it an English classic, but it has served well the religious needs of ten generations of readers and hearers."[40]

A professor from Brown University was confident that the American Standard Version of 1901 would soon replace the KJV since the new revision was "commended by Protestant leaders of all shades of belief; adopted by the American Bible Society; by colleges, theological seminaries, and training schools; read in multitudes of pulpits of all denominations; it seems destined to become the 'standard' Bible of all American Protestants."[41] But an Amherst academic disagreed because of what he called "the myopic, groping translation of the Revised Version."[42] The commentator from Canada, J. Paterson Smyth, conceded that many factors were working in favor of recent attempts to revise the KJV, but he was a better prophet as he explained why the new translations would not carry the day: "The old version holds the ground not only by the familiarity of its phrases but by its wonderful charm. It is universally accepted as a literary masterpiece, as the noblest and most beautiful book in the world."[43]

Against this torrent of praise, there were very few objections. An occasional voice reminded readers of the inadequate Greek and Hebrew texts upon which the KJV was based.[44] A local newspaper objected mildly by suggesting that social and political institutions of the English-speaking world actually owed more to ancient German and Saxon traditions than to the KJV.[45] But with one exception, systematic reservations about the version were hard to find in 1911.

The one exception was commentary from aggrieved Roman Catholics who considered the hoopla over the KJV a misreading of history and an offense to their church. Some of this wounded opinion may have been responding to Protestant commentary about Catholicism and Catholic translations included in commendations for the KJV. Many Protestant accounts, for example, quoted the comments of Frederick Faber, the convert to Catholicism best known for his hymn, "Faith of Our Fathers." Faber had once written at length about "the uncommon beauty and marvelous English of the Protestant Bible" and contended that "in the length and breadth of the land there is not a Protestant with one spark of religiousness about him whose spiritual biography is not in his Saxon Bible." But some who lauded the KJV also included Faber's conclusion that the version was "one of the greatest strongholds of heresy in this country. . . . It is part of the national mind, and the anchor of the national seriousness. Nay, it is worshipped with a positive idolatry, in extenuation of whose fanaticism its intrinsic beauty pleads availingly with the scholar."[46]

Several commendations of the version paused for a few words on the Catholic translations published before the KJV, the New Testament appearing at Rheims in 1582 and the Old Testament at Douai in 1609. They gave occasional credit to the Catholic versions for supplying words to the KJV translators like "impenitent" (Romans 2:5) and "propitiation" (Romans 3:25).[47] One or two even opined that with the Challoner revision of the Douai-Rheims Bible, English translations were moving closer together and so coming to show "that with the march of centuries men of diverse faiths are coming more and more to emphasize their common ties as befitteth brotherhood."[48] Most Protestant commentary, however, complained about these Catholic translations. They were comprehensively flawed, one author wrote, for promoting a false canon, working from a substandard text, and producing a corrupt version.[49] Many complained about the Latinized quality of Douai-Rheims English. Others criticized the prefaces and notes that merely "propagated the dogmas of Popery" and offered "a mass of bigotry, sophistry and unfairness."[50]

Catholic responses to the KJV celebrations were even harsher. American Catholic periodicals relied on English Catholic sources for some of their criticism, which included the prediction that, since Protestant higher critics were eviscerating the supernatural realities of Scripture, the Bible might "survive, indeed, for the non-Catholic, but only as Homer survives, a classic collection of beautiful myths and legends, with little appeal to the spirit and no authority over heart and intellect."[51]

The Jesuit periodical *America* summarized a blast from the Liverpool *Catholic Times* that described how Wycliffe "plagiarized" earlier Catholic texts and tried to "pervert the Bible," how Wycliffe's Bible unleashed "anarchy and communism preached by the Lollards," how Tyndale's Bible was an English "corruption from a badly translated German one," and how Tyndale filled his margins with "most abusive and inflammatory notes assailing all the sacred teachings and the worship of the Catholic Faith." This summary of early Protestant versions was much different than the hagiography coming from Protestants: "Tyndale was not burnt at the stake for anything to do with religion, but for fomenting by his writings . . . political turmoil and fanaticism against the authorities of Church and State." This same critique did concede that although Protestant translators had incited "revolutionary horrors," nonetheless the KJV "certainly deserved the eulogiums bestowed upon it as to its pure and elegant English language and style." But, of course, those superior qualities resulted from heavy dependence upon the Rheims translation. In sum, to the Catholic Church "alone we owe the bible-today, and from her pulpit all who attend, both Catholic and Protestant will hear to their great spiritual profit the doctrines of the bible and the preaching of Christ crucified."[52]

Another Catholic account of biblical translation appeared in a pamphlet by the Right Reverend Henry Graham (1874–1959), who began life as a Church of Scotland minister but then converted and eventually became a Catholic bishop. It was published in the United States in April 1911 under the title, *Where We Got the Bible: Our Debt to the Catholic Church*. The foreword by J. M. M. Charleson of Pasadena, California, pointed to the "almost unanimous recognition of the immense debt which the world owes to the Catholic Church for the gift of Sacred Scriptures." The American went on that "as the dust and darkness of the 'Reformation' fade away before the growing light of truth, people are coming to understand better . . . the partial Bible that was issued by the Reformers, as if it were the complete and genuine Word of God." As perhaps in recognition of the celebrations underway as he issued the pamphlet, Mr. Charleson also noted that "the general crowd is still largely under the influence of the falsehoods of the past three hundred years, their understanding darkened, and their passions periodically roused by well-meant, perhaps, but really calumnious, writings and mob-oratory."[53] The pamphlet itself explained that the Catholic Church was responsible for the existence and preservation of the Bible, that the church was its best protector, that the self-identified champions of the Bible in Britain, America, and Germany actually undermined it, and that the church opposed individual inter-pretation because such interpretation never brought certainty but only division and strife.

The reprise of ancient Catholic-Protestant disputation was an anom-aly in the great outpouring of commendation that marked American cel-ebrations of the KJV tercentenary. Yet as historically informative and factually accurate as many of the anniversary pronouncements were, only a few commentators paused to consider in any detail broader ques-tions about what they were celebrating.

Latent in the effusive commentary was a conundrum, especially for those who thought of Scripture both as God's revealed word and as a fixture of American culture. The conundrum resulted from the dual role played by the King James Version as a mainstay of Protestant tradition and a central element in the American imagination. Because Protestant traditions had flourished in the American environment and because Protestants had done so much to shape that environment, the one preeminent Protestant Bible came to exist as an omnipresent cul-tural force. As a result, biblical vocabulary, biblical images, and biblical literary styles exerted a powerful sway in culture at large. In fact, they could be used with great effect by Americans who deliberately subverted the moral universe that the vocabulary, images, and literary styles had been created to serve.

Even more problematic could be the eager use of biblical words, images, and styles by those who saw themselves aligned with the moral substratum underlying the text of the King James Version. The United States in which the KJV enjoyed a ubiquitous presence was always sus-ceptible to civil religion, it regularly witnessed manic political combat, and it was the scene of much anti-intellectual populism. The preemi-nence of this particular version in this particular nation created the fol-lowing conundrum: the extraordinary deference to the KJV monopoly meant that this one biblical text served Americans splendidly as a source for Christian doctrine, for reproof, for correction, and for instruction in righteousness, and that it also thoroughly furnished many Americans unto good works in society. Yet at the same time, this particular version in this particular nation fed a biblical civil religion that subordinated God to Caesar, enabled a manic rhetoric that unleashed an out-of-control biblicism, and stoked an anti-intellectual populism that substituted biblicism for thought.

Roosevelt, Wilson, and Bryan

The esteem in which the King James Version was held, as well as problems related to that esteem, were revealed sharply by the major addresses that Theodore Roosevelt, William Jennings Bryan, and Woodrow Wilson delivered to commemorate the KJV. The first of the speeches was given by Theodore Roosevelt on March 26 as the centerpiece of a lecture series at Pacific Theological Seminary in Berkeley, California. As famed leader of the "Rough Riders" during the Spanish-American War, governor of New York, and then president of the United States from 1901 to 1909, Roosevelt was probably the nation's most celebrated public figure. Next came the speech on May 4 in Chicago by William Jennings Bryan, the three-time presidential candidate of the Democratic Party (1896, 1900, 1908) and the era's most widely traveled popular speaker. Only three days later, the sitting governor of New Jersey added his perspective before a great crowd of 12,000 in Denver. Woodrow Wilson, who served as president of Princeton University from 1902 to 1910, had already gained a nationwide reputation for his efforts as a progressive reforming governor. His Denver speech was part of a national tour to explore the possibilities of a presidential run.

The next year Wilson did secure the Democratic Party's nomination for president and was vigorously supported in the fall campaign of 1912 by Bryan. Wilson won the election in large part because Theodore Roosevelt mounted a third-party campaign to regain the White House from William Howard Taft, who had served as Roosevelt's secretary of war and was his handpicked successor as the Republicans' presidential nominee in 1908. After Wilson was elected, he appointed Bryan as his secretary of state.

In the speeches from 1911, Roosevelt and Wilson hailed the King James Version for its prominent role in shaping America's democratic civilization; Bryan also mentioned that theme, but stressed even more the Bible's character as Christian revelation. The speeches by Roosevelt and Wilson were classics of American civil religion; Bryan's address was an exemplary instance of populist biblicism.

To Roosevelt, the KJV was "the book to which our people owe infinitely the greater part of their store of ethics, infinitely the greater part of their knowledge of how to apply that store to the needs of our everyday life." As a good historian, the former president took time to show how much the KJV used earlier translations, but he was also characteristically dramatic in what he wanted to say about this one version: "No other book of any kind ever written in English—perhaps no other book ever written in any other tongue—has ever so affected the whole life of a people as this authorized version of the Scriptures has affected the life of the English-speaking peoples." Roosevelt based his conclusion less on specific Christian reasoning than on broad humanitarian appeal. He urged his auditors to study the Bible, not necessarily "as an inspired book," but as an essential volume for every person "who seeks after a high and useful life."[54]

What could readers derive from reading the King James Version? In answering this question, Roosevelt quoted from "the great scientist Huxley," who had called it "the Magna Charta of the poor and the oppressed . . . the most democratic book in the world." To Roosevelt, the democracy that Bible reading encouraged was a robustly moral enterprise: "I ask you men and women to treat the Bible in the only way in which it can be treated if benefit is to be obtained from it, and that is, as a guide to conduct." Roosevelt readily conceded that the Bible's content was important for dogma and that its language was important aesthetically. But, for him, all other purposes fell far short of the ethical, and so he closed with these words:

> Of course if you read it only for aesthetical purposes, if you read it without thought of following its ethical teachings, then you are apt to do but little good to your fellow-men; for if you regard the reading of it as an intellectual diversion only, and, above all, if you regard this reading simply as an outward token of Sunday respectability, small will be the good that you yourself get from it. Our success in striving to help our fellow-men, and therefore to help ourselves, depends largely upon our success as we strive, with whatever shortcomings, with whatever failures, to lead our lives in accordance with the great ethical principles laid down in the life of Christ, and in the New Testament writings which seek to expound and apply his teachings.[55]

Woodrow Wilson's speech to the Denver throng was just as forthright. As Wilson summarized matters to a correspondent immediately afterwards: "I spoke on the Bible and Progress, and the great audience moved me deeply. The Bible (with its individual value of the human soul[)] is undoubtedly the book that has made democracy and been the source of all progress."[56] To Wilson, as to Roosevelt, the King James Version inculcated a particular kind of morality—it had revealed "men unto themselves, not as creatures in bondage" but as "distinct moral agent[s]." And so he could argue that "not a little of the history of liberty lies in the circumstance that the moving sentences of this book were made familiar to the ears and the understanding of those peoples who have led mankind in exhibiting the forms of government and the impulses of reform which have made for freedom and for self-government among mankind."[57]

What Wilson called "the people's book of revelation" was for him a foundation of American democracy but also a judge of it. In words very similar to what Roosevelt told his California audience—that America's greatness lay not in its wealth but in its ideals[58]—Wilson exalted the Bible as the source of what distinguished the United States in the world: "We do not judge progress by material standards. America is not ahead of the other nations of the world because she is rich. Nothing makes America great except her thoughts, except her ideals, except her acceptance of those standards of judgment which are written large upon these pages of revelation." At the end of his address, Wilson, like Roosevelt, conflated what he wanted to say about the Bible as a general guide for American civilization and his own stance as a Christian reader of the Scriptures:

> America was born a Christian nation. America was born to exemplify that devotion to the elements of righteousness which are derived from the revelations of Holy Scripture.
>
> Ladies and gentlemen, I have a very simple thing to ask of you. I ask of every man and woman in this audience that from this night on they will realize that part of the destiny of America lies in their daily perusal of this great book of revelations—that if they would see America free and pure they will make their own spirits free and pure by this baptism of the Holy Scripture.[59]

Roosevelt and Wilson were making bold claims for the influence of the King James Version on American life. They, along with many others in 1911, expressed a common awareness that the KJV had occupied a large place at the center of American public life so long as there had been an American public life. To them, this one version of the Scriptures was a taproot of American democracy and a fountain of American ideals. What remained after the Bible's service to democracy and American ideals, what it might mean for Scripture to challenge democracy or American ideals, were subjects they did not address.

The trajectory of Bryan's speech differed considerably.[60] Unlike Roosevelt and Wilson, Bryan did speak much about the Bible's character as a primarily spiritual book. In the combative style for which his stump-speaking was known, Bryan began by stating that "atheists and materialists have assailed the Bible at every point," including its "facts . . . prophesies . . . account which it gives of creation . . . miracles." In response, Bryan reminded his listeners of Elijah's challenge to the priests of Baal and then proposed "a Bible test." There could be, he averred, no better time for such a contest than when "we are celebrating the three hundredth anniversary of the King James translation." And so Bryan posed the question that structured his speech: "Is the Bible the work of man or is it an inspired book?"[61]

Bryan began his answer by acknowledging that Scripture came from only "a single race" that inhabited only a tiny plot of land and knew only antiquated technologies—no "printing presses" or "the learning of the schools." Yet from such a limited, obscure location came the Bible, whose "characters grapple with every problem that confronts mankind, from the creation of the world to eternal life beyond the tomb." From this same unpropitious place, moreover, came also "the foundation of our statute law" (the Ten Commandments), "the rules for spiritual growth" (the Sermon on the Mount), the world's best "code of morality," and—above all—"the story of him who is the growing figure of all time, whom the world is accepting as Saviour and as the perfect example." Bryan expanded his case by arguing that humankind had advanced in every domain of life "except in the line of character-building." In that one vital area, however, "wherever the moral standard is being lifted up . . . the improvement is traceable to the Bible and to the influence of the God and Christ of whom the Bible tells."

Up to a point, Bryan sounded like Wilson and Roosevelt in praising Scripture for its utilitarian value—"back of the progress of the present day is the code of morals that Christ proclaimed." But then he went further for an explicit theological claim of the sort the others did not make: "And back of that code of morals is the divine character of him who is both Son of God and Saviour of Mankind." Bryan closed his address by contrasting the stance of the Bible-believing Christian with "the followers of

Buddha . . . the followers of the Arab prophet . . . the followers of Confucius . . . the materialist . . . the atheist." Against this array of alternatives, Bryan boldly offered his response: "To the doubts and 'I don't knows' of the agnostic, the Christian, Bible in hand, answers: 'I believe.'"

While Bryan echoed some of the ethical injunctions of Roosevelt and some of the political emphases of Wilson, his main points were not only more directly religious, but also more explicitly Christian. They were also more characteristically populist. While neither Wilson nor Roosevelt delivered an academic address, both took some time for their popular audiences to sketch a little history and elaborate nuances of their arguments. Bryan did not.

In addition to what these three statesmen said about the Bible on the occasion of the KJV tercentenary, it is helpful for positioning the KJV in American society more generally to remember that a deep familiarity with Scripture served them powerfully at key moments in their political careers. For Bryan, striking use of a biblical image secured his place as a major figure in American public life. The image came at the conclusion of his speech to the Democratic National Convention in 1896, which featured an ardent appeal for the free coinage of silver as a means to overcome a national economic crisis. He ended with these memorable words: "Having behind us the producing masses of this nation and the world, supported by the commercial interests, the laboring interests, and the toilers everywhere, we will answer their demand for a gold standard by saying to them: You shall not press down upon the brow of labor this crown of thorns, you shall not crucify mankind upon a cross of gold."[62]

Roosevelt, likewise, was expert in deploying biblical language for political purposes. His great speech accepting the Progressive Party's nomination for president in 1912 addressed a standard array of the day's economic and political problems. But his peroration climaxed with a powerful biblical image: "Our cause is based on the eternal principles of righteousness; and even though we who now lead may for the time fail, in the end the cause itself shall triumph. . . . To you men who . . . have come together to spend and be spent in the endless crusade against wrong . . . to you who gird yourselves for the great new fight in the never-ending warfare for the good of humankind, I say in closing . . . We stand at Armageddon, and we battle for the Lord."[63]

For his part, Woodrow Wilson used a biblical notion of "covenant" as his central theme for taking the United States into the First World War and even more directly in announcing his goals for a League of

Nations.[64] Wilson's single-minded devotion in promoting the league also took on a scriptural aspect.

As political leaders, Roosevelt, Bryan, and Wilson promoted policies that were to them as biblical as the language they exploited so compellingly.[65] These policies fleshed out what they described as a commitment to "righteousness" and arose from their conviction that the ideals of democratic liberty could be translated into reality. The worldview behind their confidence in positive government came in considerable part from their reading of Scripture.

All, for example, were foes of corruption. All tried to use government to protect at least some of those most in need of protection. In their era, progressive support for an active government came mostly from Roosevelt's wing of the Republican Party, which provided his avenue for promoting reform of the civil service and of the police during his years in New York. As president, he drew on the same sources for energetic efforts to clean up the civil service, protect the public against monopolies, and preserve western land for public use.

When Wilson became president in 1913, he justified many of his appeals for new legislation by the necessity to help people in actual need. This motive led him to back restrictions on corporate trusts, to create a Federal Reserve for ensuring stability in banking, to secure an eight-hour day for railroad workers, and to establish the first national standards protecting child labor.

Although Bryan's populism was constrained by the Democratic Party's need to placate the segregationist policies of its southern wing, he was a lifelong champion of women, children, and the working poor. An especially poignant episode at the end of his life testified to the reputation Bryan had won as an advocate for the powerless. When he was enlisted by the state of Tennessee to help prosecute John Scopes for teaching evolution in a high school classroom, the organization that was funding Scopes' defense had second thoughts. It was the American Civil Liberties Union (ACLU), several of whose leaders were great admirers of Bryan for his public advocacy on behalf of the defenseless, to which the ACLU was also committed.[66]

A similar effort to promote biblical ideals inspired the international efforts of these leaders. As presidents, Roosevelt and Wilson were renowned for using the United States' rising power to promote peace among nations and liberty for oppressed peoples. Roosevelt in 1906 was awarded the Nobel Peace Prize for his success at brokering peace in a war between Japan and Russia. Wilson was even more admired for the idealism of his Fourteen Points, the plan he proposed toward the end of World War I to create an international peacekeeping order that would make destructive warfare impossible. Bryan, as secretary of state, was so dedicated to peaceful resolution of international disputes that he resigned his position when he concluded that Wilson's actions toward Germany violated the principle of noncombative neutrality.

In short, the record of these three notable Americans included many efforts to act morally at home and abroad. In considerable measure they practiced as politicians what they preached about the King James Version in the spring of 1911.

Yet the limits of their approach to Scripture have become increasingly evident with the passage of time. Roosevelt (throughout his life) and Wilson (after he became president) were both champions of what their era called the Social Gospel. Both shared much with clerical activists like Washington Gladden who defined the biblical "Kingdom of God" as primarily a set of ethical axioms. With such ethical axioms often came a reformulation of historical Christian teaching keyed more to what the spirit of Scripture seemed to be saying in the late nineteenth century than what it had said to generations stretching back in time. In keeping with that spirit, Roosevelt and Wilson mostly practiced a Christianity guided by the norms that progressives—right thinking, scientifically informed, and politically energized—hoped would reform the world through their own efforts.

Even as the two presidents continued to draw inspiration from Scripture, their civil religion changed traditional convictions about what scriptural religion meant. For the biblical sense of sin as an ever-present reality threatening even the best efforts of the most noble political actors, they substituted a nearly utopian confidence in what disciplined human effort could accomplish by itself. Instead of a biblical sense of humanity joined alike before God's law and alike before the offer of salvation, they allowed the era's theories on race, eugenics, and Social Darwinism to delude them into thinking that "Anglo-Saxons" or "Teutonic peoples" had qualitatively surpassed all others. This thinking had an immediate effect on their racial attitudes. Although Roosevelt made a few moves toward treating the races fairly—for example, by welcoming the black leader Booker T. Washington to the White House—neither leader followed biblical teachings on human equality with respect to blacks, Native Americans, or Asian Americans. For the Bible's words of warning and reassurance for all nations, they substituted supreme confidence in the United States as uniquely qualified to lead the world through sheer moral effort to a new day of universal peace.

Woodrow Wilson's stance was particularly troubling. Shortly after his election in 1912, Francis Grimké wrote him a congratulatory letter, not so much for his electoral triumph as for having recently published an article in the *Expositor* on the importance of Bible study in Sunday schools. Grimké told Wilson that since he was "a colored man," Wilson doubtless knew that "the triumph of the Democratic Party has always been attended, more or less, with a sense of uneasiness on the part of the colored people for fear lest their rights might be interfered with." But Grimké's mind was "greatly relieved" when he read Wilson's article. The reason was patent: "I said to myself, No American citizen, white or black, need have any reasonable grounds of fear from the Administration of a man who feels as he does, who believes as he does in the word of God, and who accepts as he does, without any reservation, the great, eternal, and immutable principles of righteousness for which that Word stands."[67]

Yet it was not to be. Wilson soon re-segregated the nation's civil service, which prompted another letter from Grimké that upbraided the president for an action that was "undemocratic . . . un-American . . . un-Christian [and] is needlessly to offend the self-respect of the loyal black citizens of the Republic."[68] Wilson also gave in to racism during the next major American celebration of Scripture. In 1916 the president responded positively when invited to participate in a 100th anniversary celebration for the American Bible Society to be held at the Daughters of the American Revolution building in Washington. Yet before the event could take place there was, in the words of a Bible society official, "one difficult corner to turn—the color question." This official explained to the staunchly segregationist president that, as a national organization, "having an Agency among colored people with a colored minister at its head, we have certain obligations which we cannot avoid."[69] Despite this sense of duty, it came to pass on May 7, 1916, that, because of unrecorded backstage maneuvering, the president addressed the society with no blacks on the platform. On that occasion, the same Wilson who in 1911 had praised the King James Version because of "How these pages teem with the masses of mankind! . . . These are the annals of the people—of the common run of men," now spoke loftily of how "the Word of God" was "weaving the spirits of men together" throughout the whole world."[70]

To his credit, Bryan on this score was somewhat diffident. Perhaps because of the many defeats he suffered in his political life, perhaps because of his cooperation with conservative forces in his Presbyterian denomination, or because his approach to Scripture made more room for a theological appreciation of Jesus, Bryan was less prone to thinking that progressive effort by itself would succeed in reforming the world. These reasons may explain positions where his views shied away from the other two. For example, Bryan was somewhat more alert to a biblical sense of sin as an ever-present reality threatening even the best political efforts. He was less prone to racism than the strongly segregationist Wilson, and his later campaigns against Darwinism were aimed directly at the Anglo-Saxon Social Darwinism that Roosevelt accepted. His resignation as secretary of state showed that he was more capable of seeing how the biblical story might conflict with American political ideals as well as support them.

But if Bryan's attachment to the Bible allowed him to keep some distance from the civil religion of Roosevelt and Wilson, it did not protect him from the anti-intellectual excesses of populism. Bryan retained a strong sense of the Bible's ability to challenge as well as define America. He did not, however, succeed in showing how that challenge could be mounted responsibly in an age of increasing pluralism about Scripture within Christian communities and increasing religious pluralism in the nation at large. For much of his adult life, Bryan earned his living as a public speaker; one of his most frequently repeated speeches was an address on the person and work of Christ entitled "The Prince of Peace."[71] In his later years, as is well known, Bryan became a leader in the crusade against Darwinism. Both "The Prince of Peace" speech and his anti-Darwinism activities have more to commend them than suggested by stereotypes from the likes of H. L. Mencken.[72] Yet they also lacked a consistent effort at explaining how Bryan's biblical Christian faith could be foundational for the public life that he also approached in biblical terms. He did not or could not explain how a scriptural faith could avoid both the ideological Americanism of civil religion as developed by Wilson and Roosevelt and the biblical demagoguery that some of his own speeches promoted.

The speeches of these three leading statesmen on the King James Version were highlights in the commemorations of 1911. From one angle, they testified to the durability, integrity, and moral depth of the Bible in American public life. From another, they showed that platitudes, even when biblical, were platitudes still.

Complexity

Only a few commentators in 1911 addressed the question of implications for Christian use of the Bible when a Bible like the KJV became a prominent cultural artifact. To be sure, several elegant statements did emphasize that the KJV became dominant only because it delivered the words of life. One Methodist put it like this:

> Among all classes and ranks this book of the people has healed broken hearts, has hushed the voice of weeping, has been bread to the hungry, waters to the famishing, has encouraged the despairing, has strengthened the faint, has charmed childhood and has been a staff to feeble age, has shed light on the pilgrim's path and winged men's thought and hope to a larger, fuller, better life, where there shall be no more curse, and death shall be no more, neither sorrow, nor crying, neither shall there be any more pain; for the former things have passed away.[73]

A Presbyterian expressed the same conviction: "The deeper reason for the paramount influence of the English Bible in English literature" is that "good shepherds [were] bent on feeding the flock of God with the wholesome necessaries of the spiritual life. . . . With eternity ever before their minds they gave the English folk not only Saxon diction but spiritual ideas so that the way of life was made luminous and real to their readers."[74]

Yet such expressions did not lead on to further reflection about how the popularity won by the KJV *because* it provided such spiritual riches may have doubled back to *undercut* the ability of this version to provide spiritual nourishment. Probing the critical possibilities of hypocrisy, misplaced allegiance, or unintended spiritual consequences was left to a very few.

A subject very much pertinent to the world in 1911 was the role the King James Version might be playing in propping up imperial conquest, an issue that has been addressed much more directly in our own postcolonial age than it was in 1911.[75] When empire did come into focus in 1911, it was usually spoken of approvingly, as by the American who commended what the Marquess of Northampton said when he presented a ceremonial Bible to King George as part of tercentenary celebrations: "The growth and strength of the Empire owe much to the English Bible."[76]

One person in 1911, however, did draw the contrary conclusion— that talk of the KJV, in fact, hypocritically masked the designs of empire. Roger Casement was a Protestant-raised Anglo-Irish consul in the British foreign service who came to despise his employer for oppressing colonial Africa and also came to regard the subjugation of Ireland as the key to Britain's world dominance. Casement would become notorious during World War I for plotting to secure an Irish-German alliance against Britain, plotting for which he was eventually executed for treason. In August 1911, he looked upon celebrations of the KJV as only another noxious example illustrating an "English mentality . . . that whatever England does is divinely ordained." Casement mocked the sentiment of the KJV celebrations that claimed "The British Bible" as "the first and greatest of British investments," upon the moral dividends of which "was founded the imperial greatness of this Island Empire." His ridicule was boundless: "The British Bible was the Bible that counted. It was the bible upon which the sun never sets, the bible that had blown Indian mutineers from its muzzle in the 'fifties and was prepared to-day to have a shot at any other mutineers, Teuton or Turk, who dared to dispute its claim that the meek shall inherit the earth." The truth was rather that the British empire was founded upon the ability to "ravage . . . sack . . . and plunder" that it had displayed in subduing Ireland.[77] Needless to say, Casement's sentiments echoed not at all in the American observances of 1911.

A different sort of critical reflection came more gently from the most interesting Catholic comment on the celebrations of that year. In a general essay on Protestant tercentenary commemorations, the American Jesuit A. J. Maas found a great deal to praise in the King James Version, especially "its marvelous felicity of style . . . chaste, dignified, and impressive, and of a rhythm which is always melodious and grateful to the ear." Maas spent much of his essay trying to explain that the Catholic Church had never been opposed to the Bible as such, but only to the unchecked use of Scripture that lead on to "violence and anarchy" by "enemies of order and disturbers of society."[78]

In his defense of Catholic attitudes toward Scripture, Maas also paused to make a more general point. As he observed the Protestant celebrations that verged toward adulation of the KJV, he worried that "the Authorised Version is to a certain extent substituted for the Bible itself or for the Christian truths it conveys." In particular, he complained that George V had spoken of the KJV's "inexhaustible springs of wisdom, courage, and joy." Surely, the priest responded, those are qualities belonging to the Bible itself: "The Authorised Version is at best the faucet through which Biblical truth is communicated."[79] Maas was touching an issue of generic Christian, rather than particular Catholic, concern. But it too was an issue that others at the time did not pursue.

A third critical reflection addressed directly the question of how much the KJV's cultural authority depended on its religious power. Anticipating C. S. Lewis' later prediction that this translation would fade when the religion it represented declined, an author in the *Princeton Theological Review* put the issue forthrightly: "The literary reputation of the English Bible is the consequence and not the cause of its power. The true cause of its whole influence is the conviction, bred into the bone of English Christendom, that it is the very Word of God and the ultimatum of Deity. If once that conviction be impaired, we need not fancy that its literary power and influence will not wane. . . . When men cease to believe in its full divine authority, they will presently find plausible reasons for denying its supreme value as literature."[80]

Fox was raising an important issue, but several of the voices that joined in commemorating the King James Version showed that his prediction was faulty. As we have seen, Theodore Roosevelt breezed past dogma to focus on ethics. Others recommended the KJV for its professional value, "not as a religious book, but as a manual of utility, of professional preparation and professional use for the journalist";[81] affirmed that "aside from the religious teachings in it, it is a great literary achievement";[82] or spotlighted its effect on "English character" that is "not merely religious (that goes without saying) but even social and political."[83]

Perhaps even more typical were statements that recognized the primal religious character of the King James Version but went on to discuss its social, political, ethical, and literary effects as if the latter posed no complications at all for the former. Thus, one author, after dwelling at length on the KJV's historical importance for individual believers, affirmed that "its secondary service to society" was "even more important" for "helping to realize the exalted ideals and beneficent tendencies of those social institutions which at the last have grown up, if not wholly yet chiefly, under the inspiration and sanction of the Gospel itself."[84] Another writer posed the connections just as unambiguously: "The one end of the Bible is, indeed, to tell the world about God and the great salvation. But while it has done this, it has done more, supplying rhetoric with powerful and happy diction, and enriching literature with noble thoughts and images and the fine arts with memorable subjects."[85]

The enthusiasms of 1911, in other words, made it difficult to step back for broader consideration of what the KJV's popularity meant for religious traditions that were splintering in contentions over how to understand the Bible and a culture that was rapidly throwing off the marks of a Bible civilization.

Assessment

In conclusion, it may seem petty or carping to pose a contrast between the Christian and the cultural effects of the King James Version. If only a fraction of the great religious and cultural good ascribed to the KJV in the American celebrations of 1911 was warranted, perhaps we too in 2011 should simply join in the cheering.

Yet the fact that many of the words in the 1911 celebrations were lost in a fog of American or British or Anglo-Saxon civil religion, that the specter of manic biblicism could be glimpsed in the acrimonious exchanges between Catholics and Protestants, and that some of the celebrations verged over into populist anti-intellectualism means that critical questions are not entirely a presentist concern.

The question about anti-intellectualism centers on a complexity that has continued to characterize American popular religion. For many American believers, and not exclusively lowbrow believers, the KJV opened the door of paradise and ushered them into the very presence of God. As they read, heard, and heeded its words, millions were rescued, blessed, inspired, and empowered. Insofar as the wide prevalence of the KJV opened these benefits to almost all, the story looks like a straightforward account of spiritual advance. Yet precisely because the advance was so widespread, the story has become complicated. With the words of the KJV in their heads and the self-confidence in their hearts that they have been redeemed through the word alone, American Bible-believers have accomplished great good, but also have become fertile ground for creation science, encouraged vast quantities of runaway apocalypticism, and fueled the many theological eccentricities that are rife in American popular Christianity.

The civil religion problem can be explicated with reference to Theodore Roosevelt and Woodrow Wilson. For Roosevelt, the King James Version provided ethical energy for bringing the whole world closer to the ideal condition achieved by the United States as the summit of Anglo-Saxon civilization. For Wilson, the KJV provided the political wisdom for bringing the whole world closer to the same ideal condition. While the activities of Roosevelt, Wilson, and many more who thought as they did testified to the version's triumph in American civilization, they also testified just as eloquently to the hijacking of the KJV for nationalistic or ideological purposes.

The problem of manic biblicism came from the same complexity. When the language of the KJV was everywhere the common public language, it was very easy to bestow a sacred aura on public discourse. Yet the sacralization of public rhetoric led easily to an absolutization of public principle. And the absolutization of public principle led easily to the demonization of opponents, which in turn promoted crusading at home and abroad. In other words, the manic note that from the beginning has never been far beneath the surface of American public life owes something to the extraordinary currency of the King James Version at all levels of society. Whether it was loyalists to Great Britain in 1776 attacked as minions of Satan or the antichrist, Southerners (and Northerners) in the era of the Civil War excoriated as raving infidels for their arguments in favor of (and against) slavery, union organizers in the wake of World War I depicted as nihilistic "Reds," John Kennedy's campaign for president in 1960 luridly portrayed as a plot to deliver the United States into the hands of the pope, religiously inspired contributions on issues of public policy scorned as "fascist," or proposals for government-sponsored health care dismissed as "communist"—the prevalence of the King James Version in the nation's culture must share some of the responsibility.

Assessment of the 1911 celebrations of the KJV call for a combination of discrimination, appreciation, and criticism that has been difficult for Americans to bring to bear on our own situation. When the phrases of the KJV came naturally to one and sundry, it was easy for believers to assume that it was the nation's responsibility to do the business of the church and the church's responsibility to do the business of the nation. It was easy to confuse literary influence with spiritual influence. But those assumptions and confusions could become a threat to Christian integrity as easily as they could become a danger to civic peace.

A notable foreign visitor in the 1930s concluded his commentary on American Christianity with something like that criticism. After spending two periods of study in the United States, Dietrich Bonhoeffer wrote an essay on American religion when he had returned to Germany. In it he praised much that he had seen, but he also observed that the American separation of church and state was linked to an extraordinary "participation of the churches in the political, social, economic, and cultural events of public life." He could just as easily have been speaking about the nation's love affair with the King James Version. To Bonhoeffer, the nature of that synergy made him ask whether American Christians grasped the negative criticism of the Christian gospel. As he put it toward the end of his 1939 essay, American believers "do not understand that God's 'criticism' touches even religion, the Christianity of the churches and the sanctification of Christians, and that God has founded his church beyond religion and beyond ethics. . . . In American theology, Christianity is still essentially religion and ethics. But because of this, the person and work of Jesus Christ must, for theology, sink into the background and in the long run remain misunderstood, because it is not recognised as the sole ground of radical judgment and radical forgiveness."[86] Following Bonhoeffer, it could be asked about 1911 whether praise for the KJV represented the triumph, the defeat, or a strange combination of both for the history of Christianity in America.

Five

THE KING JAMES BIBLE, MISSION, AND THE VERNACULAR IMPETUS

Lamin Sanneh

*T*ranslation of the Bible into the vernacular has had important unintended consequences not only for culture and society generally, but also, notably, for subject and colonized populations. Bidding fair to the scruples of the Enlightenment regarding the intellectual inferiority of illiterate cultures, the proponents of vernacular Bible translation produced the first systematic documentation of non-Western languages, including languages with no written form. Access to the Bible became the cutting edge of literacy and national awakening in many indigenous societies. Indeed, biblical literacy in the mother tongue was a catalyst for broad cultural transformation, affecting family life, personal motivation, popular mobilization, interethnic encounter, and national identity. Under conditions of colonial rule, biblical literacy became an unexpectedly potent weapon *against* the suppression of local agency. Rather than reinforcing the power of overlords, it induced sentiments of cultural and national autonomy, as biblical themes provided new paradigms for political aspiration and models for education, citizenship, and human dignity. The transformation in such cultures has altered the face of global Christianity by giving it distinct and various indigenous features.

My purpose here is not so much to discuss the role of the KJV in bringing the gospel to indigenous societies as to reflect on the King James Version of the Bible as the example par excellence of vernacular Scripture as a means of indigenous encounter with the gospel. It is easy to forget the extraordinary excitement with which the "Englished" Bible, in its various early forms, was met in its day, or the revolutionary impact of the King James Version on all of society as it found its way into household use.[1] Having the Scriptures in the mother tongue is arguably no less important or less revolutionary in non-English and developing-world contexts.

On the Christian view, providing the Bible in the tongue of the people is a requisite phase of the divine instruction of the human race, with the diverse, multiple languages of the world the appointed and indispensable means by which God chooses to bring into existence communities of faith. As Adolf Deissmann has put it, as the message of God to humanity, the New Testament was written in the simple style of the carpenter's and tentmaker's language, which rendered it suitable to be the book of all the peoples of the world.[2] There is no such thing as a church without language or without the Scriptures. In spite of the barriers of natural separation among us (often reinforced by cultural systems), God remains accessible to all through the spoken and written word, allowing our divisions to be overcome and our aspirations to be directed toward a common purpose. God woos us in tones and accents that accord with our primal self-understanding. The response of faith is born of a living encounter with a personal God. On any credible view, Christianity is recognizable only in the embodied idioms and values of the cultures in which we find it, allowing Christians to speak and respond with the facility of the mother tongue, and mother-tongue speakers to express faith and trust in God's universal promises. As a distinctive religion, Christianity is in principle invested without prejudice or favoritism in the particularities of national life, and flourishes in, not in spite of, those particularities. The premise of Bible translation is that no culture is inherently impermeable or alien to its message, nor is any society indispensable or exceptional as its audience. It will be evident that this premise carries implications for religious, linguistic, and cultural initiatives above and beyond the specific, technical concerns of translators. The creation of the King James Bible vindicated that premise with respect to the culture of England. In the process of its wider dissemination as an example of a successful vernacular translation, the King James Bible became a model of the impact of Scripture on other cultures.

Christianity and Translation

By general consent the German Reformation is recognized as the major impetus behind the modern movement of vernacular Bible translation, though in fact Bible translation is as old as Christianity itself. Yet the Reformation story, in providing the lens through which modern writers have tended to consider the subject, has sometimes obscured Christianity's universal nature and historic character as a translated and as a translatable religion. There is inherent irony in the fact that Christianity's European (especially its English) forms of discourse are often given normative status in rendering the language of Jesus, with a corresponding disinclination to welcome the expression of faith in the tongues of the peoples of the wider world, including Asia and Africa. This irony is compounded when one reflects on the persecution attendant on early efforts to translate Scripture into English.

The story of John Wycliffe (d. 1384), who guided a vernacular translation by some of his Oxford colleagues, is illustrative. Wycliffe was condemned as a heretic; forty years after his death his body and bones were exhumed by ecclesiastical order and burnt, with instructions for his ashes to be so disposed as to leave no trace of the man. Thomas Fuller (d. 1661), the historian, was moved to make amends for this effort to obliterate Wycliffe's memory. "Thus this brook [the river Swift] hath conveyed his ashes into the Avon; the Avon into the Severn; the Severn into the narrow seas; they into the main ocean. And thus the ashes of Wyclif are the emblem of his doctrine, which now is dispersed all the world over."[3]

Scriptural translation is not alien to Christianity even though in much of its premodern history it has been attended by the opprobrium of heresy. After all, Tertullian (ca. 160–ca. 240), who converted to Christianity in 195, expressed support for distribution of the gospel in the languages of the peoples of the world, as did Irenaeus (ca. 130–ca. 200) and numerous others after them, including Otfrid von Weissenburg in the ninth century.[4] The translators of the King James Bible cite Theodoret of Cyrrhus (d. ca. 458) to the effect that by his time Scripture had been translated into the languages of the Greeks, Romans, Egyptians, Persians, Indians, Armenians, Scythians, Sauromatians, "and, briefly, into all the languages that any nation useth." In the list of subsequent translations they include Gothic, Arabic, Saxon, French, Slavic, and Dutch. "So that, to have the Scriptures in the mother tongue is not a quaint conceit lately taken up . . . but hath been thought upon, and put in practice of old, even from the first times of the conversion of any nation; no doubt, because it was esteemed most profitable to cause faith to grow in men's hearts the sooner, and to make them able to say with the words of the Psalm, 'As we have heard, so we have seen' (Ps. 48:8)." All this suggests the role of the vernacular Bible in providing a measure of stability for the scattered communities of faith across space and time. This was especially true in the age following the collapse of the Roman Empire, including the centuries of the ascendancy of Islamic power. The language of faith was in specific ways often more meaningful than political identity.

Rather than seeing the different languages of the world, including English, as obstacles that the church must overcome to establish the faith, Christianity became invested in local languages and remote idioms whose authentic forms could nonetheless be seen as having in some mysterious sense anticipated the gospel. Accordingly, the translators of the King James Version could affirm in their preface their "desire that the Scripture may speak like itself, as in the language of *Canaan*, that it may be understood even of the very vulgar."[5] Translation into the common, local idiom reflects, and is emblematic of, the very incarnation by which the "word became flesh and dwelt among us."

That is the fundamental case the King James Bible translators affirmed, reflecting the argument of the Apostle Paul (1 Corinthians 14) that Scripture was intended to be understood in all languages, not just "Hebrew the ancientist, not Greek the most copious, not Latin the finest," all of which can seem "barbarous" to those who do not understand them.

> Nature taught a natural man to confess, that all of us in those tongues which we do not understand are plainly deaf. . . . Therefore as one complaineth that always in the Senate of Rome there was one or other that called for an interpreter; so lest the Church be driven to the like exigent, it is necessary to have translations in a readiness. Translation it is that openeth the window, to let in the light . . . that removeth the cover of the well, that we may come by the water; even as Jacob rolled away the stone from the mouth of the well, by which means the flocks of Laban were watered. Indeed without translation into the vulgar tongue, the unlearned are but like children at Jacob's well (which is deep) without a bucket or something to draw with.

The experience of Pentecost (Acts 2:1-13) had among its disconcerting effects the loosening and anointing of Gentile tongues, and scriptural translation extends the recognition of those tongues and voices as an enduring witness to God's unforgettable promises. If Pentecost was a novel experience, the truth to which it bore holy witness was not new; it was a sign and confirmation of God's sovereign design of universal

redemption and reconciliation. The one God is "in all the world" by virtue of, not in spite of, the sundry and manifold tongues of witness that
are cultivated (and yet to be cultivated) in Scripture, worship, prayer,
and devotion. In that witness no language is forbidden, and none is
prerequisite.

This theological view of language is far more radical in its unquali-
fied welcome of language, any language, than a purely utilitarian view
in which languages of scale weigh more heavily in the balance of merit.
Before God, all languages are equal in their merit, as in their demerit,
for which reason none has an inbuilt advantage or disadvantage. All
languages share in the consequences of fallen human nature, just as by
virtue of Bible translation all languages share equally in the benefits of
God's intervention in Christ. Scriptural translation is not an exercise in
linguistic perfection; it is a willing and attentive inquiry into God's mind
and purpose for us. "We never thought," the KJV translators declared,
"from the beginning that we should need to make a new translation, nor
yet to make of a bad one a good one; (for then the imputation of *Sixtus*
had been true in some sort, that our people had been fed with gall of
dragons instead of wine, with wheal instead of milk;) . . . To that purpose
there were many chosen, that were greater in other men's eyes than in
their own, and that sought the truth rather than their own praise."[6] Undeterred by the pitfalls of human fallibility, the translators, like the biblical
writers themselves, set to work with the unwavering confidence that their
commission was from God. It is in that sense that the Bible is *sui generis*.
A focus other than that may produce a technically correct translation,
but not the Bible as the heritage of faith. Referring to the Septuagint, the
pre-Christian translation of the Hebrew Scriptures into "familiar" koine
Greek that was widely known not only in the Mediterranean basin but
also in Asia, parts of Europe, and Africa, the King James translators
reflected on both its providential suitability and its imperfections:

> Therefore, the word of God, being set forth in the Greek, becometh
> hereby like a candle on a candle-stick, which giveth light to all that
> are in the house; or like a proclamation sounded forth in the market-
> place, which most men presently take knowledge of; and therefore
> that language was fittest to contain the Scriptures, both for the first
> preachers of the Gospel to appeal unto for witness, and for the learn-
> ers also of those times to make search and trial by. It is certain, that
> the translation was not so sound and so perfect, but that it needed in
> many places correction; and who had been so sufficient for this work
> as the Apostles or apostolick men? Yet it seemed good to the Holy

Ghost and to them to take that which they found . . . rather than by making a new, in that new world and green age of the Church, to expose themselves to many exceptions and cavillations, as though they made a translation to serve their own turn; and therefore bearing witness to themselves, their witness not to be regarded.

What the KJV translators here say "seemed good to the Holy Spirit"—authoritative use of an imperfect vernacular translation like the LXX—did not always seem good to everyone else. For some, the entire Reformation emphasis on vernacular translation was suspect, or even reckless, in that it "put [the Bible] into the hands of the commonality and interpreted no longer by the well-conditioned learned, but by the faith and delusion, the common sense and uncommon nonsense, of all sorts of men."[7] (Such a bias echoes the strictures of Galen [d. 200], the Greek physician, against the ancient Christians, namely, that they were intellectually uncouth.[8])

Yet it is hard to see how Christianity qua Christianity can be cultivated or faithfully transmitted in any other way. A religion shut up in the language in which Jesus actually preached, taught, and worshipped had never been available, and was never mandated by Jesus or by the apostles. Christianity is encountered only and always in a translated, and, therefore, in a comprehensible form, with interpretation its handmaid. And it is difficult to maintain fidelity to the vernacular ethos of Scripture by flouting the rule of making sense to "the simple reader." Tyndale pressed the argument memorably: "I wish," he said, "that even the weakest woman should read the Gospel—should read the Epistles of Paul. And I wish that these were translated into all languages so that they might be read and understood, not only by Scots and Irishmen, but also by Turks and Saracens. . . . I long that the husbandman should sing portions of them to himself as he follows the plough, that the weaver should hum them to the tune of his shuttle."[9] The approach allowed Tyndale to deploy what Donald Coggan calls "his almost uncanny gift of simplicity . . . a true nobility of homeliness."[10] For his own reasons, Johannes Kepler echoed the sentiment when he declared, "The Bible speaks the language of everyman."[11]

Strength in Weakness

The KJV triumphed in spite of its well-rehearsed translation flaws. None was quicker off the mark to call attention to these flaws than the erudite maverick scholar Dr. Hugh Broughton, who wrote to the king's attendants condemning the Bishops' Bible of 1568, saying it should be burnt as flawed and worthless. "The cockles of the sea shores," he noted caustically, "and the leaves of the forest, and the grains of the poppy, may as well be numbered as the gross errors of this Bible, disgracing the ground of our own hope." The new (King James) translation, he asserted confidently, "might well give place to the Alcoran [of the Muslims], pestered with lies" as it was.[12] The first edition of the KJV contained several typographical errors. In addition, numerous amendments were made to the text within a very short space of time: for example, the phrase "approved to death" was changed to "appointed to death" (1 Corinthians 4:9). In 1629 the injunction to "runne with patience unto the race" was corrected to "run with patience the race" (Hebrews 12:1). In some versions, printers' errors changed the meaning of the words. An egregious example was the 1631 edition where the printer omitted the word "not" in the seventh commandment, resulting in "Thou shalt commit adultery" (Exodus 20:14). The 1638 edition compounded these problems with a host of printing errors, prompting William Kilburne to write an essay titled, *Dangerous Errors in several late Printed Bibles to the great scandal and corruption of sound and true religion* (1659). In one case involving a printed Bible in England in the 1650s, Kilburne claims to have found 20,000 errors. All this is to say that the KJV was far from being an overnight success. Not a single member of the Pilgrims to Plymouth in 1621 arrived with a copy of the KJV. Instead, they brought with them Henry Ainsworth's version of the Psalms. Ainsworth was minister of a nonconformist congregation in Amsterdam between 1593 and 1622;[13] his work was part of the reason why there were calls in Parliament for a bill to regulate Bible translation. Such a bill passed in 1653.

Despite its early trials, however, the King James Version soon replaced the Bishops' Bible as the version adopted in the English churches. The Geneva Bible continued to be printed until 1644, after which it fell into disuse. Even without receiving final authorization by Convocation, by Parliament, or by the king, the KJV assumed ascendancy as the Bible of English-speaking peoples. As Bishop Westcott wrote in 1868, the KJV gained its status by its own internal character rather than by an external edict.[14] It transcended the circumstances of its creation, warts and all.

In his panoramic survey of English literature in the seventeenth century, Douglas Bush of Harvard notes that although we are accustomed to cooperation in scholarship and science, we do not associate great literary work with committees. Yet the King James Bible "was produced by an organization worthy of Salomon's House."[15] The translators were not literary figures in their own esteem. What distinguished them was that "they had a collective ear and taste and, above all, they had intense and reverent zeal." The Bible they created "is the grand proof in English that in the greatest writing literary beauty is not a main object but a by-product."[16] In the King James Bible literary beauty arises from language that is wrapped in devotion and humility and offered in faith as a wor-shipful tribute to God. In the conclusion to their preface, the translators took leave of their labors in words resonant with dignity, balance, and economy. "It is a fearful thing to fall into the hands of the living God; but a blessed thing it is, and will bring us to everlasting blessedness in the end, when God speaketh unto us, to hearken; when he setteth his word before us, to read it; when he stretcheth out his hand and calleth, to answer, Here am I, here we are to do thy will, O God. The Lord work a care and conscience in us to know him and serve him, that we may be acknowledged of him at the appearing of our Lord Jesus Christ."[17]

Gift of Tongues

The KJV demonstrated that the Bible could be made English—that it could indeed speak to English readers as "their book"—because the Bible is universal. The concreteness of its rugged idiom and lucid figures com-bines with sublime rhythm, giving a divine account of who we are and why we are here. The language of the Bible—strong and pointed in its simplicity, broad and open in its appeal, and searching in its lessons—enlists the commitment of believers in the ordinary course of their daily lives without the necessity of ecclesiastical jurisdiction or overview. "A soldier on duty here; a trader pursuing his work there; a prisoner bear-ing witness in his cell—it was thus that the Gospel spread."[18] The ad hoc, fragmentary nature of the spread of Christianity was considerably improved by the organization of missionary and Bible societies in the modern era, but the lay character of the agents remained dominant in the vast majority of cases. The principle of voluntarism sparked the rise of the modern missionary movement both in its Protestant and Catholic forms, while in both cases the most effective means for the propagation of the gospel was by local agency: evangelists, catechists, lay readers, colporteurs, exhorters, elders, deacons, students, teachers, nurses, sol-diers, miners, farmers, traders, and civil servants. This gave the mod-ern Christian movement a decisively indigenous, voluntary orientation, and that orientation has been expanded and strengthened by missionary Bible translation.

The widespread tribute to the KJV acknowledges that from there "we descend for a moment to a chain of foot-hills, or [to] an ant-hill,"[19] a view not too uncharitable to apply to the onrush of short-lived anodyne English translations, and of the taste for secret gospels, that clogged the twentieth century. By contrast, translations of the modern mission field represented not so much a descent into banality as a plunge into untested waters. Along with societies with a written tradition, such as China, Japan, India, and the Muslim world, there were innumerable others without a written culture where obstacles to evangelism were much greater. With no orthography, alphabet, or historical documents, oral cultures presented a formidable challenge to the whole logic of a religion of the book. And the resources one depends on for dealing with written cultures unfamiliar with the gospel are woefully inadequate for dealing with illiterate cultures. Off the beaten track, new tools have had to be invented, new structures and habits of investigation created—all of them requiring skillful recourse to local institutions, ideas, and values that had never before been systematized or documented. Missionaries have had to cope not only with strange, unfamiliar sounds and usage, but also with nuance and allusions in languages for which they have had to develop, almost literally, new ears. We know from missionary correspondence what a crushing burden this puts on the shoulders of even the most able and willing, and how long and arduous is the effort to make headway.

In this situation, the lessons of the KJV, and of its precursors in Coverdale and Tyndale, are invaluable. The confidence of the translators that it is the desire of the living God "that the Scripture may speak like itself, as in the language of *Canaan*, that it may be understood even of the very vulgar," is crucial in the quicksand of new mission frontiers. Even though the translators of the KJV were working with available literary resources, including other translations, they staked the reputation of their translation on its being accessible in the language of the people, without the shibboleths of an artificial linguistic decorum, an approach that fits well the condition of unwritten vernaculars. The KJV brought out the strength and beauty of the simple and the ordinary; missionary vernacular translation can and should do the same. The KJV and its many literary tributaries gave us imperishable gems in language, rolling as easy on the tongue as on the ear; such color and music are characteristic of oral cultures. Among numerous examples that could be cited, consider this verse from Song of Solomon: "The flowers appear on the earth; the time of the singing of birds is come, and the voice of the turtle is heard in our land" (2:12). Or this: "Behold the fowls of the air: for they sow not, neither do they reap, nor gather into barns. . . . Consider the lilies of the field, how they grow; they toil not, neither do they spin: and yet I say unto you, That even Solomon in all his glory was not arrayed like one of these" (Matthew 6:26, 28-29).

Such passages call us back to the countryside, to the earth and its teeming life, showing the Bible to have its roots in the earthy preoccupations of our existence. This accessible and familiar character of the language of the KJV inspired Wordsworth to write:

> But to outweigh all harm, the sacred Book,
> In dusty sequestration wrapt too long,
> Assumes the accents of our tongue;
> And he who guides the plow or wields the crook,
> With understanding spirit now may look
> Upon her records, listen to her song.

Across the mission frontier lay much hidden treasure waiting to be unearthed and gathered into the corpus of a shared spiritual heritage. That could be done only if one possessed a good ear and a keen eye and still had one's feet firmly planted in the soil. The KJV was a triumph of the colloquial over the recondite, of the warm voice over the cold pen, and as the people's book it gave impetus to forays into remote and exotic regions to reclaim the people's heritage as part of the tribute of all to the living God. The KJV rejected the prickly scruples of theologians about what were called "ethnical and heathenish distinctions." The key to the Bible is prayer, not learning, said Thomas Taylor in 1619.[20] The idea of prayer is at the root of language, and the poetic imagination that one encounters in the Psalms in the KJV finds an analogue in a fragment of an ancient pre-Columbian Quechua hymn dedicated to *Viracocha*, the Creator, as captured in this felicitous translation:

> The wind lifts up
> The tops of the trees
> And waves each branch
> In tribute to thee.
>
> From the shadowy woods
> The birds sing out
> To render praise
> To the Ruler of all.

The flowers show forth
In brilliant array
Their vivid colors
And pungent perfumes.

The cliffs are dressed
In glowing green,
And the canyon walls
With flowers gleam.

Caution is necessary in assuming any particular Bible translation to be the silver bullet to settle religious differences. To start with, the tumultuous early reception of various English Bibles, including the King James Version, should dispel any lingering doubts on that score. Anyone acquainted with the subject will be aware of the contentions that arose about how to read and treat Scripture, and the KJV in particular. For another, printers added their share of errors to the blemishes of translation without the meaning of Scripture being compromised. Without the seal of non-translatability that distinguishes the Qur'an (requiring it to be performed in Arabic alone), the vernacular Bible comes to us as witness that the "word became flesh," bearing the crown of thorns. Its message is not that the word became book, tied up in syllables. In that way, the appeal of vernacular Bible translation to popular lay use in matters of religion proved impossible to curtail or to control, restrictions and prohibitions notwithstanding. To say the gospel should not be translated is like saying that we cannot see the sun in its own light. In Thomas Taylor's view of the Bible, as we have seen, devotion and faithfulness have primacy over privilege and hierarchy. Understood in its personal rather than sacerdotal sense, the idea of prayerful reading of the Bible was consistent with the emergence of the idea of the individual as a free social agent.[21]

Translation is the original language of Christianity, it bears repeating, and if that fact strikes people as somewhat disconcerting, no less so are the implications of this fact for difference, variety, diversity, and adaptation, or, indeed, for the very idea of Scripture itself. In this respect, the Bible is quite unlike the Qur'an, the Muslim Scripture that, according to the doctrine of *i'jáz*, is inseparable in any religious sense from its original Arabic.[22] Qur'an translation occurs widely without yielding on the uniquely revealed status of its Arabic medium whose incorruptible sanctity is preserved in distinctive letters and syllables, what tradition considers "the limbs of the divine." Because it has no intrinsic merit, translation is at best extraneous. A logical outcome of this position has been the absence of interest in developing the vernacular as a medium of Islamic worship, pilgrimage, and devotion. If Protestant Christians have sometimes promoted the KJV, or, in the case of Catholics, the Vulgate, as in this sense the equivalent of the Qur'an, this reflects the high regard for the prestige of the KJV and the Vulgate in their respective communities more than it describes the actual status of the Qur'an for Muslims. That the KJV for so long occupied such a preeminent and enduring place in the lives of English-speaking Christians throughout the world demonstrates the force of the longing for a normative text in religious life. The scramble by rival translations to move into the ground once—and, in some quarters, still—dominated by the KJV has continued to this day, but is unlikely to be successful. Meanwhile, the work of providing new indigenous translations of the biblical text for people groups throughout the world continues apace.

Translation in Africa

Insofar as the New Testament is itself a translation and interpretation of the preaching and teaching of Jesus, the history of its translation into other languages is necessarily an exercise in intercultural understanding. This is a subject that John Peel, a British sociologist, discussed in his Marett lecture at Exeter College, Oxford, in 1993.[23] In that lecture Peel developed a theory of a narrative paradigm, construing missionary Bible translation as a critical instrument for giving people groups a way of contextualizing their existence, of placing within a larger story the arch of actions, memories, and experiences that spans their life. Most importantly, biblical meta-narrative bestows knowledge of an outcome, and so frames history and identity in a way which is strikingly different from that of the chronicle, with its linear enumeration of events.

Thus understood, the Bible became the paradigmatic narrative—in African societies, for example—with power to console and to inspire, and insight to anticipate a conclusion, and thus the means to infer meaning and purpose. The gospel made people "literate" as to meaning in their lives, allowing them to read what God has in mind for them and for their neighbors. Thus could the nineteenth-century Yoruba pastor, Samuel Pearse, despairing of events ravaging his hometown, Badagry, a festering slave port, speak of the house of God there being deserted "as a cottage in a vineyard, as a lodge in a garden of cucumbers," citing Isaiah 1:8, and of his own unrequited labors by referring to the words of Luke

5:5: "Like the Galilean fishermen, we have toiled all night and caught nothing." With his copy of the King James Bible at his side, Pearse had a fund of pithy, handy passages with which to reflect on his personal and historical circumstances.

Pearse was a disciple of Samuel Ajayi Crowther (ca. 1806–1891), the foremost African churchman of the nineteenth century. Crowther (the name adopted at his baptism as a teenager) described his rescue from slavery and his eventual return to his native Yorubaland in the narrative style of the biblical story of Joseph, but with Samuel as model. The story of his eventual reunion with his mother, Afala, after nearly thirty years of separation, Crowther readily conflated with the relevant Old Testament narrative. He baptized his mother as Hannah, so that as Samuel he was now reunited with his by then elderly mother in the family of faith. The biblical passage in 1 Samuel 1:2 and following, with its striking African analogues, has the polygamous Elkanah, the Ephraimite, limping ungainly between two wives, the barren but favored Hannah, and Peninnah, blessed with children. Stigmatized by Peninnah, the tormented Hannah pleads with God for a child to save her honor, saying she will devote the child to God's work. The son she later bears she names Samuel, and, as promised, consecrates him to God's service. So too an old African woman, Afala, rendered "childless," as it were, by the cruelty of slavery, had her implicit prayer answered and regained her son, now Samuel, a priest of God, the most important African churchman of the nineteenth century. Crowther announced his public vocation as apostle of antislavery with the words of Isaiah in the King James translation: "For Zion's sake will I not hold my peace, and for Jerusalem's sake I will not rest, until the righteousness thereof go forth as brightness, and the salvation thereof as a lamp that burneth."[24]

In that work Crowther was scrupulously uncompromising. At a public meeting in his native Nigeria he confronted the people "from a sense of duty," he said, asking them "to put an end to the trade in human flesh and blood. Conscious of the justness of the cause I was expounding, I could do it with perfect calmness of mind, and free from apprehension of the displeasure of those against whose interest I was speaking."[25]

For Crowther and his African contemporaries it was the KJV that supplied the dignified language of religion and the norms of translation, of which Crowther was the distinguished African leader. He translated and published portions of the Bible into Yoruba between 1850 and 1851; a complete New Testament appeared in 1862, and the first complete Bible in 1884. Crowther's Yoruba New Testament translation was the first in an African language—done by an African with African materials for African use. His Bible, rendered in the Oyo dialect, became the Yoruba KJV, and is as revered and honored today as it ever was. A common criticism is that Crowther's translation has so dominated the field that it has discouraged a fresh and more contemporary version to be undertaken. It is a backhanded compliment, a clear acknowledgment of the strength and durability of the translation. For his linguistic labors, Crowther turned field anthropologist long before the discipline existed. Yet even given the standards of those antediluvian days his method of inquiry can withstand today's stringent tests. His edition of the Yoruba *Grammar and Vocabulary*, published in 1852, had the benefit of extensive consultations with leading linguists of the day, including Professor Samuel Lee of Cambridge, Professor Max Müller of Oxford, and Professor Carl Lepsius of Berlin, whose orthography helped open avenues into the documentation of several Nigerian languages, including Hausa, Kanuri, Igbo, and Ijaw. Crowther reflected on the challenges of reducing a language to writing for the first time, saying he did so by working diligently to get behind colloquial speech and slang. To do that he befriended informants without respect to their religious affiliation, and, in his words, "watched the mouth of elders," noting "suitable and significant words" and pondering how they would have been uttered with what David Livingstone called "the eloquence of the native assembly."[26] When he came upon words that were on the verge of extinction, Crowther said their historical value persuaded him to retain them because, in time, transfused with the merits of Christian usage, "to the rising generation, they will sound sweet and agreeable." He continued: "In tracing out words and their various uses, I am now and then led to search at length into some traditions or customs of the Yoruba."[27] When his house burned down in a fire in 1862, his collections of language research, all eleven years' worth, were lost. To him that work was more valuable than anything money could buy, and its loss was like the death of a dream. Undeterred, Crowther continued his work in language and Bible translation. Eventually his revised dictionary was published in 1870.

Few people anywhere saw more clearly the imperative and value of local custom and culture for vernacular Bible translation, and few were more assiduous in cultivating an indigenous approach to the enterprise. In important ways Crowther was the Tyndale of Africa; his extraordinary labors were like the KJV project writ small. Even in his lifetime he was perforce a legend, what one historian called "missions' greatest propaganda weapon" in the antislavery cause.[28] Like Tyndale, Crowther considered his translation work his legacy to his countrymen. Writing to London in January 1860, he pleaded with the Church Missionary Society, his employer, to allow him to relinquish leadership of the mission to Nigeria. His age and declining health, he appealed, had made travel particularly onerous. When approached to be consecrated as the first African Anglican bishop, he again pleaded to be exempted. "I should like to spend the remainder of my days among my own people, pursuing my translations as my bequest to the nation."[29] London would not budge in either case. Crowther would soldier on against European missionary colleagues who resented his leadership. Their resentment reflected the complex and shifting relations between Europeans and subject populations in the nineteenth century, and the often divergent approaches to biblical translation and evangelism. Checkered as it was, Crowther's career was a strong endorsement of the indigenous cause.

On the issue of appropriating local custom and culture for Bible translation, Crowther addressed in 1869 a meeting of clergy under his direction, giving them instructions about the background research necessary for communicating the gospel. He said he knew opinions differed on the subject, but insisted that it was no part of Christian witness to despise local culture just because of its unfamiliar and elemental expressions. It would be wrong and unproductive to fabricate or impose a replacement. Instead of condemning indigenous entertainments as immoral, indecent, and corrupting, for example, he argued that they should be studied for the value that sustained them.

The gospel is invested in the vernacular materials that preceded it, whose cultivation boosted knowledge of salvation among unevangelized populations. Crowther made it a rule consistently to employ terms already in use rather than to invent new ones, including customs and diversions: "Of these kinds of amusements are fables, story-telling, proverbs and songs which may be regarded as stores of . . . national education in which [people] exercise their power of thinking." "Their religious terms and ceremonies should be carefully observed," he added; "the wrong use made of such terms does not depreciate their real value, but renders them more valid when we adopt them in expressing Scriptural terms in their right senses and places from which they have been misapplied for want of better knowledge."[30] When it is true to its calling, Christianity is not sent to eradicate or replace indigenous culture, Crowther insisted.

Hence the invaluable role of local agents for mission. More than "college-trained men," Crowther pointed out, the real agents of the spread of the gospel were "farmers, carpenters, merchants, masons, court messengers, stewards on ships and the like by profession . . . as men of proven character."[31] The cause of the vernacular Bible spawned confidence in local agency, and the fact that Scripture in the vernacular loses nothing of its divine merit, as the KJV translators emphasized, offered a moral challenge to the presumed entitlements of colonial suzerainty. Cranmer was invoked in this context to support calls for creating an African liturgy to consolidate the gains of having a vernacular Bible.[32]

If the key to the Bible is prayer, as Thomas Taylor declared, the key to having the Bible in the mother tongue is vernacular worship and liturgy. While still living in Freetown, Sierra Leone, where he was resettled after his miraculous rescue from a slave ship in 1822, Crowther was at the center on the occasion of the first celebration of the Yoruba liturgy in 1844. The surviving account portrays the occasion as historic.

> A large number of Africans crowded thither to hear the words of the prayer and praise for the first time in their own tongue in an English church. "Although it was my own native language," says Rev. S. Crowther, "with which I am well acquainted, yet on this occasion it appeared as if I were a babe, just learning to utter my mother-tongue. The work in which I was engaged, the place where I stood, and the congregation before me, were altogether so new and strange, that the whole proceeding seemed to myself like a dream . . . At the conclusion of the blessing, the whole church rang with *ke oh sheh*—so let it be, so let it be!"[33]

Continuities, Parallels

Several writers have called attention to the fact that the vernacular Bible is a catalyst for linguistic and cultural change, in the case of the KJV giving rise to sayings, maxims, and proverbial phrases that fell naturally from the lips even of the unlearned and the irreligious. The KJV, as the American biblical scholar A. T. Robertson observed, put a new flavor into the vernacular and lifted it to a new elevation and dignity of style to unify and glorify the language.[34]

That Robertson's statement can be applied also to other vernacular translations is confirmed by numerous testimonies emanating from the field, as Crowther's example illustrates. We hear it from Ghana, where the Rev. J. G. Christaller, a German linguist, served with the Basel

Mission. A distinguished pioneer of African languages, Christaller is regarded today in Ghana as an important advocate of Akan dialects and culture, in particular the Twi language. He did more than anyone else to establish the study of Akan on secure scientific foundations. Between 1871 and 1881 he was absorbed in mammoth tasks of translation and interpretation, carrying off the entire enterprise with rare distinction. He completed a translation of the Bible in 1871, wrote a widely acclaimed dictionary and grammar of the Twi language in 1875, and crowned it in 1879 with an invaluable compilation of 3,600 Twi proverbs and idioms. He developed a deep and abiding love for the Akan people. In the preface to his collection of proverbs he wrote:

> May this Collection give a new stimulus to the diligent gathering of folk-lore and to the increasing cultivation of native literature. May those Africans who are enjoying the benefit of a Christian education, make the best of the privilege; but let them not despise the sparks of truth entrusted to and preserved by their own people, and let them not forget that by entering into their way of thinking and by acknowledging what is good and expounding what is wrong they will gain the more access to the hearts and minds of their less favoured countrymen.[35]

Christaller repeats the plea of many missionaries that educated Africans should fit themselves for the special task of indigenization to which the success of the Christian cause was tied. Natural entitlement does not constitute an inborn advantage in this field. Bible translation fits people with new and fresh eyes to see what God would see, and thereby alters perspective in a radical way. Christaller demonstrated this in his *Twi Dictionary*, published in 1881, which has been hailed as an "Encyclopaedia of Akan Civilization."[36] Christaller helped found the Christian Messenger in Basel in 1883, a paper devoted to the promotion of Akan life and culture. From 1905 to 1917, when this publication was transferred to Ghana, it published articles in Twi, Ga, and English, and covered local events as well as international news such as the Russo-Japanese War of 1904, Halley's Comet in 1910, and the sinking of the Titanic in 1912. The use of the vernacular to report on world news and to inform its readers about local affairs was a major contribution, allowing its audience to keep abreast of happenings in the wider world without literacy in the European languages. As a pioneer in indigenous publishing it deserves far more attention than it typically receives in accounts of African journalism.

Among the greatest tributes to Christaller was that paid by J. B. Danquah, the founding spirit of modern Ghanaian nationalism, whose own work was the inspiration for Kwame Nkrumah, the founder of modern Ghana. An ethical philosopher, Danquah was enamored of the idea of the Akan having originated in the Near East; his *Akan Doctrine of God* is a dense Kantian treatise that attempts to expound the Akan worldview in the schematized terms of the social system and religious psychology—a sort of philosophical functionalism. Its very recondite brilliance, however, condemned the book to early obsolescence. In this volume, Danquah acknowledged Christaller as its source and antecedent. He said Christaller's work was "the Old Testament," the foundational Scripture of the Akan, and that his own attempt was "the New Testament," which depended on the earlier enterprise. It was high praise, indeed, yet richly deserved. With the assistance of his local colleagues, Christaller supplied an interactive cultural map of Akan life and thought, with horizons of new possibilities. He would surely have been delighted that a native Ghanaian, C. A. Akrofi, should continue his work, producing in 1960 a new Twi Bible.[37]

Another notable Ghanaian who was deeply influenced by Christaller was the Reverend David Asante of Akropong. He was trained at Basel from 1857 to 1862, and ordained in 1864. As Christaller's protégé, Asante acquired his enthusiasm for the vernacular translating works from German and English into Akan, including John Bunyan's *Pilgrim's Progress*. Asante was clearly a major national figure. "But such is the preoccupation of Ghanaian biographers with 'merchant princes' and nationalist firebrands that, outside the small circle of the Presbyterian Church and an entry in the *Encyclopaedia Africana*, not much is known of such pioneers as Asante. Yet in the translation of the Bible and in his other books he helped to introduce new concepts, new words and phrases into Ghanaian literature."[38] As one who should know, Asante wrote in 1866 paying fulsome tribute for Christaller's sterling achievement with the beautiful translation of the Psalms. At last, Africa could hail her own Coverdale.

The Psalms are translated perfectly and brilliantly. Nobody can read this translation without deep feelings of awe. They resemble in many ways the songs of mourning (*Kwadwom*) in our Twi language; the Twi people will be glad to read them. May the Lord give His blessing to your labours. I want to congratulate you personally and in the name of Africa. May the Lord give you strength for more such work.[39]

Bible translation, as Bruce Metzger has observed,[40] has become rather commonplace in our time, and so, inevitably, something of the mystique of the craft, as well as the excitement and controversy that greeted the publication of England's most famous biblical version, has been lost. Perhaps the centuries-long triumph of the KJV is unrepeatable, or even unnecessary, but we have seen signs of new stirrings in Africa and elsewhere to indicate that the old wells are far from exhausted, that fresh fields of translation may yield yet new and welcome veins of truth and beauty.

Conclusion

It is appropriate to conclude these investigations with an appeal for appreciation of the work done in Bible translation in anticipation of what the future may yet hold in store. An Irish missionary on furlough from Nigeria was on a visit to Newcastle-upon-Tyne when he saw for the first time the "Flying Scotsman," as the London-Edinburgh train was called. He could express his wonder only with the help of the KJV. "Old things are passed away, and all things are become new."[41] He proceeded to fantasize about the dawn of a quiet but inexorable social revolution that would sweep the old order away. We need not be that exuberant to appreciate the changes in religious outlook ushered in by the Christian cultivation of the vernacular worldwide. Writing in 1860 in the *New York Tribune* about the extraordinary impact of Christian missions in Hawaii, Richard H. Dana, Jr., called us to reflect as follows:

> It is no small thing to say of the Missionaries of the American Board
> . . . that in less than forty years they have taught this whole people
> to read and write, to cipher and to sew. They have given them an
> alphabet, grammar, and dictionary; preserved their language from
> extinction; given it a literature, and translated into it the Bible and
> works of devotion, science and entertainment.[42]

Six

REGIONS LUTHER NEVER KNEW
Ancient Books in a New World

Philip Jenkins

*T*he history of the King James Bible is a tale of choices, of roads taken and not taken. Which Greek version was the best source for particular parts of Scripture? Which Hebrew tradition? Which manuscripts carried authority? Most fundamentally, which books should be included or excluded? Decisions that the church made in James' time, and particularly decisions made by the translators and publishers, would carry great weight for later Christian belief and practice.

The apocryphal books offer a powerful example. Surprisingly, perhaps, in light of the disfavor in which these works stand among modern Protestants, seventeenth-century believers were quite open to reading works such as Judith and Tobit, while remaining suspicious of their seemingly Catholic aspects. The Anglican Thirty-Nine Articles had been clear about relegating these texts to a secondary status—"the Church doth read for example of life and instruction of manners: but yet doth it not apply them to establish any doctrine"—but at least faithful believers read them, including strict Puritans. The King James Bible thus incorporated the Apocrypha between the Old and New Testaments. But this somewhat marginalized status would prove perilous, as it suggested a sub-biblical quality, and those texts lost some of their status over time. In 1826, critically, the British and Foreign Bible Society decided not to print the Apocrypha with their Bibles, effectively closing access to those books for the emerging Anglophone Christianity of Africa and Asia. Thus even a minor denigration of a text could in the long term have potent consequences for what King James' translators termed "the farthest parts of Christendom."

This example points to an aspect of the translation process that perhaps we take for granted, namely the strict conservatism of the King James scholars in deciding the canon. Although in 1611 we are still centuries away from higher criticism and the ruthless standards by which later scholars would weigh a biblical book in the balance and find it canonically wanting, the intellectual ferment of the Reformation had posed serious challenges to the commonly accepted limits of Scripture. Martin Luther, especially, had raised real concerns about several familiar New Testament works, and his immense influence among seventeenth-century Protestants might conceivably have resulted in granting these works some kind of associate status in the canon.

Very fortunately, in light of later events, the King James translators made no such decision. And the full wisdom of that conservatism, that inclusiveness, would not become apparent until our own day, and the present age of global Christian expansion.

The Farthest Parts of Christendom

If the Bible claims an eternal quality, then the readership of that book changes dramatically over time. As is well known, the shape of the "Christian world" is very malleable. A hundred years ago, Christianity was decidedly a Euro-American faith. Combining Christian numbers in Europe and North America, these continents accounted for 82 percent of all believers in 1900, and even by 1970, that figure had fallen only to 57 percent. But that situation was changing rapidly. According to the World Christian Database, just since 1900, the number of Christians in Europe has grown by 29 percent, a substantial figure. In Africa, though, the absolute number of recorded believers grew in the same period by an incredible 4,930 percent. The comparable growth in Latin America was 877 percent. The number of African believers soared, from just 10 million in 1900 to 500 million by 2015 or so, and (if projections are correct) that number will reach an astonishing 1 billion by 2050.[1] Put another way, the number of African Christians in 2050 will be almost twice as large as the total figure for all Christians alive anywhere on the globe back in 1900. By 2050, in contrast, Euro-American Christians could make up around a quarter of the global total. That is a revolution indeed.[2]

It is also a revolution with profound implications for Bible readership, as the spread of Christianity has created vast new markets for Bible translation and reading. By far the largest importers and consumers of Bibles are now outside the West—in Brazil, China, India, Nigeria, and Indonesia. Allowing for nuances of translation, different communities are reading the same Bible, but they are reading it very differently than it is read in Euro-American churches. Some years ago, in my book *The New Faces of Christianity*, I discussed some of the most significant themes in Bible interpretation that surface in many of the newer churches.[3]

Of course, I was not suggesting that these themes are uniform, any more than there is a homogeneous reality called Southern Christianity. The concepts of "South" and "Third World" are enormous generalizations, which ignore not only the distinctions between countries but the regional differences within such vast states as China or Brazil. Yet it is not absurd to compare churches in very dissimilar societies, provided that they share significant features that distinguish them from the traditional Christian heartlands. In many African and Asian countries, for instance, churches are largely made up of Christians relatively new to the faith, either first- or second-generation converts; this characteristic affects styles of worship and faith. The same holds true for recent Latin American converts to surging evangelical or Pentecostal denominations. Furthermore, across the global South, Christians live alongside numerous members of other creeds, possibly as small minority populations, and therefore always have to bear in mind the risk of hostility from these neighbors. New Christians, moreover, carry with them a substantial cultural baggage from these other religions, whether from traditional primal worship or from one of the great world faiths. In all these ways, Christians in the newer churches operate on assumptions very different from believers in the United States or Germany.

With these points in mind, it is legitimate to speak of distinctive ways of reading the Bible. We can see those differences in approaches to several books that, to say the least, did not attract the lively enthusiasm of the Protestant reformers. To the contrary, Martin Luther especially disliked them, and would have been happier had they been removed from the canon. Today, though, these books have a lively presence and popularity worldwide because they speak to contemporary issues and concerns in ways that the reformers could not have understood. Semi-seriously, I offer an excellent ground rule for understanding attitudes to books of the Bible in Africa especially: if Luther hated it, it goes down very well in Africa.

Hence my title. In 1782 William Cowper imagined a Celtic druid comforting the defeated warrior-queen Boadicea. Not to worry, he promised, the Roman oppressors too will fall, and a new global (British) empire will arise, far greater than anything the Romans ever imagined:

> Regions Cæsar never knew
> Thy posterity shall sway,
> Where his eagles never flew,
> None invincible as they.

Comforted, she returns to the fight:

> Empire is on us bestow'd,
> . Shame and ruin wait for you.[4]

My agenda here is less triumphalistic, with no comparable talk of empire: Rather, I will focus on the renewed popularity of books that were once disparaged in regions Luther never knew. The words of the Reformation translators—and especially of the English Bible—resonate in ways that the translators could not have suspected.

Luther's *Antilegomena*

Luther famously drew a distinction between those New Testament books that were regarded as unquestionably canonical (the *Homologoumena*) and those that were disputed, the *Antilegomena*, a category that included the Epistle to the Hebrews, James, Jude, 2 Peter, 2 and 3 John, and Revelation. Luther's criteria for doubt were largely rooted in sound historical scholarship, but also included a large measure of his personal theological prejudice. If a book did not fit his views, then it hardly belonged in the New Testament, and that was particularly true in the case of James, which (he thought) contradicted Pauline teachings. As Luther wrote,

> I think highly of the epistle of James, and regard it as valuable although it was rejected in early days. It does not expound human doctrines, but lays much emphasis on God's law. Yet to give my own opinion without prejudice to that of anyone else, I do not hold it to be of apostolic authorship, for the following reasons:
> Firstly, because, in direct opposition to St. Paul and all the rest of the Bible, it ascribes justification to works, and declares that Abraham was justified by his works when he offered up his son . . . This defect proves that the epistle is not of apostolic provenance.
> Secondly, because, in the whole length of its teaching, not once does it give Christians any instruction or reminder of the passion, resurrection, or spirit of Christ. It mentions Christ once and again, but teaches nothing about Him. . . .
> *The epistle of James, however, only drives you to the law, and its works.*[5]

Perhaps, thought Luther, the epistle's problems lay in its mixed origins, which mangled apostolic teachings:

> [James] mixes one thing with another to such an extent that I suspect some good and pious man assembled a few things said by disciples of the apostles, and then put them down in black and white; or perhaps the epistle was written by someone else who made notes of a sermon of his.[6]

Luther also disliked or rather distrusted Revelation, partly because it failed to present what he saw as the core of Christian truth, but also because the book so entranced radicals, millenarians, and social revolutionaries in his own day. In 1522, he wrote that individuals should make their own minds up about Revelation, although as for himself,

> I miss more than one thing in this book, and it makes me consider it to be neither apostolic nor prophetic. First and foremost, the apostles do not deal with visions, but prophesy in clear and plain words, as do Peter and Paul, and Christ in the gospel. For it befits the apostolic office to speak clearly of Christ and his deeds, without images and visions. Moreover there is no prophet in the Old Testament, to say nothing of the New, who deals so exclusively with visions and images . . . I can in no way detect that the Holy Spirit produced it. . . . Finally, let everyone think of it as his own spirit leads him. My spirit cannot accommodate itself to this book. For me this is reason enough not to think highly of it: Christ is neither taught nor known in it. . . . Therefore I stick to the books that present Christ to me clearly and purely.[7]

Of the Epistle to the Hebrews, Luther felt that "it cannot in all respects be compared to the Apostolic Epistles," and he famously suggested Apollos rather than Paul as the author. He was also worried that the epistle seemed to grant no forgiveness for a second apostasy, placing limits on God's grace.

Jude, finally, he disliked because it seemed unnecessary, virtually a doublet or précis of 2 Peter. "Although I value this book," he wrote, "it is an epistle that need not be counted among the chief books which are supposed to lay the foundations of faith."[8]

Accordingly, Luther placed four rejected books (Hebrews, James, Revelation, and Jude) at the end of his translation, and he was followed in this by both Tyndale and Coverdale—although the King James Version permitted no such doubts.

Africa's Epistle

Viewed from the modern world, though, such theological caution seems misplaced. In different ways, each of these books exercises a potent appeal in modern churches, because they all speak to the conditions in which people live—in conditions of poverty, social fragility, and political oppression; a world in which vestiges of older religions still flourish; a world of complex religious coexistence. Each speaks to lively modern debates—on syncretism, on political resistance, on Christian living.

Let us for instance take Hebrews, which has a mixed reception in the Western world. Although many modern readers know passages from Hebrews—the cloud of witnesses, or the definition of faith as the evidence of things not seen—they see little relevance in much of the book's argument. The epistle assumes deep knowledge of the Jewish temple ritual, and it describes how this has been superseded by the once-and-for-all sacrifice of Christ, who is now the ultimate high priest. The author knows a great deal about sacrifice, not just its religious significance, but also the practical minutiae: he knows that the sacrificial blood is not just shed, it is sprinkled.

However rich the argument, though, the complex discussion of sacrifice and thus of priesthood seems to have no contemporary value. Surely, it is a matter for historians curious about how early Christians defined themselves against Judaism? Euro-American readers might turn with surprise to the account of Hebrews in the work of Kwame Bediako, one of the most influential of African theologians, who uses the intriguing heading "The Epistle to the Hebrews as OUR Epistle"—that is, as Africa's. Bediako, after all, worked in an African society where the idea of blood sacrifice is deeply entrenched and forms the backdrop to any Christian theological debate over atonement and justification. For Bediako, "The value for us of the presentation of Jesus in Hebrews stems from its relevance to a society like ours with its deep tradition of sacrifice, priestly mediation and ancestral function."[9] In Ghana, where sacrifice marks the turning points of the year, "the traditional purificatory rituals of Odwira, repeated year after year, have in fact been fulfilled and transcended by the one, perfect Odwira that Jesus Christ has performed once for all . . . The Odwira to end all Odwiras has taken place through the death of Jesus Christ."[10]

Hebrews thus becomes a powerful argument in current controversies, particularly in drawing strict lines against syncretism. It is a decisive weapon for those African Christians appalled at the idea that importing some form of blood sacrifice into the churches would represent a form of "meaningful inculturation." In the massive *Africa Bible Commentary*, Kenyan theologian Samuel Ngewa writes that,

> We need to know about our heritage, including the sacrifices in our traditional religions. We must however always keep the right perspective. These sacrifices are a contact point for the presentation of the supreme sacrifice, that is, Christ.[11]

Ethiopian scholar Tesfaye Kassa recalls that:

> The message of Hebrews was a great encouragement for many believers during the Communist era in Ethiopia (1974–1991). . . . [Hebrews] still speaks to all who face the challenges posed by Orthodox religious syncretism, African traditional religions, the day to day temptations of worldly passions and, in Muslim countries, the pressure of extremely difficult situations. The Letter to the Hebrews calls on believers to make a bold commitment to Christ in the face of public abuse, imprisonment and the loss of their property.[12]

Interestingly, other African scholars find profoundly modern relevance in another short text that Luther disparaged, namely Jude. One of Africa's leading biblical scholars is Tokunboh Adeyemo, who finds in Jude a stirring call to action among second-generation believers who are tempted to compromise with the surrounding culture and its pagan religions—a situation as threatening in Africa in 2011 as in the Mediterranean world around 100 AD. As Adeyemo writes, "In the face of religious pluralism, Christo-paganism, widespread syncretism and theological liberalism that denies the divinity of Christ, there is an urgent demand for people ready to defend the Christian message in Africa today." How, for example, should Christians respond when "a resistance movement that is fighting to overthrow an elected government claims to be Christian but mixes witchcraft and magic with the Bible and has a leader who claims to be the messiah"? "May the church in Africa heed Jude's call to defend the faith!"[13]

Incidentally, the enthusiasm of both Bediako and Kassa for Hebrews quite unconsciously recalls a truly ancient African linkage for this letter, which no later than the third century was especially popular in the Roman churches of Carthage and North Africa. That great African theologian Tertullian not only prized Hebrews, but also shared the sense of his church that this was in fact the Letter of Barnabas.

The Epistle of Straw

Other books of Luther's *Antilegomena* have had equally interesting after-lives. If Luther found little of value in James, that epistle has enjoyed a vast resurgence in global South churches, where it benefits considerably from its wisdom genre. Although James forms part of the New Testament, it very much bears the imprint of the Old, and it uses and comments on traditional wisdom texts, including Proverbs and Ecclesiastes. However much wisdom themes surface elsewhere in the New Testament, James is its only entire work of Wisdom literature. Moreover, the authorities and examples cited in the epistle itself are Old Testament figures particularly beloved in these churches: Job as an ideal of innocent suffering, Elijah as a model miracle worker, and Abraham as the type of unquestioning faith.

The roots in Wisdom literature are particularly important. Biblical Wisdom literature grew out of social settings that are immediately recognizable today, in their intense social stratification, in the omnipresence of poverty, and, above all, in the transience of life. Because they speak so exactly to real-world conditions, texts like James appeal not only to millions of global South Christians, but also to members of other faiths who share the same social and economic circumstances. Arguably, James may be the single biblical book that best encapsulates the issues facing global South churches today, and its influence is as evident in Asia and Latin America as in Africa. James is much cited in contexts of spiritual healing, of persecution and resistance, of activism and social justice, and even of interfaith relations.

Especially in the African Initiated Churches, James is a great source for sermon texts. Studying West African churches in the 1960s, Harold W. Turner noted that James was the most-cited work in sermons, perhaps because in both form and content it so much resembled familiar Wisdom literature, with all its "aphorisms, epigrams and similes."[14] Although Turner was describing conditions in one region some decades ago, the influence of James is still obvious across the spectrum of African churches. The ambitious recent work, *The African Bible,* remarks that "James addresses things that concern African cities. . . . In a continent that experiences much suffering, the concerns in James' letter are very much ours also."[15] When Solomon Andria summarizes James' teaching, he cannot refrain from meeting a proverb with a proverb: "The rich are easily noticed and gain the respect of leaders. Then the poor find themselves shoved to one side because, as the proverb says, 'thin cows are not licked by their friends.' "[16]

In its combination of literary styles, no less than in the themes it addresses, the epistle offers much to global South churches. James was written for emerging churches still trying to define the distinctions between Christian and non-Christian worlds, and it offers a set of rules for life as an unpopular Christian minority in a hostile non-Christian culture. One African commentary notes that "James uses a particularly friendly way of addressing his Christians on the day to day problems they (and we too) are likely to meet."[17] To take a pressing example, how far should worldly distinctions of wealth and power be reproduced within the Christian community? Undoubtedly, James speaks directly to class issues, though the revolutionary activist interpretation is by no means the only possible reading. The text is directed at poor believers who must face constant stress and temptation without facing despair and without envying the rich, whose fate is in God's hands. In passages with an apocalyptic tone, James reminds his listeners that the lot of the rich deserved little of their attention, since God will sweep away the wealthy at the coming judgment. Yet poor global South Christians need not be actively leftist or revolutionary in their politics to find solace in such words, as they are constantly deluged with the images of wealth and success presented by Western media and advertising.

Above all, the letter demands that the Christian life be manifested in practical deeds rather than affirmations of faith. The emphasis on deeds rather than words does not mean that these churches fail to appreciate ideas of salvation by faith alone, as Luther assumed. Rather, they identify with James' assumption that Christians are joining the church from a mainstream community with radically different values, pagan or secular, into which Judeo-Christian ideas have not yet begun to penetrate, so that church members need practical lessons in living in an alternative society.

James also provides guidance for spiritual healing, one of the centerpieces of the Christian appeal in much of Africa and Asia. Not only does it promise healing, but it provides specific instructions, telling believers to seek healing in prayer and anointing by elders of the church. James' influence can be seen in the widespread practice of anointing with oil. This is a trademark of independent healing churches like Nigeria's Aladura, for whom healing is and has always been their main raison d'être, but anointing is widely used across denominations. In West

Africa's booming Winners Chapel, the text from James is reinforced by a battery of Old Testament passages, and the anointing oil is sometimes credited with miraculous powers. West Africa's Mosama Disco Christo Church offers a concise summary of healing texts in its articles of fundamental belief. After declaring forthrightly, "We believe in divine healing," the document lists James 5:14-15 alongside other classic passages from the Gospels. The strictly mainstream Anglican Church of Nigeria also recommends "Bible passages for certain life situations," presenting a deeply religious interpretation of sickness and health. Naturally enough, James 5 is prescribed to justify and sanctify the practice of healing through prayer.

However, African Bible scholars read James carefully, noting that the oil must not be regarded as miraculous in its own right: as Andria stresses, "It is the prayer of faith rather than the repetition of special formulas that brings miraculous healing."[18]

The Bible's Wisdom literature is especially popular because of its profound sense of the transience of life. From many beloved passages in the Epistle of James, one of the most used African sermon texts is James 4:14, which seems uncannily relevant to the conditions of everyday life: "Ye know not what shall be on the morrow. For what is your life? It is even a vapor, that appeareth for a little time, and then vanisheth away." In the New International Version, the NIV, life is a mist. Echoes of this text often resurface in paraphrased form. In the Sudan, which for some forty years suffered repeated civil wars and the vicious persecution of non-Muslims, one Christian chorus teaches the grim truth that "You are here today but tomorrow you'll be here no more / Our only hope is Jesus Christ, so receive him now." After catastrophes such as the 2004 tsunami, sermons in South and East Asian churches made great use of James.[19]

James between Faiths

Its breadth of appeal gives a special meaning to the familiar classification of James as a catholic or universal epistle. James has very little that would offend the strictest Muslim, and indeed, much of its content echoes the Quran. Particularly appealing is the letter's attitude toward the future and its assumption that all worldly conditions are transient. So uncertain is life that James specifically warns against even saying that you are planning to do something or travel somewhere, because you do not know if you will live to do it. Any such plan should be accompanied by the provisional phrase "If God wills," an exact parallel to the Muslim custom of inserting "Inshallah" when expressing any plan or intention. In Latin America, the equivalent phrase, and a sentiment much heard, is "Si Dios quiere." James portrays God as "compassionate and merciful," a familiar Muslim characterization (5:11). The epistle has been proposed as a basis for missionary inroads—for Christians seeking to convert Muslims and vice versa. Just as plausibly, it offers common ground for interreligious dialogue.

Quite apart from Islam, James can be read in various religious contexts. One remarkable claim about James concerns the cryptic reference in 3:6 to *trochos tes geneseos*, usually translated as "cycle of nature." The term may derive from Greek mystery religions, but translated as "wheel of birth" (which is plausible), the phrase sounds distinctly South Asian, either Hindu or Buddhist. R. S. Sugirtharajah remarks, "If there is any influence of Eastern ideas, it is here that it is visibly prominent."[20]

James acquires its greatest value as a bridge between faiths in a Buddhist context. In 1974 Kosuke Koyama saw the letter as an invaluable tool in his quest for a distinctively Asian manifestation of Christianity. Drawing upon his experiences as a missionary to Thailand, Koyama advocated a popular-oriented water-buffalo theology that could speak to the overwhelmingly poor masses who were unacquainted with Christian tradition. He imagines welcoming the Apostle James to Thailand, where his epistle fits well into traditional concerns, so much so that it reads like a translation of a traditional Buddhist sutra.[21]

In so many ways, James speaks appealingly to an Asian audience. As Koyama says, "You are very good in the use of picture language . . . These images remain with us."[22] Just as important, Koyama's James speaks to familiar religious concepts, particularly transience: "All decays! All is transient!" He also praises detachment and self-control. James makes it clear that evil stems from within the individual, from misdirected desires and passions that must be combated, and that anger and intemperate speech give rise to much conflict. "'Bridle your tongue,' your letter says to us. Right indeed!" As in many premodern cultures, Koyama's James knows the very high value that attaches to speech, and the vital necessity of judging one's words.[23] As *The African Bible* remarks of James, "From the African point of view the words of 3:1-12, 4:11-12 call for special reflection. Here we are reminded of the importance of words in African communities. The word can be a medicine but it can also be a poison."[24] Also reflecting the values of traditional societies, the apostle praises the virtues of slowness—"listeners should be slow to speak, and slow to become angry." As Koyama notes, a Thai audience might remark, "We like this word 'slow,'" and all the more so as society modernizes and accelerates.[25]

Supporting the notion of James' appeal to Buddhists, the current Dalai Lama provided an admiring introduction for a recent reprinting of the text. He finds strong linkages between James and the Tibetan Buddhist genre of *lojong,* or mind training—a term that could serve as an excellent alternative name for the wisdom genre. Like Koyama, the Dalai Lama dwells on James' praise of the virtues of slowness, "be swift to hear, slow to speak, slow to wrath." This is "the most poignant verse of the entire letter." The Dalai Lama goes on to remark that the declaration that "your life is a vapor" "beautifully captured" the basic and seemingly universal doctrine of transience. James, in short, is excellent Buddhism. Or rather, it excellently captures the social realities underpinning faith across many global South societies.[26]

Revelation

Given Luther's political situation, surrounded as he was by revolutionary fanatics, it is not surprising that he was suspicious of Revelation, and of the extravagant claims of self-styled prophets. (Interestingly, though, given his distrust of private judgments, one main reason for his suspicion was highly individual and subjective: "My spirit cannot accommodate itself to this book.") In modern times, Revelation enjoys huge success as a critical guide informing Christians' decisions about how to live in the political circumstances they must endure.

Like Hebrews, Revelation speaks abundantly to cultures that know the concept of sacrifice. In fact, only readers in a culture familiar with sacrificial tradition are in a position to appreciate fully the numerous allusions to this practice throughout the New Testament. A quick search of the New Testament produces over ninety uses of the word "blood," not counting cognates or related concepts such as "altar" and "lamb," so it is scarcely an exaggeration to describe the text as soaked with images of sacrifice and redemptive blood. The goriest texts of all are precisely Hebrews and Revelation, which between them account for 40 percent of these references. The same two books account for nine of the New Testament's twenty-one uses of the word "altar."

The same Old Testament elements that give Hebrews an African feel are also present in Revelation. Fidon Mwombeki, a Tanzanian Lutheran leader, writes of the many ways in which that book speaks clearly to

Africans. For modern Africans, as for the original audience of Revelation, "The dead are still living in the other world, and they influence the life of those in this world."[27] He discusses the exalted picture of God and the common belief that the future can be seen through visions, dreams, and revelations. Moreover, he writes, "the dominant symbols of the lamb, the throne, the blood, and the animals are common in African religious symbolism. The sacrificial blood, as well as innocent human blood crying from the ground (Revelation 6:10), correspond to present-day African beliefs. No one in Africa can expect to get away with shedding innocent blood. At the same time, the lamb as the animal of sacrifice slaughtered for the sins of humanity is a dominant symbol both in Revelation and in African beliefs."[28]

But it is the political content that gives Revelation its greatest modern appeal—or perhaps anti-political would be a better term. The biblical account of Revelation exercises an immense fascination across the political spectrum. Given its portrayal of secular states as deceptive, evil persecutors, and cities as the seats of demonic forces, the book's appeal requires little explanation. For many on both left and right, it reads like a political science textbook. From a liberation theology perspective, Brazilian scholar Gilberto da Silva Gorgulho remarks, "The Book of Revelation is the favorite book of our popular communities. Here they find the encouragement they need in their struggle and a criterion for the interpretation of official persecution in our society."[29] Revelation is eminently suitable for a society that lives constantly with disasters and violence. As Kenyan scholar Elias Githuka stresses, this message is exactly suited for modern Africa:

> The persecution has continued in modern times in countries like Uganda under President Idi Amin, in Chad under President Tombalbaye, and it is still continuing in countries like Ethiopia and Eritrea. It flares up sporadically in other countries too. Those who convert from Islam to Christianity often face severe discrimination and sometimes even death. The main aim of persecution is not to destroy the individuals who are persecuted but to eliminate the faith they profess.[30]

Revelation exists to strengthen believers facing these threats. Churches in Sudan, subject to decades-long mass martyrdom, read the book for its promise that whatever may ensue in this world, God's justice will ultimately prevail.

Such a message was no less newsworthy for Ugandan Christians in the 1970s in the years of the Amin dictatorship. At one point, the small "Redeemed Church" faced imminent persecution and likely extermination. Its followers naturally turned to Revelation to make sense of their plight, and in one service, they read this passage: "And when they shall have finished their testimony, the Beast that ascendeth out of the bottomless pit shall make war against them, and shall overcome them, and kill them." The preacher continued, "By these words we are comforted." The "comfort" in such nightmarish images might seem slight indeed, except that now the listeners have been reminded of two things. They understand the diabolical nature of the Amin regime, and by the same token, they also know the end of the story, that the beast will be annihilated.

The message of Revelation is simple: however overwhelming the world's evils might seem, God has triumphed and will triumph. In China, Christians turned to Revelation for hope during times of persecution, above all during the phantasmagoric horrors of the Cultural Revolution. According to K. K. Yeo, "By means of the motifs of visionary transportation to heaven, visions of God's throne room in heaven, angelic mediators of revelation, symbolic visions of political powers, coming judgment, and new creation, Chinese Christians see the final destiny of this despaired world in the transcendent divine purpose. . . . It is the hope portrayed in the Book of Revelation that sustains Chinese Christians to endure to the end."[31]

Elsewhere, too, Revelation speaks plausibly to a modern audience. The modern development of apocalyptic theology reached new heights in the South African churches of the 1980s, when government opponents portrayed the apartheid regime, and its religious allies, according to the most harrowing texts of Revelation. Preaching at the funeral of civilians killed by South African authorities, Desmond Tutu chose as his text Revelation 6, in which the martyrs cry out, "Lord, how long?" So burningly relevant were such texts that, as Tutu remarks, they "seemed then to have been written with our particular situation in mind." Though the government exercised a draconian censorship, they had missed such incendiary items as Revelation: "The book they should have banned was the Bible."[32]

Though other global South crises and confrontations fail to stir the Western media as much as South Africa did, apocalyptic visions still shape African Christianity. One Ghanaian author notes, "In Africa today there are still marks of the 'Beast'—pain and suffering arising from ethnic conflicts and civil wars, corruption in high places which results in unnecessary deaths on our roads, political assassinations, high increase in crime on our streets, extreme poverty and hunger which dehumanizes many Africans."[33] But Revelation exercises a widespread influence, and passages and images from it appear in the oddest contexts. To announce a routine committee meeting, one Nigerian church naturally uses a weighty and quite threatening text from Revelation: "The biannual meeting of the Standing Committee of the Church of Nigeria kicks off Tuesday this week in Maiduguri with the theme, 'I know your works' (Revelation 2 and 3)."[34]

Reading Cleanly

In making these observations, I am certainly not arguing that Western churches have an obligation to accept every word of African biblical interpretation, or vice versa. Because Ghanaians read Hebrews so lovingly and intuitively does not mean that Germans are obliged to have the same reaction. Different books speak differently to various audiences.

In fact, in understanding this diversity of voices, we could do worse than to follow the advice of Martin Luther himself, who had to deal with European contemporaries intoxicated by the Scriptures they had discovered with such awe and excitement. The attitudes of these early modern Christians, in fact, closely resembled those of first- and second-generation Christians in the emerging nations of Africa and Asia, still in the first throes of an intense love affair with the Bible. Inspired by the Scripture, some of Luther's extreme contemporaries wanted to import it wholesale into the modern world, using Old Testament law codes to rule a Christian society.

Trying to calm his rivals, Luther urged that modern believers should be very careful in how they read Scripture, and especially in how they apply it in their own day. They should "read cleanly":

> From the very beginning, the Word has come to us in various ways. It is not enough simply to look and see whether this is God's word, whether God has said it; rather we must look and see to whom it has been spoken, whether it fits us. This makes all the difference between night and day. . . . The word in Scripture is of two kinds: the first does not pertain or apply to me, the other kind does.[35]

The words of the Bible do not apply to all. Passages addressed to David as king might be relevant to kings, but not to the rest of us, and we would be mad to pretend they do. More generally, for Luther, large sections of the Bible—especially the Hebrew law codes and rules of ritual purity—did not apply literally to Christians, who lived under the different arrangements prevailing under Christ. That did not mean that the Old Testament was repealed or obsolete, but people had to seek in it what was relevant to them.

The medieval scholastics had a useful rule: *Quidquid recipitur ad modum recipientis recipitur,* or roughly, "What people hear depends on who is doing the hearing." We see (and hear) things not as they are, but as we are. Looking at changing attitudes to the Bible, we see above all how audiences and readerships change over time. You cannot turn the Christian world upside down—as has occurred within our lifetimes—without radically revising the terms on which new believers read the Scriptures. We can only be grateful to the King James translators for maintaining the library of faith in its broadest terms, for the benefit of generations yet unborn.

Seven

THE QUESTION OF ELOQUENCE
IN THE KING JAMES VERSION

Robert Alter

*I*f there is a single attribute large numbers of readers attach almost reflexively to the King James Version, it is most likely eloquence. The warrant for this attribution is abundantly evident. Eloquence, a term associated with oratory, especially delivered orally, suggests a powerful marshalling of the resources of language to produce a persuasive effect, and that quality is manifested in verse after verse of the 1611 translation. It is an intrinsic quality of this English rendering of the Bible that no doubt has been heightened by the virtually canonical status the King James Bible came to enjoy and by the performance of passages from it in ecclesiastical settings or on other solemn occasions. If it became almost a convention in Hollywood films of the 1930s and 1940s to introduce a sonorous recitation of the Twenty-Third Psalm in deathbed scenes, this biblical illumination of the cinematic moment was surely felt to be appropriate because the beautifully cadenced language of the King James Version of that psalm is such a moving expression of trust in God even in life's darkest moments.

The eloquence of the 1611 translation nevertheless deserves some scrutiny in regard to its sources, its nature, its relation to the original language of the Bible, and the degree to which it may or may not be pervasive in these English renderings of the biblical texts. Let me propose at the outset that the eloquence of the narrative prose and the eloquence of the poetry are not cut from the same cloth, however much readers tend to lump them together, something they may be encouraged to do by the fact that the King James Bible provides no typographical differentiation between poetry and prose. For the prose, the committees convened by King James adopted a translation strategy, adumbrated by Tyndale a century earlier, meant to create close equivalents for the Hebrew diction and syntax, and that resulted in a particular kind of forceful effect which was new in English. An exemplary instance is the beginning of the report of the flood in Genesis 7:17-21.

> And the flood was forty days upon the earth; and the waters increased, and bare up the ark, and it was lift up upon the earth. And the waters prevailed, and were increased greatly upon the earth; and the ark went upon the face of the waters. And the waters prevailed exceedingly upon the earth; and all the high hills, that *were* under the whole heaven, were covered. Fifteen cubits upward did the waters prevail; and the mountains were covered. And all flesh died that moved upon the earth, both of fowl, and of cattle, and of beast, and of every creeping thing that creepeth upon the earth, and every man.*

It should be said that the flood story, though it shares certain features with other kinds of narrative prose in the Bible, is not entirely typical because in its solemnity and in its rhythmically choreographed account of portentous primeval events it has—both in the passages drawn from the J and, even more, from the P document—a kind of epic grandeur. That, of course, is precisely an occasion for the exhibition of eloquence, which is finely exploited by the 1611 translators. The parallel syntax of the Hebrew, elsewhere deployed for other purposes, here is used to present a stately parade of clauses linked by "and" that report the sequence of momentous acts in which the whole earth is covered by the waters of the flood. Laying everything out in these parallel structures is not, I think, a natural way to package units of syntax in English, though it became a viable option for literary English after the King James Version. The King James translators, by following the syntactic contours of the Hebrew, achieved a new kind of compelling effect, at once lofty and almost stark. The antithetical strategy of modern translations of the Bible by sundry scholarly-ecclesiastical committees has been to repackage the syntax of the original in order to convey a sense that it might have been written in the twentieth century. What is lost in eloquence is palpable.

Compare, for example, "And the waters prevailed, and were increased greatly upon the earth; and the ark went upon the face of the waters,"

---

* Emphasis in biblical quotations is original throughout.

with the rendering of the Revised English Bible: "The ark floated on the surface of the swollen waters as they increased over the earth." The modern version is clear—the pursuit of perfect clarity being one of the great fallacies among modern translators of the Bible—and has a certain succinct tidiness, but it loses all the high solemnity of the King James Version. Instead of the report of three actions in grand sequence conveyed by three verbs—the prevailing and the increasing of the waters and the movement of the ark over the waters—the "prevailing" of the flood is tucked into an adjective, "swollen," and the increase of the waters is relegated to a subordinate clause, with the movement of the ark now "logically" placed at the beginning of the sentence. An epic movement, in sum, has been reduced to a prosaic notation.

Beyond considerations of syntax, much of the force of the 1611 translation derives from the kind of diction to which it generally adheres, at least in the narrative prose. There is a good deal of evidence that the writers of ancient Hebrew narrative, by a tacit consensus of literary convention, used a deliberately restricted vocabulary. Synonymity, which is often rich and inventive in biblical poetry, was rigorously avoided, and a lexicon of primary terms rather than fancy literary ones was generally favored. By and large, the King James translators honor this ancient commitment to plain diction and the repetition of terms. Note in our passage how "the flood was forty days upon the earth" and how "the ark went upon the face of the waters." The taut eloquence of the narrative inheres partly in the use, faithful to the original, of such simple primary terms—here, the verbs *to be, to go.* Alas, modern translators, evidently feeling that this is not the way *they* would have written the story, have not been able to resist the temptation of improving the original. Thus, as we have seen, in the Revised English Bible, the ark is made to "float," not "go," upon the waters, and in a still more fanciful exercise of editorial license, the New Jewish Publication Society translation has the ark "drift." (Are we certain that Noah's craft was rudderless?)

Other word choices in the 1611 version work equally well, even if one might have marginal reservations about a few of them. For the most part, as is evident here, a homespun Anglo-Saxon vernacular is favored, which is a good English equivalent of the plain diction of the Hebrew. Elsewhere, the use of such polysyllabic Latinate terms as "iniquity," "tribulation," "countenance," and "habitation" might be questioned, though all those words by now bear the authoritative weight of the canonical. In our passage, "prevailed" is an interesting if slightly odd choice, probably dictated by the fact that this same Hebrew verb is used elsewhere for prevailing in battle, though the local sense seems to be something like "surged." Another reiterated verb, "increased," is a fair enough rendering of the Hebrew and is idiomatically right in context, though a small opportunity is missed in not using "multiplied," the English equivalent for this Hebrew verb that is employed in the creation story, for there is a pointed irony that the same activity of multiplication initially applied to human procreation is now attached to the destruction of all living things. The King James translators, of course, had no notion of reiterated thematic key words as a formal literary device in biblical narrative, and so their choices sometimes reproduce the device and sometimes, as here, obscure it. Their language in this case, as in so many other instances, nevertheless does capture a great deal of the evocative driving force of the original. Throughout the translation of the Bible's narrative prose, the emulation in English of the Hebrew's plain diction and parallel syntax conveys the paradoxical sense of a discourse at once plain and elevated.

The case of poetry is more complicated. Biblical poetry uses a noticeably richer vocabulary than does the narrative prose, and at least some of it appears to be specialized poetic vocabulary, sometimes incorporating archaic terms and archaic grammatical forms. Because semantic parallelism between the two—in some instances, three—parts of the poetic line is fundamental to the system, the poets play with many different possibilities of synonymity, though it also should be said that usually the ostensible echoing of the first half of the line in the second half involves some sort of heightening, intensification, or even narrative development. The structure of biblical Hebrew, in which subjects, objects, and pronominal references can all be packed into a single word through prefixes, suffixes, or conjugated forms, lends itself to a terrific compactness, a feature repeatedly exploited, rhythmically and otherwise, by the poets. The compactness is a special challenge for translators because the structure of English is so radically different, and the King James translators do not appear to have paid much attention to the conciseness of the original, focused as they were on the literal meaning of the Hebrew words and not on how they sounded. This did not prevent them from achieving effects of great eloquence in rendering the poetry, but it was often not a Hebrew eloquence, as I will try to show.

The one bit of poetry from the King James Version that most native speakers of English know by heart is this line from the Twenty-Third Psalm: "Yea, though I walk through the valley of the shadow of death,

I will fear no evil." It is certainly eloquent, but is the eloquence biblical? I argue that it is not, the difference being between a wonderfully expansive utterance and a powerfully succinct one. The English deploys seventeen words, with twenty syllables. (That ratio neatly reflects the degree to which the translation on the whole aptly chooses short, simple words.) The Hebrew here shows just eight words, eleven syllables, and sounds something like this: *akh ki-'elekh begey tsalmavet lo' 'ira' ra'.* The English makes evocative use of a string of three noun phrases, "through the valley of the shadow of death," which has the effect of spinning out the skein of the beleaguered walker's trajectory through the valley to the very brink of death. The Hebrew has not a single "of" and only one preposition, itself no more than a particle attached to the beginning of the word that means "valley." "Shadow of death" (some scholars, but not I, think it means merely "darkness") is a single word, more or less like "deathshadow," and "valley" is joined to it in what amounts to a genitive structure that dispenses with "of." The English version, though not set as verse, feels like a line of poetry, but it is a kind of free-verse poetry that is almost an anticipation of Walt Whitman. One thinks of all those lengthy lines of Whitman's that sweep on grandly across the page from left margin to right, and it is surely relevant that Whitman was influenced by the King James Version, and in particular by Psalms.

This microscopic example tells us something about the general character of the translation of poetry in the King James Version. It often reads magnificently as English verse—one recalls, among a host of memorable instances, many of the Psalms, the voice from the whirlwind in Job, the haunting poem on mortality at the end of Ecclesiastes. Eloquence seems the proper attribute for these renderings of ancient Hebrew poetry, yet, as in the line from the Twenty-Third Psalm, the eloquence is more Jacobean than biblical—orotund, expansive, at times exhibiting a relish in the accumulation of ringing words and syllables, whereas the Hebrew is compact and incisive.

Let me venture a general qualification about the admired eloquence of the seventeenth-century translation. Because the translators were constantly concentrating on the words, straining to work out the most precise English equivalents for each of them, they did not, as I have noted, pay a great deal of attention to the sound of the words, which, as in all poetry, is inseparable from their meaning. Intermittently, intuitively, they do appear to have listened to the sounds, as attested by the fine rendering of the great prose-poem that opens the book of Ecclesiastes, where

there is good evidence that the translators were picking up the mesmer-
izing music of the Hebrew. But more often than most readers choose to
remember, the translators exhibit an indifference to the cadences and the
compactness of the Hebrew, blunting its pointed expressiveness.

Because we think automatically of eloquence when we think about
the King James Version, we tend to overlook its lapses, the places where
the language audibly stumbles. Here are the two lines of poetry that constitute the ninth verse of Psalm 30: "What profit *is there* in my blood, when
I go down to the pit? Shall the dust praise thee, shall it declare thy truth?"
The compact diction of the English is admirable throughout these two
lines, and the rendering of the second line, with its emphatic parallelism
("praise thee," "declare thy truth") is perfectly apt. Yet something has gone
awry rhythmically in the first of these two lines. The Hebrew sounds like
this: *mah betsa ' bedami / berideti 'el shaḥat.* There are exactly three words,
three accented syllables, in each half of the line, with a pounding allitera-
tion of *m*'s and *b*'s in the first half. The King James translators could have
reproduced the strong rhythm—an expression of the speaker's desperate
insistence—by writing, "What profit in my blood." Fearful, however, that
they might be obscuring an implied meaning, they felt obliged to add the
words "is there," indicating by the italics that these are merely implied
(in the first edition, it would have been smaller font in roman against the
boldface gothic of the surrounding words). The consequence is to break
the rhythm of the line. The second half of the line, "when I go down to
the pit" is a precise representation of the meaning of the three Hebrew
words, but the problem with expressive sound has been magnified: it is
not merely that we are given seven words for three but that the entire
clause is rhythmically slack, the strong cadenced poetry of the original
devolving into a prose amble.

The King James translators are at their best when they hew closely
to the evocative simplicity of the Hebrew diction, as is evident in the
example from the flood story, or even, despite the problems of rhythm,
in the two lines from Psalm 30 that we have been considering. These
learned churchmen—some of them conversant in Arabic, Syriac, and
Aramaic as well as Hebrew and Greek—of course viewed all of Scripture as sacred, and the assumed context of the sacred at times led them
astray in their translation choices, either producing a kind of eloquence
that is rather unbiblical or actually compromising the overall effect of
eloquence. Memorably, at the beginning of the creation story, they have
God place a "firmament" between the waters above and the waters below.

"Firmament" is a medieval astronomical term (Chaucer uses it), and it in fact has a certain etymological warrant because the Hebrew *raqia'*, conceived by the ancients as a vast celestial slab, derives from a verb that means "to pound out," though I am not entirely sure the King James translators were aware of the etymology. But it is something of a mouthful as an English word for "sky" and qualifies as what the Elizabethans called an inkhorn term, thus introducing an element of erudite fussiness of which there is no hint in the original. That element is even more evident when the word is used in poetry, as at the beginning of Psalm 19: "The heavens declare the glory of God; and the firmament sheweth his handywork." One might justifiably claim that this line of English poetry has real grandeur, but the presence of "firmament," where the Hebrew simply says "sky," imparts a note of formal elevation not intended by the ancient poet.

The reverential view of the Bible often leads the translators to opt for ecclesiastical or theologically fraught terms that give the biblical language a coloration fundamentally alien to it. In the fourth verse of Psalm 19, it is said of God that in the heavens "hath he set a tabernacle for the sun." Now, what God sets up in the heavens is actually a tent, the ordinary word for the prosaic dwelling, often made of black goat skins, which Bedouins and migratory pastoralists like Abraham used for shelter. "Tabernacle" enters the celestial scene because the translators are thinking ecclesiastically. It may be a nice flourish, but it falsifies the original, where three plain words—"in-them" (one word in the Hebrew), "set," and "sun"—are matched by the plain word used for the sun's dwelling, *'ohel*, "tent." A similar elevation of an ordinary Hebrew dwelling-place is observable in Psalm 18:11: "He made darkness his secret place; his pavilion round about him *were* dark waters *and* thick clouds of the skies." The first half of this line, up to the semicolon, seems to me just right. The second half runs into the difficulty of sprawling rhythm that we noted before, reflected in the unnecessary words in italics. More to our present purpose, "pavilion" is a suspect choice for the Hebrew *sukkah*, which means a "shelter," in some instances the rough thatched shelter set up by a watchman in a vegetable patch. What the learned divines of the seventeenth century obviously felt was that for the Lord of Hosts in his celestial setting something grander, something more imperial, was called for, and so they gave us "pavilion," which adds an impressive clarion note but is quite unlike the original.

In addition to these instances in which the King James Version introduces alien gestures of elevation, it also imposes an alien theological
frame of reference through some of the English terms it uses. This was
inevitable because the translators, after all, regarded both Testaments as
inspired repositories of Christian faith. Let me mention just one recur-
rent instance. The 1611 translation abounds in "salvation," especially in
Psalms. "God of my salvation" is a wonderfully resonant phrase, and
one is loath to give it up—even I am, though I have rigorously excluded
it from my own English version of Psalms. "Salvation," we all recognize,
is a theologically loaded term, sometimes pointing to a vast eschatological horizon and sometimes to a dramatic transformation of the condition
of the individual soul that will remain in effect for all eternity. In the
world of ancient Israel, however, with its unflagging commitment to the
here-and-now, the word *yeshu'ah*, which is consistently rendered as "salvation," as well as the verb that is cognate with that noun, plainly suggest
getting out of a tight fix, whether in battle or in other situations of danger
or distress. Thus, the verb in question means something like "rescue,"
and, however it may grate on canonically tuned ears, the reiterated epithet for God actually means "God of my rescue." The God of my salvation, of course, is a deity who more comfortably dwells in pavilions than
in shelters and who erects a tabernacle, not a tent, in the sky for the sun.

All this may sound, especially at this moment of four-century anniversary celebrations, like ungenerous carping, but I want to stress that
what I have been saying does not constitute a stylistic critique of the King
James Version. The kinds of terms about which I have been raising questions in fact often contribute to the general eloquence of this canonical
translation. The problem is that in numerous places, by virtue of such
momentary elevation of diction, the style becomes grandiloquent, which
is fine in its own right but is nothing like the original.

It is worth pursuing more broadly what the King James Version does
with biblical poetry. Its rendering of the prose narratives of course affords
many moving moments, but it is above all in the poetry that we feel we
are being swept up by a grandeur of language that seems distinctive
among all the possibilities of literary English.

Melville's attunement in *Moby-Dick* to the poetry of the King James
Version is deeply instructive in this regard. His aspiration, which his own
contemporaries did not fathom, was to create an American prose epic that
would have the cosmic reach of *Paradise Lost* and Shakespeare's tragedies
and the Bible itself. And so his language is sometimes high-Miltonic,

more often, especially at moments of narrative intensity, Shakespearean, and very frequently biblical—all intermingled with a good deal of pungent American vernacular. But unlike other American writers whose styles bear the imprint of the King James Bible, Melville was drawn preponderantly to the poetry and not to the prose of Hebrew Scripture. He may not have fully perceived it as poetry, given the prose typography in which the translation presents it, but that would have been very much to his purpose, since he aspired to write poetic prose. What is formally interesting is that, just as he internalized the iambic cadences of Shakespeare and Milton, producing many lines of prose that are fully scannable, he also internalized the semantic parallelism that is the foundation of the biblical poetic system, creating many lines built from emphatically parallel clauses that read like lines of biblical verse. What he sensed in biblical poetry was precisely its eloquence. If the stark and explosive poetry of *King Lear* in the night storm on the moor gave him a lexicon for representing the searing experience of men in an open boat on the tossing ocean in pursuit of a whale, then Psalms, Job, and the Prophets offered him both a stylistic register for reaching from sky to abyss and a poetic vehicle for hammering insistence in the inter-echoing clauses of the parallelistic verse. Here is an evocation of Ahab's torment, which reads like a lost verse from the book of Job, though there is no actual allusion: "He sleeps with clenched hands; and wakes with his own bloody nails." Again, in describing the vat in which whale-blubber is rendered on the deck of the Pequod, Melville writes, "It smells like the left wing of the day of judgment; it is an argument for the pit." Despite two American colloquial touches here, this is a sentence that scans as a line of biblical poetry, and it would not be out of place in Isaiah. I invoke the instance of Melville because it is always a strong testimony to genuine eloquence when a literary work can engender a kindred eloquence in a later writer. The 1611 translation made a difference not only in the subsequent history of English poetry but also, on both sides of the Atlantic, in the evolution of English prose.

The book of Job is the ultimate test of the power and imperfection of any translation because it is the pinnacle of biblical poetry, manifesting a forcefulness, a formal virtuosity, and a vigor of inventive metaphor that make it one of the most brilliant achievements in all of ancient Mediterranean poetry. It must be said that the Hebrew text of Job swarms with difficulties, at least in part because the ancient scribes, not entirely understanding the rich and sometimes exotic language they were transcribing, frequently scrambled it. One should not, then, fault the King James translators for failing to make sense of the many cruxes in the book—their modern counterparts have done only somewhat better. But quite apart from any consideration of deciphering or reconstructing corrupted texts, how well did the 1611 translators convey the grandeur and the formal subtlety of the poetry of Job? The broad-gauge answer has to be that their own poetic performance was impressively successful, or countless English readers, Melville among them, could scarcely have responded as they did to the strong poetry of Job's anguish or to the grand panorama of creation in the voice from the whirlwind. One must thus begin with the general assumption that the translation of Job is a prime piece of evidence for the splendid and enduring eloquence of the King James Version. Nevertheless, some qualifications are in order. To pull this picture into focus, let us consider what the seventeenth-century translation does with Job's great death-wish poem in chapter 3, which opens the whole poetic argument of the book. Here are the first eleven lines of the poem, typographically presented as in the King James Version. For convenient reference, the verse numbers are incorporated in the quoted passage.

3. Let the day perish wherein I was born, and the night *in which* it was said, There is a man-child conceived.

4. Let that day be darkness; let not God regard it from above, neither let the light shine upon it.

5. Let darkness and the shadow of death stain it; let a cloud dwell upon it; let the blackness of the day terrify it.

6. *As for* that night, let darkness seize upon it; let it not be joined unto the days of the year; let it not come into the number of the months.

7. Lo, let that night be solitary, let no joyful voice come therein.

8. Let them curse it that curse the day, who are ready to raise up their mourning.

9. Let the stars of the twilight thereof be dark; let it look for light, but have none; neither let it see the dawning of the day.

10. Because it shut not up the doors of my *mother's* womb, nor hid sorrow from my eyes.

11. Why died I not from the womb? *why* did I *not* give up the ghost when I came out from the belly?

12. Why did the knees prevent me? or why the breasts that I should suck?

13. For now should I have lain still and been quiet, I should have slept: then had I been at rest.

Some, but not all, of this is quite wonderful, amply confirming the 1611 translation's reputation for compelling eloquence. Among much to admire here, one might single out the way this version captures the driving force of the triadic Hebrew line in verse 5: "Let darkness and the shadow of death stain it; let a cloud dwell upon it; let the blackness of the day terrify it." "Stain" is a particularly fine English choice for a relatively rare Hebrew verb that means "to besmirch" or "to foul." Accuracy in grasping the original is not the subject of our consideration, but this passage happens to contain one of the egregious errors of the King James Version, which it may be instructive to note. The cursers who in this version are "ready to raise up their mourning," whatever that might mean, in fact are "ready to rouse Leviathan." The mistake arose because *livyatan*, Leviathan, has a homonym that means "their mourning." The translators, even without knowing what we do through archeological discoveries about Leviathan as a fearsome sea monster in Canaanite mythology, might have realized that they had gotten it wrong because what they construed as a possessive suffix would be a feminine plural, whereas the context requires a masculine plural. In any event, the result was that they missed the first introduction of the fabulous beast that will play a climactic role at the end of the poem in the speech from the whirlwind. One other error in the passage is the result of uncharacteristic timidity on the part of the seventeenth-century translators. The phrase "the dawning of the day" in verse 9 should be "the eyelids of the dawn." Faced with a bold and striking metaphor, they apparently were unable to imagine how the dawn could have eyelids, and so they erased the figure entirely—as, alas, many modern translations continue to do.

The canonical English version certainly contains strong poetry, but it is a loose kind of poetry in which the rhythm often goes slack. The beginning of verse 9, "Let the stars of the twilight thereof be dark," involves an unnecessary proliferation of syllables and words, even in seventeenth-century usage, to represent three Hebrew words, three beats. The translators could easily have rendered this as "Let its twilight stars be dark." The fact that they did not may reflect a fondness for orotundity, a kind of eloquence perhaps more rhetorical than poetic. In the next verse, an awkwardly extraneous word is the consequence of their commitment to absolute literalism: "Because it did not shut up the doors of my *mother's* womb." The Hebrew says simply "my womb," but since Job could not have a womb, the obvious meaning is the womb he inhabited for nine months, which of course was his mother's. This minor difficulty could have been obviated by translating the phrase as "the doors of the womb," but because the Hebrew noun shows a first-person possessive suffix, the translators felt obliged to represent it, adding the awkward "mother's" in italics to indicate that it is a word merely implied in the Hebrew.

Verse 11 is an example both of the splendid felicity of the 1611 translation and of its lapses into ungainliness. The Hebrew has four words in the first half the line and just three in the second half, with four beats against three. The English rendering of the first half of the line could scarcely be surpassed: "Why died I not from the womb?" These seven monosyllabic words, with three accents, perfectly convey the forceful compactness of the Hebrew. As a translator, I envy the freedom of my seventeenth-century predecessors to deploy the rhythmically concise inversion, "died I not," where modern usage compels one to settle for "did I not die." But in the second half of the line, the translation becomes unhinged: "*Why* did I *not* give up the ghost when I came out of the belly?" The entire clause is arhythmic, and it offers a full sixteen words for the three in the Hebrew. This version reflects a certain literalist impulse of clarification—note the supplying of the italicized "why" and "not," which are quite unnecessary—and though "give up the ghost" is a fine old phrase, there surely are more compact English synonyms for dying. It is hard to resist the inference that the King James translators often relished the proliferation of words, a stylistic habit that could generate a kind of eloquence, though not, I think, here, but an eloquence antithetical to the original.

It has not been my intention to expose the stylistic beauty of the King James Version as merely a long-standing cultural delusion. The impressive power of the canonical English Bible is surely secure, and it continues both to nourish us as readers and to provide a wealth of resources for English writers. My argument has been rather that we all tend to remember books selectively just as we remember almost everything else selectively. Having been moved by the lofty dignity, the poised cadences, and the plain directness of the King James Version in many passages, we are inclined to imagine in recollection that the entire translation is like that. In point of fact, the grandeur of the 1611 version is not infrequently interrupted by stylistic lapses, awkwardness, and patches of gratuitous wordiness. Job 3:11, which we have looked at closely, is a microcosmic instance of the ups and downs of the King James Version, the first half of the line beautifully felicitous, the second half, a long stumble. But even when the translation is flawlessly eloquent, the nature of the eloquence is often quite different from the biblical original. It comes closest to the biblical style, as I tried to illustrate at the outset, in the narrative prose. Its treatment of the poetry, on the other hand, owes its eloquent force sometimes to an echoing of the images and the formal configurations of the original, and sometimes, rather more often, to its transformation of the original into a different mode of expression that draws on indigenous English patterns of expression.

This amalgam of disparate cultures and styles resulted in a great many sublime passages that have illuminated the inner lives and enchanted the poetic ears of English speakers for four centuries. One particularly memorable instance is the 1611 rendering of the anonymous prophet of the Babylonian exile—the sweetest of biblical poets—whose writings are appended to the book of Isaiah. Let me cite just two verses, four lines of poetry, from the beginning of Isaiah 40. After a verse that is one of those left-footed moments involving two misconstructions ("Speak ye comfortably to Jerusalem . . . that her warfare is accomplished"), this is how the King James translators make the Hebrew poet sing in English: "The voice of him that crieth in the wilderness, Prepare ye the way of the Lord, make straight in the desert a highway for our God. Every valley shall be exalted, and every mountain and hill shall be made low: and the crooked shall be made straight, and the rough places plain." This is sonorous English poetry that lifts the spirit, as truly eloquent language can do. One readily sees how it helped inspire the soaring music of Handel's *Messiah*; how it, and passages like it, ignited answering sparks in the celebratory verse of Whitman, Hopkins, and Hart Crane. Though the King James Bible may not be altogether what reverential recollection makes of it, after four hundred years its grand language still rings strong.

Eight

THE WORD THAT ENDURETH FOREVER
A Century of Scholarship on the King James Version

Beth Allison Barr

"*I*f everything else in our language should perish it would alone suffice to show the whole extent of its beauty and power."[1] When Thomas Macaulay penned these words about the King James Version in 1868, the world was a different place. Queen Victoria was still in the early years of mourning the death of her beloved Albert; the United States was still staggering from the devastation caused by the Civil War; technology was still eight years from Alexander Graham Bell's telephone; and only a handful of versions of the Bible existed. Yet, despite a century of historical change churning around it and a proliferation of English translations chipping away at its distinctiveness, the King James Version—in at least one important way—has remained the same. A century of scholarship indicates that even as we have gained more insight into its origin and a more realistic understanding of the extent of its influence, the King James Version continues to endure as "the Bible of the heart."[2]

In a lecture series delivered at the Brooklyn Institute of Arts and Sciences to mark the 300th anniversary of the King James Version, Cleland Boyd McAfee helped set the stage for the next century of KJV scholarship. On the one hand, he reflected the laudatory tones of Macaulay, describing it as "the Book of greatest literature," "the Book of mightiest morals," and "the Book governing history." On the other hand, he emphatically reminded his audience that "the King James version is not the Bible," it is just a version of the Bible.[3] Thus McAfee approached the King James Version in a balanced way, as he both recognized its importance and emphasized its limitations. Recent scholarship echoes this methodology. Alister McGrath, in his 2002 survey of the history of the King James translation, provides a clear example. He argues that the KJV translators did indeed create a "literary milestone." Since he explains the translation's extraordinary success through the ordinary business of printing and bookselling, however, McGrath presents the triumph of the King James Version as mostly accidental. Nonetheless, McGrath concludes that we can and should still celebrate the translators' enduring work, both in the "superb translation of the Bible that they intended to create, and the classic work of English literature that was an accidental, yet most welcome, outcome."[4]

This tempered portrayal of the King James Version as remarkable yet historically explicable stems, at least in part, from a better understanding of how the 1611 translation was created. Studies by Ward Allen, Edward Jacobs, and David Norton have demystified the translation process. Instead of a romanticized picture of the "greatest scholars" analyzing and debating in an orderly, harmonious, and almost divinely inspired way, scholars have pieced together from the surviving notes of the KJV translators themselves a more realistic and messier depiction of what really happened within the translation companies.[5] David Norton sums up these findings, arguing that—from beginning to end—translating the King James Version was more "muddled" and individualistic than previously thought, and was "as much about committee politics as it was about accuracy."[6] Further scholarship has focused on illuminating the lives of the translators. It suggests that, despite various personal idiosyncrasies, the "learned men" had the education necessary for translating biblical manuscripts. David Daiches, after a brief comparative analysis of the translation of Isaiah in English Bibles with the Hebrew text, claims that the King James Version "preserves a surprising number of traditional Jewish renderings" and is overall "as accurate a rendering" of the Bible as could have been produced.[7] Gordon Campbell agrees with this, stating in his memorable fashion: "It would be difficult now to bring together a group of more than fifty scholars with the range of languages and knowledge of other disciplines that characterized the KJV translators. We may live in a world with more knowledge, but it is populated by people with less knowledge."[8] From the lives of the translators to the process of translation, scholarship during the past century has so enriched our understanding of the making of the 1611 King James Version, that now—when we attempt to visualize the translation process—we are no longer looking through a glass darkly.

Just as peering through the words left behind by the translators in copies of their notes and in the margins of their revisions sheds light on the inner workings of the translation committees, peering through the words chosen by novelists and poets and everyday people sheds light on the continuing influence of the King James Version. While most scholars agree that it has clearly influenced English literature (and hence Western culture), many have qualified the extent of that influence. C. S. Lewis startled many of his readers in the mid-twentieth century by stating that the literary "influence" of the KJV has been exaggerated. In his words, "the Authorised Version as a strictly literary influence has mattered less than we have often supposed."[9] Although Lewis presents a more pessimistic portrayal than most, recent scholars do seem to have heeded his cautionary tone. David Burke, for example, praises the KJV for its "many euphonious phrasings and the distinctive cadences of its prosody" that continue to echo in modern literature and language. Yet his caution that the translators acknowledged their engagement in a "thoroughly human" effort as they stood "on the shoulders of those who have gone before them" reminds us that the specific influence of the King James Version is difficult to separate both from the general influence of the Bible and the preceding influence of other English translations (such as Wycliffe and Tyndale).[10] Even David Crystal, who has counted 257 idioms in the English language stemming—at least to some degree— from the KJV, cautions about overestimating its influence. While 257, he claims, is a "notable" number, it is still a restrained number and does not reflect the hundreds or thousands of KJV phrases that some might have thought existed. Moreover, Crystal claims, only 18 of the 257 idioms stem uniquely from the King James Version.[11]

By narrowing the definition of "influence" and acknowledging the debt owed by the KJV to previous English translations, modern scholarship has painted a more limited picture of how it has shaped the English language. At the same time, modern scholarship has broadened the viewpoint from which we study the influence of the KJV. Essays from the recent collection edited by Burke and the even more recent collection edited by Hannibal Hamlin and Norman Jones demonstrate how the King James Version affected both African American and Jewish traditions and even spread into the postcolonial world by riding the coattails of education. Thus even with a more modest understanding of the influence of the KJV in the English-speaking world, scholarship during the past century has established it as a significant and even global influence.

In sum, from 1911 to 2011, scholars have gained a more nuanced understanding of both the origin of the King James Version and the extent of its impact. The result of this deepening awareness seems two-fold. First, it has led to increased anxiety about the future of the KJV. From McAfee's unrequited plea specifically to reintegrate the King James Version into the basic fabric of society (the school, home, church, and media) to Robert Alter's lament a century later that its influence in American culture has waned significantly, the consensus suggests that the translation's 400th anniversary might double as a swan song.[12] Hamlin and Jones convey exactly this fear in the introduction to their essay collection. The "new discoveries of ancient texts and other advances in understanding the Hebrew, Aramaic, and Greek originals, along with demands for Bibles that speak in more contemporary language, have rendered the KJB obsolete for many. . . . Indeed, in creating *The King James Bible after 400 Years*, we have more than once been led to wonder whether we weren't creating a kind of elegy for the KJB at the end of its four hundred years."[13]

Second, even within this atmosphere of concern for the survival of the King James Version, scholarship accentuates the powerful hold that it has exerted throughout the past 400 years. In 1910 Albert Cook wrote of the English people believing almost in the "literal inspiration of the very words which composed it."[14] In 1977 Gustavus Paine proclaimed that "millions could unite in their respect for the King James words when they could unite on almost nothing else."[15] In 1982 Olga Opfell described the growing popularity of the 1611 translation as "so widespread that for many persons it was *the* Bible, the only version they recognized."[16] In 2010, Gordon Campbell presented the KJV as "the centre of the religious culture of the English-speaking world. It is valued by everyone who is a Christian by conviction or background, even by those who for one reason or another use another translation."[17] Finally, in 2011 Leland Ryken has claimed that, "between 1700 and 1975, any consideration of biblical influence on public life, politics, education, music, and art is actually a consideration of the King James Bible."[18] While the past century has witnessed critical advances in the study of the KJV, attitudes about its emotional appeal and the momentous role it has played in literature, culture, and even history have remained very much the same. David Norton's assessment of it in 2011 as "the most important book in English religion and culture" sounds strikingly like Thomas Macauley's praise in 1868: "If everything else in our language should perish it would alone suffice to show the whole extent of its beauty and power."[19] Thus, at least in scholarship about the King James Version of the Bible, the word does indeed seem to endure forever.

* * *

Allen, Ward. *Translating for King James: Notes Made by a Translator of King James' Bible*. Nashville, Tenn.: Vanderbilt University Press, 1969.
Reprint, 1993.

Heralded as a "classic of biblical scholarship," this text first made available the private notes of John Bois, a member of the Cambridge company of King James Version translators and one of the twelve reviewers of the manuscript in 1610 before it was printed in 1611. Allen discusses Bois' role in the translation, describes the survival of his notes in the collected papers of William Fulman, and demonstrates the authenticity of the Fulman manuscript as a product of the final editing process for the King James Version (1610–1611). Allen argues that this is significant because it shows that the final editing of the KJV did indeed take only nine months (as contemporary accounts claim, but modern scholars have doubted this time frame) and because it illuminates the thought processes of the men responsible for the final manuscript of the King James Version—especially their search for "rhetorical majesty." In addition to Allen's introduction to the Fulman manuscript and a translation of John Bois' notes, *Translating for King James* also contains an appendix of the references cited by John Bois and Anthony Walker's contemporary account of the life of John Bois.

Allen, Ward S., and Edward C. Jacobs. *The Coming of the King James Gospels: A Collation of the Translators' Work-in-Progress*.
Fayetteville: University of Arkansas Press, 1995.

Allen and Jacobs examine the annotations of the KJV translators to detail the creation of the Authorized Version of the New Testament. Drawing from the notes of John Bois, a manuscript from the Second Westminster Company, and the 1602 Bishops' Bible used by the translators, they first provide an analysis of the scribes and their revisions and second provide a collation of the Gospel annotations, the Bishops' Bible, and the resulting King James Version. Thus readers can follow the progress of the translators as they constructed at least some of the King James Version.

Allen and Jacobs argue that the annotations found in the 1602 Bishops' Bible stemmed from three main scribes (who are easily discernible) and two primary stages of revision (although they claim that a third stage of revision occurred before the final version of the 1611 Bible). They also demonstrate that the translators relied on several previous translations, including the Bishops' Bible, the Geneva Bible, the Rheims Bible, the Tyndale Bible, and the Coverdale Bible. As Allen and Jacobs conclude, "the journey of the translators to the Authorized Version of 1611—a journey that begun in 1604—was long, complex, and arduous. And the debts of the translators to earlier English Bibles were substantial" (29).

Alter, Robert. *Pen of Iron: American Prose and the King James Bible.* Princeton, N.J.: Princeton University Press, 2010.

Just as a pen of iron recorded the sins of Judah, Robert Alter contends that the equally strong pen of the King James Version left its mark on American authors. In this short text that began as a lecture series at Princeton, Alter underpins his case studies of *Moby-Dick*, *Absalom, Absalom*, and *Seize the Day* with an overview of the literary impact of the King James Version. For example, in his analysis of Samuel Bellow's *Seize the Day*, Alter shows how "the language used to articulate the anguish of this hapless average sensual man [Wilhelm] in the middle of the twentieth century harks back to the urgent cries for help registered in those Hebrew poems written more than two and a half millennia earlier" (145). Alter argues that the King James Version appears as a "scarlet thread" in some American literature, such as the easily discernible biblical influence in *Moby-Dick* (with such characters as "Ahab" and "Ishmael," and language echoing the Psalms). At other times it just forms a background to the text, "variously receding, disappearing, and reappearing," to give the narratives "weight and resonance" (145). Thus, from Abraham Lincoln's Gettysburg Address to William Faulkner's *Absalom, Absalom*, Alter shows that the prose style as well as the content of the King James Version has significantly influenced how American authors have approached their writing. He laments that this influence has waned with the proliferation of English Bible translations and with a general decline in cultural knowledge about the Bible.

Barker, Henry. *English Bible Versions: A Tercentenary Memorial of the King James Version*. New York: New York Bible and Common Prayer Book Society, 1911.

Printed after Barker's death by the New York Bible and Common Prayer Book Society in honor of the third century of the King James Version, this Bible handbook was intended to provide a comprehensive survey of biblical texts and translations for introductory students. "The same and not the same," Barker concludes about similarities and differences among the biblical versions he examined, including the Old Testament Hebrew, the Septuagint, the Vulgate, various English versions, the Douay Version, the King James Version and its subsequent printings, and even the American Standard Edition (269). In the course of this sweeping overview of the history of translating the Bible, Barker traces the history of the King James Version. He begins with its inception at the Hampton Court Conference and the support of King James for one "uniform" translation. He discusses the organization of the translation committees, the qualifications of the translators, and the rules they were to follow. Finally, he explains the acceptance of the title "Authorized Version" and the triumph of the King James Version over other English versions within less than 50 years, and briefly—but exhaustively—demonstrates its significant influence within English culture and religion. He writes: "It has been remarked that: 'English literature has been formed largely on the Bible of 1611. Our great works, whether in prose or verse, bear the plain stamp of its language. No master of style has neglected its charms' " (178). Barker justifies the need for continued revisions of the King James Version because of its many defects (such as Greek tenses that were "misconceived, misinterpreted, and confused") and because of the discovery of biblical manuscripts since the 1611 edition (190–91). He explains that as "good as it is," the King James Version "might be made better" (193). Barker thus expresses qualified admiration for the King James Version. He claims that through God's providence, the 1611 edition was created at a time when "the English language was at its best" (177). Yet he also recognizes the need for continued revisions of Bible translations. Barker includes several useful tables and appendices, although much of his information is now dated.

Bobrick, Benson. *Wide as the Waters: The Story of the English Bible and the Revolution It Inspired*. New York: Penguin, 2002.

The King James Version, according to Bobrick, played a significant role in the development of modern democracy. Bobrick argues that the social and religious "revolution" which produced the Bible in English also undermined traditional views about authority—first by severing the link with papal authority, and second through its emphasis on free thinking and equality, challenging the idea of monarchy. "The growth of independent thought in the interpretation of the Bible was symptomatic of a larger spirit of questioning and inquiry which marked the age," claims Bobrick. "Without the vernacular Bible—and the English Bible in particular, through its impact on the reformation of English politics—there could not have been democracy as we know it, or even what we call today the 'Free World'" (268–69). Bobrick traces the rise of the English Bible, including chapters on Wycliffe, Tyndale, Bible publication in England under the later Tudors, and the making of the King James Version. Bobrick's argument is very broad-brush and often leans on a simplistic understanding of the late medieval church and a romanticized view of John Wycliffe and the English Reformation. But *Wide as the Waters* provides a good, readable introduction to the production of the King James Version and includes five appendices: a selective chronology through the seventeenth century, a selective chronology of the Bible in English through the Revised Standard Version, a selective comparison of translations in English Bibles, a listing of the translations by company, and Richard Bancroft's rules of translation.

Brake, Donald and Shelly Beach. *A Visual History of the King James Bible: The Dramatic Story of the World's Best-Known Translation*. Grand Rapids, Baker Books, 2011.

In this beautifully illustrated volume, Brake's purpose is three-fold: first, to trace the story of the KJV from its birth at the Hampton Court conference and in the previous flourishing of English Bibles through its modern revisions and adaptations; second, to demonstrate visually the evolution of the KJV through the eighty-nine images that he includes, ranging from photographs of Hampton Court to the Geneva Bible and modern Textus Receptus to papyrus fragments and KJV Civil War Bibles; third, to demonstrate the "unparalleled influence" of the KJV while simultaneously emphasizing its position as a Bible version that points to God instead of being a divine text itself. "The translators themselves spurned the worship of the text they produced, for God alone is worthy of our worship. Yet the King James Version stands as a translation of unparalleled influence. . . . As such, it is certainly worthy of the valued place it holds in the history of Christian faith and the history of the world" (246). Brake tempers his clear admiration for the KJV with a straightforward presentation of the early English Bibles, the translation process of the KJV, and the reception of the KJV followed by its subsequent printings and spread throughout the world. On the one hand, Brake adds very little new to scholarship about the KJV. His discussion, although sound, lacks nuance (his presentation of the rules of translation, for example, omits analysis about how the rules were practiced). On the other hand, Brake speaks graciously to those who may be troubled to discover the human side of the KJV translation and provides a very reader-friendly text that is full of useful and accessible information as well as visually stimulating.

Burke, David G., ed. *Translation That Openeth the Window: Reflections on the History and Legacy of the King James Bible.* Atlanta, Ga.: American Bible Society, 2009.

A gathering from two symposia celebrating the 400th anniversary of the King James Version, one held at the annual meeting of the Society of Biblical Literature and the American Academy of Religion in 2003 and the other at Saint Paul's Lutheran Church in New York City in 2004, this collection of essays cautiously praises the extraordinary achievements of the King James Version while gently critiquing misunderstandings that have followed it. David Burke's introduction clearly reveals this two-pronged approach. He praises the KJV for its "many euphonious phrasings and the distinctive cadences of its prosody" that continue to echo in modern literature and language (ix). Yet he also cautions that the translators were very aware that they engaged in a "thoroughly human" effort. "They know that they stand on the shoulders of those who have gone before them, and they do not see themselves as exceptional or providentially guided in greater measure than those who have preceded them in translation work" (xv). On the one hand, this volume covers familiar ground with essays exploring the English Bibles preceding the KJV, the making of the KJV, and its influence on the English language. On the other hand, this volume also broadens the conversation about the version in several valuable ways. From a close examination of the marginal notes included in the KJV (which includes recognizing the gender-inclusive language used by the 1611 translators), to considering its influence on both African American and Jewish traditions, to a critique of KJV-Onlyism, this volume emphasizes how relevant the King James Version continues to be in the modern world.

Butterworth, Charles C. *The Literary Lineage of the King James Bible, 1340–1611.* Philadelphia: University of Pennsylvania Press, 1941.

While acknowledging the debt the King James Version owes to previous English Bibles, Butterworth argues that its literary genius flows from the King James translators themselves. "Compared with its predecessors, the King James version shows a superb faculty of selection and combination, a sure instinct for betterment. It bespeaks a readiness of mind, a keen and elastic intelligence" (242). Butterworth substantiates this argument through a comparison of "every important variation" of ten scriptural passages, taken from a study of forty-five passages, within the English translations preceding the King James Version. The selected passages are Genesis 37:12-28; Ruth 1:8, 14-18; Job 39:19-25; Psalm 23; Proverbs 30:18, 19, 21-31; Isaiah 35; Wisdom of Solomon 7:24-30; Matthew 6:24-34; Luke 1:46-55; and 1 Corinthians 13. Butterworth also traces the history of the English Bible from Wycliffe through the King James Version (including a discussion of Catholic versions), briefly discusses the emergence of the English language and the influence of the Bible, and provides an overview of the making of the King James Version, concluding that it was "based on a conscientious study of the original Scriptures as they were known in 1611" (214). He also includes three appendices: the comparison of scripture passages, an analysis of which English Bible versions contributed most to the six sections of the King James Version, and a bibliography of the printed editions of English Bibles from the eighth through the sixteenth centuries (followed by a bibliography of secondary texts on the history of the English Bible).

Campbell, Gordon. *Bible: The Story of the King James Version 1611–2011.* New York: Oxford University Press, 2010.

In this "affectionate biography" that accompanies a new edition of the King James Version itself, both commissioned by Oxford University Press, Campbell argues that other Bible translations "may engage the mind, but the King James Version is the Bible of the heart" (vi, 275). In his first five chapters, Campbell follows a much-trodden path: he traces the history of the English Bible before the King James Version, discusses the ordinary men (at least ordinary for their day) who were called out by their king to perform an extraordinary task, and describes the "triumph" of the 1611 translation and printing of the first edition—although he admits that the initial reception of the King James Version was, at least by some, markedly lukewarm (2). He clearly admires the accomplishment of the translators, noting that they were "vastly more scrupulous" than their predecessors and emphasizing both their erudition and remarkable ability collectively to produce a version of the Bible that has endured for so long. Campbell then turns to a familiar yet less traveled road, marching through 400 years of the subsequent printings, misprintings, and revisions of the King James Version in England and in the United States. Drawing from examples such as the Scofield Reference Bible of 1909, he shows how the KJV was continuously reinvented by later generations and thus became "the most widely owned and used translation in the United States" (270). Campbell acknowledges the literary impact of the version, demonstrating its presence in our everyday speech when we are at our "wits' end" or complain about a "thorn in the flesh" (271). Yet he seems to argue that the primary significance of the King James Version lies in its religious influence. It is "the centre of the religious culture of the English-speaking world," states Campbell. "It is valued by everyone who is a Christian by conviction or background, even by those who for one reason or another use another translation" (273–74). Campbell concludes this broad survey with two appendices: the first an annotated bibliography of the translators and revisers, and the second a copy of the preliminaries to the 1611 edition.

Carson, Don A. *The King James Version Debate: A Plea for Realism.*
Grand Rapids: Baker, 1979; reprint 2001.

Carson respects the significant influence the King James Version has exerted on the Christian world since the seventeenth century, but attempts to demonstrate that it is not "superior" to other translations. First, Carson briefly introduces biblical textual criticism and walks the reader through the challenges faced by modern translators. Second, he explains why KJV-Only proponents uphold the *Textus Receptus* and Byzantine text-type as the "best" biblical manuscripts and then demonstrates that "their interpretation of the evidence is mistaken" (43). Finally, Carson addresses arguments supporting the "stylistic superiority" of the King James Version, concluding that although it continues to be an important and revered translation, it cannot be considered the only appropriate English version of the Bible. "The plain truth of the matter is that the version that is so cherished among senior saints who have more or less come to terms with Elizabethan English, is obscure, confusing, and sometimes even incomprehensible to many younger or poorly educated Christians" (101–2). As the title of his book states, Carson is pleading for a more reasonable approach to English translations of the Bible—especially among Christians who insist that churches should only use the King James Version and perhaps even make its use a test for orthodoxy. Yet the fact that Carson felt compelled to make this argument in 1979 accentuates the unique and significant place that the King James Version continues to hold in the hearts and minds of modern Christians. Carson includes one appendix, which critiques the argument that he claims is the most "convincing" defense of the *Textus Receptus*: Wilbur N. Pickering's *The Identity of the New Testament Text*, rev. ed. (Nashville: Thomas Nelson, 1980).

Cook, Albert S. *The Authorised Version and Its Influence.*
New York: G.P. Putnam's Sons, 1910; reprint, Folcroft, Pa.:
Folcroft Library Editions, 1976.

According to Cook, the Bible is a literary classic because of its dignity of theme, "God, man, and the physical universe," its unity and earnestness of purpose, its quality of breadth, and its vigor (3). The skill of the King James translators, asserts Cook, further transformed the Bible into an English classic, "the first English classic" (1). Cook acknowledges that some of the "great force and beauty" of the King James Version did originate with earlier versions, that the King James translators benefited from the challenges faced by their predecessors, and that the general influence of the Bible in England is often hard to distinguish from the specific influence of the KJV. But, he argues, it was the King James Version which surpassed all previous translations, unified a nation, and became so beloved that the English people "may almost be said to have believed in the literal inspiration of the very words which composed it" (15, 20). Thus the King James Version increased the impact of the Bible in England, and Cook demonstrates how English literature abounds with scriptural themes, quotations, allusions, and idioms. As Cook concludes: "The influence of the Bible can be traced through the whole course of English literature and English civilization, and, more than anything else, it tends to give unity and perpetuity to both" (30).

Crystal, David. *Begat: The King James Bible and the English Language.*
New York: Oxford University Press, 2010.

Crystal's journey through the history of the King James Version begins
with the truism that " 'no book has had greater influence on the English
language' " (1). Instead of exploring the validity of this claim through literary inclusions of KJV quotations, biblical themes, or stylistic parallels,
Crystal chooses to exhibit the influence of the King James Version on
popular idioms. "There are many cases where expressions have become
so thoroughly assimilated into the language that any sense of a biblical origin is quite lost. . . . These are the clearest cases where we could
assert with confidence that the King James Bible has helped to shape the
modern English language" (5). For those who have complained about
"a fly in the ointment" or breathed a sigh of relief after escaping a metaphorical lions' den or accused a peer of acting "holier than thou," Crystal demonstrates the biblical origins of these phrases. He contends, after
having read through the Bible twice looking for specific expressions,
that the English language still preserves 257 idioms that stem (at least
to some extent) from the King James Version. His forty-two chapters
demonstrate the widespread usage of biblical idioms, including in such
varied environments as "basketball, comic strips, dentistry, engineering,
pornography, and social networking" (257). His appendices, however,
clarify that only 18 are unique to the KJV, with the remainder stemming
from pre-1611 English translations that were then carried over into the
King James Version, from expressions which predate English Bibles, or
from unclear antecedents. Crystal argues that 257 is a notable number
of idioms, stating: "When it comes to idioms, the Bible reigns definitely
supreme" (258). Yet he cautions that this is a restrained number—not the
hundreds or thousands of KJV phrases that some might have thought
existed—and also that this is a subjective number, "for not everyone will
share my intuition about what counts as an idiom" (258). Despite these
reservations, however, Crystal's study accentuates how the King James
Version continues to influence contemporary culture. Crystal concludes
with two appendices: the first lists the derivation of the 257 idioms from
six English translations of the Bible, and the second lists the number of
references made to Old and New Testament sources.

Daiches, David. *The King James Version of the English Bible: An Account
of the Development and Sources of the English Bible of 1611 with Special
Reference to the Hebrew Tradition*. Hamden, Conn.: Archon, 1968.

In this short volume, Daiches surveys both the early history of English translations of the Bible and, by using Hebrew scholarship as a
case study, the methodology and resources of the King James translators. First, he traces the translation of English Bibles from 1523 to 1611:
from Tyndale's request to be allowed to translate the Bible in 1523, to
the printing of Coverdale's commissioned Bible in 1535, to the so-called
Matthew's Bible supported by Cranmer in 1536, to Taverner's revision
of Matthew's Bible in 1539, to the publication of the Great Bible in 1540,
to the Geneva Bible of 1560, to the 1568 printing of the Bishops' Bible,
to the Rheims Bible first published by Roman Catholics in 1582, and
finally to the Hampton Court Conference of 1604 and the publication of
the King James Version in 1611. Second, he asserts that the impetus for
publishing English translations arose not only from the zeal of reformers but also from the "disinterested scholarship that is a feature of the
Renaissance" (75). To demonstrate this, Daiches surveys the survival
of Greek and Hebrew scholarship throughout Europe, emphasizes its
increased popularity during the fifteenth and sixteenth centuries (especially due to the influence of individuals like Johanne Reuchlin and the
rise of trilingual colleges), and explains the state of Hebrew scholarship
in England at the time of the King James translation. He concludes,
after a brief comparative analysis of translations of Isaiah in sixteenth-
and seventeenth-century English Bibles with the Hebrew text, that the
King James Version "preserves a surprising number of traditional Jewish renderings" and is "as accurate a rendering as the combined Christian scholarship of Europe would at that time have been able to produce"
(208). Daiches includes two appendices: the first uses Isaiah 51:1-8 to
demonstrate the amount of Tyndale's language retained in the 1611 King
James Version, and the second lists the comparative readings of Isaiah
40 used by Daiches in his analysis of the translators' methodology.

Daniell, David. *The Bible in English: Its History and Influence*.
New Haven, Conn.: Yale University Press, 2003.

In this sweeping survey (899 pages) of the English Bible from its Old English incarnation through the proliferation of translations during the latter
half of the twentieth century, Daniell observes that "there have never

been more translations into English available than there are now" (13). Daniell's goal is to show the versatility of the English Bible, its triumph despite difficult historical circumstances, and how it became accessible to the general population. Daniell carefully details the production and circulation of various English versions, but what sets his account apart is his contextualization of Bible production within the broader historical narrative. For example, he briefly traces the history of North American settlement "to give some structure to the accounts of the English Bible among those pioneers" (395). Thus he shows how English Bibles navigated the Atlantic with American colonists and circulated within the colonies. This methodology allows Daniell to argue for the centrality of the Bible within the English historical narrative, such as its role in the instigation of the Reformation and its place at the heart of the Victorian world. Daniell also shows the cultural influence of the English Bible by discussing, for example, how artistic talents like Shakespeare and Handel "interiorized" the language of the Bible and wrote it into their public performances. Daniell's meticulous chronology includes but does not focus on the King James Version. Yet his insightful discussion of the KJV, especially his recognition of its problems as a translation within his respectful admiration for its literary quality and longevity, has become an indispensable part of the scholarly conversation. Daniell's rigorous examination allows him, on the one hand, to herald the King James Version as a "phenomenon, without parallel," whose "influence cannot be calculated" (427). On the other hand, he clearly states that praise of the translation's literary quality did not begin until the eighteenth century and that despite its revered position in biblical history, "[s]ometimes the translation is wrong, or clumsy, or baffling," the "readings of the base texts are in hundreds of places now superseded by greater knowledge, or just better texts," and "[i]ts older English can confuse the tongue" (428). Hence Daniell tempers his praise of the King James Version with pragmatism and a broad historical lens.

Hamlin, Hannibal, and Norman Jones. *The King James Bible after 400 Years: Literary, Linguistic, and Cultural Influences.* New York: Cambridge University Press, 2010.

In this edited collection, Hamlin and Jones convene a wide array of scholarly voices to tell the complex story of the "single most influential book in the English language and arguably the greatest work every produced by a committee" (15). The goal of the volume is threefold: to explore the production of the King James Version, to survey its literary and linguistic influence from the seventeenth century through the modern era, and to introduce readers to the most recent scholarly discussions about its creation and reception—including often overlooked fields such as women's studies, postcolonial studies, and African American studies. Essays in the volume discuss the making of the KJV (from the origin of the English Bible through the aftermath of Tyndale), explain the significance of the "formally equivalent" translation methodology favored by the 1611 committees, tackle the "disjunction between the aesthetic beauty of the KJB as literature" and its besieged religious authority (9, 15), and demonstrate the varied uses of the version by writers such as Milton, Thomas Hardy, and even Toni Morrison. Perhaps the greatest strength of this volume is its wide-angle lens, as it shows how the KJV traveled geographically from England to the Americas to the colonies, linguistically through education and literature, and even intellectually as it faced the challenges of higher criticism and became a persistent "echo" in English literature. Yet, even while telling these multifaceted stories, Hamlin and Jones worry that the story of the KJV may be in its last chapter. The "new discoveries of ancient texts and other advances in understanding the Hebrew, Aramaic, and Greek originals, along with demands for Bibles that speak in more contemporary language, have rendered the KJB obsolete for many," they write. "Indeed, in creating *The King James Bible after 400 Years*, we have more than once been led to wonder whether we weren't creating a kind of elegy for the KJB at the end of its four hundred years" (19).

Jacobs, Edward Craney. "King James's Translators: The Bishops' Bible New Testament Revised." *Library*, 6th ser., 14, no. 2 (June 1992): 100–26.

In this technical essay intended to elucidate the primary stages of the 1611 translation process, Jacobs examines the handwriting and methodology of the annotations found in the 1602 Bishops' Bible (purchased by the Bodleian Library in 1646). As the "only known survivor" of the forty unbound Bishops' Bibles sold by Robert Barker to the KJV translation committees, the Bible's annotations reveal the actual translation process of "the learned men." Jacobs contends (like Allen Ward) that the annotations reveal three main scribes (MT, ML, and LJ) who worked across three main stages of translation during the years 1607–1610. Although most of his analysis supports the findings of Ward, Jacobs further argues that the stage 3 revisions of MT differ from ML and LJ, suggesting that they "may have encompassed some additional revisionary work, say of 1607–1608, that the company was still receiving from other companies and learned men, as well as the subsequent work of 1609 that prepared MT's work for review by the General Meeting" (102). Jacobs' analysis clearly shows the importance of the 1602 Bishops' Bible annotations, as well as the challenges involved in interpreting the annotations.

Lewis, C. S. "The Literary Impact of the Authorised Version."
In *They Asked for a Paper: Papers and Addresses*, 26–50.
London: Geoffrey Bles, 1962.

In this essay, which was delivered as the Ethel M. Wood lecture at the University of London in 1950, Lewis provocatively suggests that the literary impact of the King James Version has been overestimated and predicts that the future influence of the translation will be limited to the Christian sphere. Lewis first traces the literary impact of the Bible before 1611. He claims that ancient scholars equated Genesis with literature like Greek mythology, that medieval scholars preferred the allegorical meaning of the text to the "rustic" literal sense, and that humanists dressed up Scripture with their own ornamentation. Lewis then examines the literary impact of the King James Version. He describes five potential categories to measure its impact on English literature: the Bible as a source, the use of direct biblical quotations, the use of "embedded" or paraphrased quotations, the assimilation of biblical language into everyday speech, and biblical influence on literary style and imagery. Only the last two categories should be considered as "influence," he argues, and within those categories the King James Version has made only moderate headway. Finally, he suggests the reasons that he thinks the King James Version lacks literary influence: because its style will only be valued by certain readers (the "Romantics"), and because its religious nature trumps its literary appeal. Lewis concludes: "You can read it as literature only by a *tour de force*. You are cutting the wood against the grain, using the tool for a purpose it was not intended to serve. It demands incessantly to be taken on its own terms: it will not continue to give literary delight very long except to those who go to it for something quite different. I predict that it will in the future be read as it always has been read, almost exclusively by Christians" (49). Lewis therefore minimizes both the past and future literary influence of the King James Version.

McAfee, Cleland Boyd. *The Greatest English Classic: A Study of the King James Version of the Bible and Its Influence on Life and Literature.* New York: Harper A. Brothers, 1912.

In this study, which was originally delivered as a lecture series at the Brooklyn Institute of Arts and Sciences to mark the 300th anniversary of the King James Version, McAfee praises the creation of the King James version as the "greatest version of them all." At the same time, he recognizes its limits as a "revised version" that is not the Bible itself (242). The first chapter traces the history of English translations before 1611, beginning with the partial paraphrases and translations by Caedmon, Bede, and Orm before moving on to more familiar texts by John Wycliffe and William Tyndale. It argues that the impetus for creating vernacular versions stemmed from individual desires for an English translation and from a more general need for social reform. "It cannot be too strongly urged that the two great pioneers of English Bible translation, Wiclif and Tindale, more than a century apart were chiefly moved to their work by social conditions" (11). Second, McAfee follows the progression of the King James translation from the Hampton Court Conference to the final product in 1611. He paints a rosy picture of the "greatest scholars" analyzing and debating previous versions in an orderly manner—working not for pay but "for the joy of working"—to create an "honest" version free from "argumentative purpose," a version of "remarkable accuracy," and a version in which "language blends dignity and popularity so that it lowers the speech of none" (62, 64, 72, 88). Third, McAfee argues that the King James Version has become a singularly influential English classic that has shaped literature "in material, in idea, in spirit," and influenced history through its emphasis on "essential democracy" and "persistent moral appeal" (194, 224). Finally, McAfee accentuates the need for continued biblical revision, claiming that the influence of the Bible needs to be "magnified" in the church, the press, the school system, and the home so that its impact on modern society will wax instead of continuing to wane. Not surprisingly, McAfee is dated in many of his presumptions and historical facts. He also seems overly optimistic in his concluding plea for modern society to regard the Bible not as a "sectarian Book," but rather "the Book of greatest literature," "the Book of mightiest morals," and the Book "governing history" (286).

McGrath, Alister. *In the Beginning: The Story of the King James Bible and How It Changed a Nation, a Language, and a Culture*. New York: Doubleday, 2001.

" 'If the King James Bible was good enough for St. Paul, it's good enough for me' " (302). McGrath uses this quote to conclude his study of how the King James Version emerged triumphant from the challenges of the early modern printing world to become regarded not just as *a* successful translation of the Bible, but as *the* Bible. McGrath organizes his story of the KJV around the printing and bookselling business, discussing predecessors like the Coverdale Bible as a "landmark on the road to the King James Bible" and explaining the challenge presented by the Geneva Bible because of its "growing sales and influence" (90, 148). The trigger for the KJV—according to McGrath—was the threat the Geneva Bible posed to King James' "passionate belief" in the divine right of kings. Thus he supported a new translation that "would be a powerful factor in creating a cohesive English national identity" (171). McGrath provides a lively picture of book production in England, the "ponderous" translation process itself, and the translators' achievement of "literary excellence precisely by choosing to avoid it" (182, 253). Ultimately, he argues, the political, cultural, literary, and economic success of the King James Version was as "accidental" as it was substantial. "Without actually intending to, those translators produced a literary milestone. We can still celebrate both their achievements—the superb translation of the Bible that they intended to create, and the classic work of English literature that was an accidental, yet most welcome, outcome" (310). Thus McGrath contextualizes the success of the King James Version within the unique circumstances of early modern England. McGrath includes an appendix comparing translations from historic English Bibles and an appendix listing the major "landmarks" in the publication of the King James Version. Instead of using footnotes, he includes a bibliography of sources consulted.

Nicolson, Adam. *God's Secretaries: The Making of the King James Bible*. New York: HarperCollins, 2003. (UK edition: *Power and Glory: Jacobean England and the Making of the King James Bible*.)

A study of the King James Version, asserts Nicolson, cannot be separated from the struggles of Jacobean England. Thus Nicolson explores the making of the King James Version through an examination of the lives of the Jacobean men involved in the translation process. From King

James, who suggested first that the new translation be a "joint product" (created by a company rather than an individual), to Richard Bancroft, who rounded up the translators, to conservative ecclesiastical leaders such as Lancelot Andrewes, to ordinary Puritan folk like John Bruen of Cheshire, who served as both a country squire and parish minister, Nicolson claims that the "essence of the King James Bible lies precisely in the coming together of these mentalities, the enriched substance of Andrewes's supremely well-stocked mind lit by the fierce white light of Puritanism" (125). Nicolson also shows how the making of the King James Version was embedded in the social and political context of Jacobean England—a product of James' desire for unity, the religious unrest between the ecclesiastical hierarchy and Puritan Dissenters, the shock of the Gunpowder Plot, and the quest to create a vernacular Bible that could be understood by all yet was still majestic enough to be read aloud (as this was still an age of performance). Nicolson concludes his brief study with three appendices: an overview of the Bible as text in the sixteenth century, an annotated listing of the six companies of fifty translators (he includes Ralph Ravens and Leonard Hutton as two distinct translators), and a brief chronology of the production of the King James Version. As this is a popular history text, rather than an academic one, Nicolson does not include citations. Instead, he includes a select bibliography to direct the reader to his sources.

Norton, David. *The King James Bible: A Short History from Tyndale to Today.* New York: Cambridge University Press, 2011.

In this concise history of the development of the King James Version in all of its manifestations, Norton maintains that the KJV is "the most important book in English religion and culture" (1). Norton himself describes his outline as beginning with William Tyndale and "the Bible itself," then documents the "history of the work on the King James Bible" (which includes a detailed examination of the translators' scholarship and the first edition text) before concluding with a survey of both the successes and the failures of the version's printed history (ix). As always, Norton's meticulous research and careful reconstruction creates perhaps the clearest picture available of how the translators worked. He also highlights notable moments in the print history of the KJV, such as when the "remodeling" by Benjamin Blayney in 1769 cemented it as a literary classic and became the basis for nineteenth-century American versions, or when the success of new versions in the twentieth century finally broke the KJV monopoly. "As people became accustomed to the idea that the Bible could be in contemporary language, so many also became unaccustomed to the KJB" (198). This book streamlines much of Norton's previous scholarship, making it more accessible to a general audience.

Norton, David. *A Textual History of The King James Bible.*
New York: Cambridge University Press, 2005.

Charged by Cambridge University Press to revise their publication of the King James Version, Norton surveys KJV translations from 1611 to the present to serve as a backdrop for his *The New Cambridge Paragraph Bible.* His goal for the new Cambridge translation is to create "the most faithful presentation of the King James Bible there has ever been" (148). In order to do this, he first explores the history of the production of the King James Version from 1611 to the present. He claims that the process creating the King James Version was much less fixed than scholars have previously thought. Because of "gaps in the evidence," contributions of "individual work," and the fact that production rules were "not as literally and uniformly followed as has been imagined," Norton portrays the making of the King James Version as "a more muddled picture wherein the KJB stands partway between the orderly committee work of the Revised Version and the individualism of the Bishops' Bible" (27). Moreover, the continued production of the text has resulted in significant deviations from the 1611 version. In addition to describing the surviving texts associated with the making of the original King James Version (the 1602 Bishops' Bible, Lambeth Palace MS 98, and the notes of John Bois), Norton also discusses the significant revisions made between 1629 and 1879, explains his editorial methods (returning to the text of the translators while modernizing spelling, punctuation, and other matters of style), and includes nine appendices which illustrate the errors, variations, and changes that have occurred in the manuscripts since 1611 (including Norton's changes within *The New Cambridge Paragraph Bible*).

Norton, David. "John Bois's Notes on the Revision of the King James Bible New Testament: A New Manuscript." *Library*, 6th ser., 18, no. 4 (December 1996): 328–46.

In this technical essay intended for a primarily scholarly audience, Norton tests the reliability of the copies of John Bois' notes, taken during the revision of the New Testament, by comparing the two surviving manuscripts which preserve the notes: British Library MS Harley 750 and the Fulman manuscript. Norton concludes that the copy preserved in MS Harley 750 is probably a firsthand copy of Bois' original notes but that the differences found in the Fulman manuscript "show the superior understanding and care of Fulman as a copyist, and the degree to which he might correct his original" (334). Norton argues that the variant readings between the two manuscripts "shed light on what Bois originally wrote, and most importantly, some of them elucidate how the translators worked and thought" (330). Norton concludes with a table of the "principal variants" between British Library MS Harley 750 and the Fulman manuscript.

Norton, David. "Imagining Translation Committees at Work: The King James and the Revised Versions." In *The Bible as Book: The Reformation*, ed. Orlaith O'Sullivan, 157–68. Newcastle, Del.: Oak Knoll, 2000.

Drawing from Rudyard Kipling's fictional account of Shakespeare's contribution to the translation of the 1611 King James Version, accounts of the meetings of the nineteenth-century Revised Version translators, and the evidence remaining about the work of the 1611 translation committees, Norton attempts to provide a glimpse into how the translation committees produced the King James Version. He uses 1 Corinthians 4:9 as his test reconstruction and follows the debates of the translators about the wording of the text to its final printing. Norton argues that the working process of the 1611 translators was different than has often been portrayed. The translators, he asserts, had plenty of time to work slowly and thoroughly, subdivided the work within the companies (thus only three or four would have tackled a specific scriptural passage instead of the entire committee), and approved and rejected changes in a mostly informal manner. Moreover, the "translation decided upon was as much about committee politics as it was about accuracy" (6). Hence Norton asserts that the translation process for the 1611 King James Version was more individualistic than has previously been thought.

Opfell, Olga S. *The King James Bible Translators*. Jefferson, N.C.: McFarland, 1982.

Before Nicolson wrote his best-selling study, Opfell had investigated the "mostly unknown and unremembered" scholars "who produced this masterpiece" (in the words of Winston Churchill, vi). Her goal was to ascertain how a group of forty-nine men, divided into six different companies, successfully worked together to create "a work of art." "It is a miracle and a mystery that they could do so since group writing seldom achieves great heights," she claims (131). Beginning with a chapter on King James, Opfell discusses almost all those individuals who were involved in the creation of the 1611 text: King James, the predecessors to the KJV translators (William Tyndale, Miles Coverdale, Richard Taverner, the Puritans who created the Geneva Bible, and Matthew Parker, editor of the Bishops' Bible), each company of the KJV translators, and the final editors, writers, and printers (including Bishop Bilson and Robert Barker). She claims, in agreement with Ward Allen, that the translators mostly followed the rules outlined by Bancroft, that most of the translation had been completed by 1608, and that (although acceptance was slow at first) the "magnificence" of the 1611 version soon triumphed. She concludes with a brief discussion of the widespread influence of the King James Version followed by four appendices: a list of the forty-nine translators divided by company (she records that the inclusion of Ravens is a mistake, and that the appropriate name is Leonard Hutten), Bancroft's rules for translation, the epistle dedicatory to the 1611 text, and its preface. Also like Nicolson, Opfell includes a bibliography to direct readers to her sources but does not include citations.

Paine, Gustavus S. *The Men Behind the King James Version.* Grand Rapids: Baker, 1977. Originally published as *The Learned Men.* New York: Thomas Y. Crowell, 1959.

Like Opfell and Nicolson after him, Paine reconstructs the production of the King James Version through his investigation into the lives and deaths of the translators. He argues that probably more than fifty-four translators worked on the text. "The surmise that many aided in the translation unofficially seems justified. Many must have offered advice on verses, helped solve hard problems, and queried readings on which the chosen learned men agreed" (76). Yet, despite the many different personalities (from ecclesiastical leaders, to a seafaring adventurer, a drunken English Dutchman, and a bachelor who wrote on marriage), and despite the many distractions from their task (from lack of funding, to an unfaithful wife, and even the Gunpowder Plot), they reached an almost miraculous unity that Paine tentatively links with "direct inspiration." Paine, however, acknowledges that the translators were not always in agreement and that their translating went through several drafts—as the notes of

John Bois clearly demonstrate. Despite this, Paine concludes that unity and majestic language were the overarching themes of the 1611 Bible, writing: "Untold millions could unite in their respect for the King James words when they could unite on almost nothing else" (182). He includes two appendices: a listing of the fifty-seven translators and comparative readings among the Coverdale Bible, Geneva Bible, Revised Standard Version, the Bishops' Bible, and the King James Version. He includes a bibliography to direct readers to his sources but only rarely uses citations.

Ryken, Leland. *The Legacy of the King James Bible: Celebrating 400 Years of the Most Influential English Translation.* Wheaton, Ill.: Crossway, 2011.

In this short and accessible introduction to the King James Version, Ryken defends its literary excellence and impact on British and American culture. As we all know, the King James Version "did not suddenly appear in 1611" (29). Thus Ryken begins with a survey of its English predecessors, arguing that even though the KJV owes its greatest debt to William Tyndale, it also owes a debt to the Wycliffe Bible, whose translators (at least by the second edition) made a conscious attempt to convey the meaning of the text instead of just transposing words. Ryken emphasizes the irony that "the idea for the King James Bible was hatched at a low moment for Evangelical Christianity," yet it soon gained a reputation as the most cherished, most accurate, and most influential of English translations (54). In the remaining chapters, Ryken demonstrates how the KJV continues to influence translations of the Bible (whether the translators have wanted it to or not). He claims without hesitation that "between 1700 and 1975, any consideration of biblical influence on public life, politics, education, music, and art is actually a consideration of the King James Bible" (114). He also explains clearly how the literary masterpiece of the KJV stems from the literary nature of the Bible itself. Finally—basing his methodology on C. S. Lewis and drawing from such authors as John Bunyan, John Milton, William Wordsworth, Herman Melville, Virginia Woolf, Ernest Hemingway, and Toni Morrison—Ryken successfully establishes that even when the Bible does not reflect "the religious belief of most authors, the King James Bible has remained a pervasive literary presence" (227). In approved textbook style, Ryken includes clear summaries of each chapter and uses text boxes to highlight notable dates, quotes, questions, reviews of major points, and interesting information.

Vance, Laurence M. *King James, His Bible, and Its Translators.*
Pensacola, Fl.: Vance, 2006.

In this collection of fifteen essays about the making of the King James
Version, Vance discusses the accession of James I to the English throne,
the Hampton Court Conference, the translators and translation process,
the printing of the 1611 edition and later editions, technical aspects about
the King James text (such as the number of verses), and even a defense of
the King James Version as the version given by God because it has been
"purified seven times" (Psalm 12:6). From the style of these essays to
the material included, Vance's choice to self-publish without serious peer
review is evident. Yet, despite his specious use of evidence, forced arguments, and very clear bias toward KJV-Onlyism, Vance's essays attest to
the exalted place that the King James Version continues to hold in the
hearts and minds of modern Christians. David Norton's summary of the
scholarly value of this volume, however, should be heeded: "The KJB
Deserves Better Than This," *Library*, 7th ser., 8, no. 4 (December 2007):
452–53.

Willoughby, Edwin Elliott. *The Making of the King James Bible:
A Monograph, with Comparisons from the Bishops Bible and the Manuscript
Annotations of 1602, with an Original Leaf from the Great "She" Bible of 1611.*
Los Angeles: Plantin Press, 1956.

Willoughby weaves his account of the King James Version within a narrative about printing and politics in early modern Europe. From early
printings of the Vulgate, to the fear Willoughby claims Wycliffe's translation inspired among English bishops, to the brave determination of William Tyndale to put a copy of the Bible into every plowman's hands, to
the political maneuverings of the Tudors to the wily King James, Willoughby explains the creation of the King James Version as almost a by-
product of the social and political changes of the fifteenth and sixteenth
centuries. At the same time, he minimizes the involvement of King
James to that of a disinterested prime mover, who—if he had been more
involved—would probably have created a much less successful version of
the Bible. For example, he writes during his description of the translation
procedures that "the king's instructions, if followed, could have resulted
in nothing but a mediocre Bible, though it might have been an accurate
one" (19). All in all, Willoughby creates an impression that the KJV was
almost an accidental product: if printed Bibles had not become such an

important tool of reformers, if the revisers had really only, as Bishop Westcott commented, "arrange[d] the materials already completed," the King James Version might have been quite different (22). Thus, drawing from the manuscript evidence of the 1602 Bishops' Bible and the 1611 King James Version, Willoughby argues that the final revisers of the King James Version played a significant role in improving the work of the translators. Concluding his account with the printing of "The Great He Bible" and "The Great She Bible" of 1611 and the demise of the printing of the Geneva Bible, Willoughby reflects that even though King James had "lost interest" in the translation process and never officially authorized the version, his marginal role in the production of the King James Version had far-reaching implications (31). "King James, too, by providing a Bible without notes encouraged readers to independence of thought. Bible reading on the American frontier grew to be considered more important than public worship." As a result, Willoughby argues, "a king, to promote the doctrine of the divine right of kings, caused the publication of a best-seller which became a milestone in the march of American democracy" (31).

Wilson, Derek. *The People's Bible: The Remarkable History of the King James Version*. Oxford, UK: Lion Hudson, 2010.

Commissioned by Lion Press for the 400th anniversary of the King James Version, this succinct volume tells a familiar story of the process leading to the Hampton Court Conference of 1604 and the six translation teams charged with making a Bible both acceptable to the English monarchy and accessible to the English people. Written in a popular style for a popular audience, Wilson's engaging narrative carries the reader through a relatively solid overview of medieval Christianity, presents them with both the pre- and post-KJV highlights of the English biblical translation process, and delivers them safely to a discussion about the cultural impact of the King James Version and the challenges of modern translations. Wilson covers little new ground in his history of the KJV, but he paints a very clear picture of the world in which it was born, as well as the social context of future translations. For example, drawing from the scholarship of Eamond Duffy, he demonstrates how the clash between monarch and people over the "stripping of the altars" contributed to Puritan desire for a new version of the Bible. Likewise, he shows how the contentious intellectual debates of the nineteenth century fostered an atmosphere entrenched in supporting the KJV and hostile to updating it.

In short, as Diarmaid MacCulloch writes in the foreword, "Derek Wilson leads us further" than just the ordinary story. He explains "how this great cultural monument of seventeenth-century England took shape, and how its majestic official prose has sustained Christians across the world in very different circumstances over four centuries" (7). Perhaps the greatest strength of this volume lies in Wilson's ability to combine good storytelling with good scholarship. Wilson's overall approach to the KJV reflects that of most recent scholarship: cautiously reverential. As he concludes, "It has helped to shape the western mind; has influenced what we think and how we think. It has changed the world. Yet, we must be careful not to lapse into idolatry for, of course, the 1611 Bible is only one vehicle carrying across the centuries and millennia a cargo of ancient wisdom, piety, and truth" (202).

NOTES

Introduction

1 See David Lyle Jeffrey, "Habitual Music: The King James Bible and English Literature," in *Translation That Openeth the Window: Reflections on the History and Legacy of the King James Bible*, ed. David G. Burke (Atlanta, Ga.: American Bible Society, 2009), 181–97.

2 D. Seaborne Davies, *The Bible and English Law* (London: Jewish Historical Society of England, 1954).

3 See Martin J. Medhurst, ed., *Before the Rhetorical Presidency* (College Station: Texas A&M University Press, 2008); also Preston Jones, *The Highly Favored Nation: The Bible and Canadian Meaning, 1860–1900* (Washington, D.C.: University Press of America, 2007).

4 C. L. Wrenn, *Word and Symbol: Studies in English Language* (London: Longmans, 1967), 11.

5 Not, however, the Revised Standard Version, whose 1887 translators said in their preface: "We have had to study this great Version carefully and minutely, line by line; and the longer we have engaged upon it the more we have learned to admire its simplicity, its dignity, its power, its happy terms of expression, its general accuracy, and, we must not fail to add, the music of its cadences and the felicity of its rhythm."

6 See Collin Hansen, "The Son and the Crescent," *Christianity Today* 55, no. 2 (February 2011).

7 Problematic culturally: unlike the culture of biblical times, the expectation of virginity in a young woman is no longer reflexive. See the review by Michelle Boorstein, "Sign of the Times: Updated Bible," *Washington Post*, March 8, 2011.

8 *Encyclopaedia Britannica*, 11th ed., s.v. "Rainolds, John."

9 Wrenn, *Word and Symbol*, 12.

10   Another example of concern from a philologist in this period is that by Ian Robinson, in his detailed negative review of the Good News Bible, which he found diminished by its word choices not only divine but human transcendence. See his "The Word of God Now," *PN Review* 6, no. 5 (1980): esp. 26–27.

11   C. S. Lewis, "The Literary Impact of the Authorised Version," in *They Asked for a Paper: Papers and Addresses* (London: Geoffrey Bles, 1962).

12   *De Nyew Testament* (New York: American Bible Society, 2005), vi.

13   *Basilikon Doron* (Edinburgh, 1599; London, 1603), 143.

Chapter 1: The "Opening of Windows"

1   For some classic comments, see C. S. Lewis, "The Literary Impact of the Authorised Version," in *They Asked for a Paper: Papers and Addresses* (London: Geoffrey Bles, 1962), 26–50. More recently, see Melvyn Bragg, *The Book of Books: The Radical Impact of the King James Bible* (London: Hodder & Stoughton, 2011).

2   The conference was originally due to take place in November 1603, but had to be postponed due to an outbreak of the plague in London.

3   For recent studies of this question, see David Norton, *The King James Bible: A Short History from Tyndale to Today* (New York: Cambridge University Press, 2011). More generally, see Gordon Campbell, *Bible: The Story of the King James Version 1611–2011* (New York: Oxford University Press, 2010). Our chief source for this event is William Barlow, *The Summe and Substance of the Conference at Hampton Court* (London, 1605), which offers a colorful and highly biased account of events. For the background to this conference and an assessment of its significance, see Charles W. A. Prior, *Defining the Jacobean Church: The Politics of Religious Controversy, 1603–1625* (Cambridge: Cambridge University Press, 2005), esp. 83–89.

4   Barlow, *Summe and Substance*, 45.

5   Barlow's account of this development should be noted: "His Highnesse wished, that some especial pains should be taken . . . for one uniforme translation (professing that he could never yet see a Bible well translated in English; but the worst of all, his Maiestie thought the Geneva to be) and this to be done by the best learned in both the Universities, after them to be reviewed by the Bishops, and the chiefe learned of the Church; from them to be presented to the Privy Councell; and lastly to be ratified by his Royall authority; and so this whole Church to be bound unto it, and none other." Barlow, *Summe and Substance*, 46.

6   Olga S. Opfell, *The King James Bible Translators* (Jefferson, N.C.: McFarland, 1982), 139–40. The textual provenance of these "rules" remains unclear. For further discussion, see Alister McGrath, *In the Beginning: The Story of the King James Bible and How It Changed a Nation, a Language, and a Culture* (New York: Doubleday, 2001); and Adam Nicolson, *God's Secretaries: The Making of the King James Bible* (New York: HarperCollins, 2003). The best study of Bancroft remains the somewhat dated account of Stuart B. Babbage, *Puritanism and Richard Bancroft* (London: SPCK, 1962).

7   Norton, *King James Bible*, 54–70. The role of John Bois is especially noteworthy; see Norton, *King James Bible*, 70–80.

8   The translation of the Bible did, of course, raise issues of particular difficulty, as can be seen from Erasmus' celebrated attempt to translate the New Testament into more reliable Latin than that of the Vulgate: see Paul Botley, *Latin Translation in the Renaissance: The Theory and Practice of Leonardo Bruni, Giannozzo Manetti, Erasmus* (Cambridge: Cambridge University Press, 2004), 115–63.

9   Rick Bowers, "Thomas Phaer and the Assertion of Tudor English," *Renaissance and Reformation* 21 (1997): 25–40.

10   See especially Cathy Shrank, *Writing the Nation in Reformation England: Literature, Humanism and English Identities, 1530–1580* (Oxford: Oxford University Press, 2004).

11   Laura Wright, "The Languages of Medieval Britain," in *A Companion to Medieval English Literature and Culture, c.1350–c.1500*, ed. Peter Brown (Oxford: Blackwell, 2007), 143–58.

12   Su Fang Ng, "Translation, Interpretation, and Heresy: The Wycliffite Bible, Tyndale's Bible and the Contested Origin," *Studies in Philology* 98 (2001): 315–38.

13   The most important was Tyndale's translation of the New Testament, published at Antwerp in 1525. For the historical importance of Antwerp in this respect, see Paul Arblaster, "'Totius Mundi Emporium': Antwerp as a Center for Vernacular Bible Translations, 1523–1545," in *The Low Countries as a Crossroads of Religious Beliefs*, ed. Arie-Jan Gelderblom, Jan L. de Jong, and M. van Vaeck (Leiden: Brill, 2004), 9–32.

14   Andrew Hadfield, *Literature, Politics and National Identity: Reformation to Renaissance* (Cambridge: Cambridge University Press, 1994); Christian Schmitt-Kilb, *"Never Was the Albion Nation Without Poetrie": Poetik, Rhetorik und Nation im England der Frühen Neuzeit* (Frankfurt am Main: Klostermann, 2004), 126.

15   See the discussion in O. B. Hardison, "Tudor Humanism and Surrey's Translation of the *Aeneid*," *Studies in Philology* 83 (1986): 237–60; and Margaret Tudeau-Clayton, "Richard Carew, William Shakespeare, and the Politics of Translating Virgil in Early Modern England and Scotland," *International Journal of the Classical Tradition* 5 (1999): 507–27. The translation of Virgil into Scots was also seen as a way of promoting the status of that language; see especially A. E. Christa Canitz, "'In Our Awyn Langage': The Nationalist Agenda of Gavin Douglas's *Eneados*," *Vergilius* 42 (1996): 25–37.

16   Donka Minkova, "The Forms of Speech," in Brown, *Companion to Medieval English Literature*, 143–58.

17   For the sources of this form of English, see Laura Wright, *Sources of London English: Medieval Thames Vocabulary* (Oxford: Clarendon, 1996).

18   D. N. C. Wood, "Elizabethan English and Richard Carew," *Neophilologus* 61 (1977): 304–15.

19   See the argument of Patrick Cruttwell, *The Shakespearean Moment and Its Place in the Poetry of the 17th Century* (London: Chatto and Windus, 1954). See further Robert Cummings, "Recent Studies in English Translation, c.1520–c.1590," *English Literary Renaissance* 39, no. 1 (2007): 274–316. For the 1590s as a period of social transition, see especially Ian W. Archer, *The Pursuit of Stability: Social Relations in Elizabethan London* (Cambridge: Cambridge University Press, 1991), 9–17.

20   Alvin Vos, "Humanistic Standards of Diction in the Inkhorn Controversy," *Studies in Philology* 73 (1976): 376–96.

21   Quoted in Albert C. Baugh and Thomas Cable, *A History of the English Language*, 4th ed. (Englewood Cliffs, N.J.: Prentice-Hall, 1993), 212–13.

22   See Erroll R. Rhodes and Lians Luyas, *The Translators to the Reader: The Original Preface of the King James Version of 1611 Revisited* (New York: American Bible Society, 1997), 34.

23   For the importance of this theme, see Lawrence Venuti, *The Translator's Invisibility: A History of Translation*, 2nd ed. (London: Routledge, 2008), 1.

24   Theo Hermans, "Images of Translation: Metaphor and Imagery in the Renaissance Discourse on Translation," in *The Manipulation of Literature: Studies in Literary Translation*, ed. Theo Hermans (New York: St. Martin's, 1985), 103–35, quote at 105.

25   On which see Massimiliano Morini, *Tudor Translation in Theory and Practice* (Aldershot: Ashgate, 2006), 35–61.

26   Rhodes and Luyas, *Translators to the Reader*, 62. Cf. Acts 9:18; 2 Cor 3:15; Luke 24:45; Ps 119:32.

27   Botley, *Latin Translation in the Renaissance*, 134–35.

28   James W. Binns, *Intellectual Culture in Elizabethan and Jacobean England: The Latin Writings of the Age* (Leeds: Cairns, 1990), 209–12. Furthermore, Humphrey's work was published in Basle, which did little to make it accessible to an English readership.

29   Morini, *Tudor Translation in Theory and Practice*, 3–61.

30   For the political aspects of Shakespeare's poetry, see Cathy Shranks, "The Politics of Shakespeare's Sonnets," in *Shakespeare and Political Thought*, ed. David Armitage and Andrew Fitzmaurice (Cambridge: Cambridge University Press, 2009), 101–18.

31   See the points made by Andrew Barnaby and Joan Wry, "Authorized Versions: Measure for Measure and the Politics of Biblical Translation," *Renaissance Quarterly* 51 (1998): 1225–54.

32   Alastair J. L. Blanshard and Tracey A. Sowerby, "Thomas Wilson's *Demosthenes* and the Politics of Tudor Translation," *International Journal of the Classical Tradition* 12 (2005): 46–80.

33   Maurice S. Betteridge, "The Bitter Notes: The Geneva Bible and Its Annotations," *Sixteenth Century Journal* 14 (1983): 41–62. See further Dan G. Danner, "The Contribution of the Geneva Bible of 1560 to English Protestantism," *Sixteenth Century Journal* 12 (1981): 5–18.

34   For the importance of this text, see Casey Dué, "Tragic History and Barbarian Speech in Sallust's *Jugurtha*," *Harvard Studies in Classical Philology* 100 (2000): 311–25.

35   Gerald Bowler, "Marian Protestants and the Idea of Violent Resistance to Tyranny," in *Protestantism and the National Church in Sixteenth Century England*, ed. Peter Lake and Maria Dowling (London: Croom Helm, 1987), 124–43.

36   For further comment on this and other political influences on the translation process around this time, see David Womersley, "Sir Henry Savile's Translation

of Tacitus and the Political Interpretation of Elizabethan Texts," *Review of English Studies* 42 (1991): 313–42. See further the discussion of censorship and the maintenance of national identity in the later sixteenth century in Andrew Hadfield, *Literature, Politics and National Identity: Reformation to Renaissance* (Cambridge: Cambridge University Press, 1994), 1–22.

37 Rhodes and Luyas, *Translators to the Reader*, 54.

38 The image, due to John of Salisbury in the twelfth century (*Metalogicon* 3.4), is frequently used by writers of the English Renaissance.

39 For an analysis of the social tensions in late Elizabethan London, see Archer, *Pursuit of Stability*, 1–14.

40 Ian W. Archer, "Discourses of History in Elizabethan and Early Stuart London," *Huntington Library Quarterly* 68 (2005): 205–26.

41 Roy C. Strong, *The Cult of Elizabeth: Elizabethan Portraiture and Pageantry* (Berkeley: University of California Press, 1986), 17–55.

42 There is an excellent account, with useful contextualization of the Hampton Court Conference of January 1604, in Charles W. A. Prior, *Defining the Jacobean Church: The Politics of Religious Controversy, 1603–1625* (Cambridge: Cambridge University Press), 2005. For the reflections of such tensions in Shakespeare's works, see Maurice Hunt, *Shakespeare's Religious Allusiveness: Its Play and Tolerance* (Aldershot: Ashgate, 2003), especially 1–17.

43 H. J. de Jonge, "*Novum Testamentum a nobis versum*: The Essence of Erasmus' Edition of the New Testament," *Journal of Theological Studies* 35 (1984): 394–400.

44 Charles Augrain, "À propos du Comma Johanneum," *Moreana* 35 (1998): 87–94. The "Comma" was reintroduced in Erasmus' 1522 edition of his Greek text, following protests from many churchmen: see Robert Coogan, *Erasmus, Lee and the Correction of the Vulgate: The Shaking of the Foundations* (Geneva: Droz, 1992).

45 "For there are three that bear record in heaven, the Father, the Word, and the Holy Ghost: and these three are one. And there are three that bear witness in earth, the Spirit, and the water, and the blood: and these three agree in one" (1 John 5:7-8).

46 See, for example, Bruce M. Metzger and Bart D. Ehrman, *The Text of the New Testament: Its Transmission, Corruption, and Restoration*, 4th ed. (Oxford: Oxford University Press, 2005).

47 Theo Hermans, "Renaissance Translation between Literalism and Imitation," in *Geschichte, System, literarische Übersetzung*, ed. Harald Kittel (Berlin: Erich Schmidt Verlag, 1992), 95–116.

48 For such notions of "imitation," see Nicola Kaminski, "Imitatio," in *Historisches Wörterbuch der Rhetorik*, ed. Gert Ueding, 8 vols. (Tübingen: Niemeyer, 1992–2007), 4:235–85.

49 For such concerns in George Chapman's famous translation of Homer (1597), see R. S. Miola, "On Death and Dying in Chapman's *Iliad*," *International Journal of the Classical Tradition* 3 (1996–1997): 48–64. More generally, see Martin L. McLaughlin, *Literary Imitation in the Italian Renaissance: The Theory and Practice of Literary Imitation in Italy From Dante to Bembo* (Oxford: Clarendon, 1995); Nicholas Watson, "Theories of Translation," in *The Oxford History of Literary*

Translation in English. Vol. 1: *To 1550,* ed. Roger Ellis (Oxford: Oxford University Press, 2008), 73–91.

50   Rhodes and Luyas, *Translators to the Reader,* 59–61.

51   Anne Reeve, *Erasmus' Annotations on the New Testament: The Gospels; Facsimile of the Final Latin Text (1535) with All Earlier Variants (1516, 1519, 1522 and 1527)* (London: Duckworth, 1986), 220. The comment is best translated as "the greater the variety, the more the benefit."

52   Venuti, *Translator's Invisibility,* 101.

53   In most modern English versions, they are set in italic text: "Paul, a servant of Jesus Christ, called *to be* an apostle" (Rom 1:1). In the 1611 printing, such additions are set in Roman type, easily distinguished from the black letter of the text itself. However, the 1611 printing is not consistent in indicating such added words in this way.

54   "Then Jesus came from Galilee to John at the Jordan" (New Revised Standard Version).

55   David Crystal, *Begat: The King James Bible and the English Language* (Oxford: Oxford University Press, 2011), 75–109.

56   William Rosenau, *Hebraisms in the Authorized Version of the Bible* (Baltimore, Md.: Lord Baltimore, 1902).

57   For a classic discussion, see Albert S. Cook, "The Authorized Version of The Bible and its Influence," in *The Cambridge History of English Literature,* ed. Adolphus William Ward and Alfred Rayney Waller, 18 vols. (Cambridge: Cambridge University Press, 1907–1921), 4:37–75.

58   For essays dealing with this development, see John H. Fisher and Joseph B. Trahern, eds., *Standardizing English: Essays in the History of Language Change* (Knoxville: University of Tennessee Press, 1989); Laura Wright, ed., *The Development of Standard English, 1300–1800: Theories, Descriptions, Conflicts,* Studies in English Language (Cambridge: Cambridge University Press, 2006).

59   As noted by Janel M. Mueller, *The Native Tongue and the Word: Developments in English Prose Style 1380–1580* (Chicago: University of Chicago Press, 1984).

60   See the analysis in Drew Clark, "Hidden Tyndale in OED's First Instances from Miles Coverdale's 1535 Bible," *Notes and Queries* 45 (1998): 289–93.

61   N. F. Blake, *A History of the English Language* (Basingstoke: Macmillan, 1996), 203–35.

62   For this development, see Albert C. Baugh and Thomas Cable, *A History of the English Language,* 4th ed. (Englewood Cliffs, N.J.: Prentice-Hall, 1993), 195–247. For some interesting observations, see Laura Wright, "Third Person Plural Present-Tense Markers in London Prisoners' Depositions, 1562–1623," *American Speech* 77 (2002): 242–63.

63   Baugh and Cable, *A History of the English Language,* 238–40.

64   To mention only one example: "prevent" (see 1 Thess 4:15) means "to go before" in Tudor English, whereas its modern sense is "to hinder" or "to stop."

65   One might note here the translations provided by Coverdale (1535), the Great Bible (1539), the Geneva Bible (1560), and the Bishops' Bible (1568).

66 Henry Owen, *Observations on the Four Gospels* (London: St Martin's, 1764). For comment, see Matthew C. Williams, "The Owen Hypothesis," *Journal of Higher Criticism* 7 (2000): 109–25.

67 Interestingly, the Vulgate offers a much more consistent translation, which (very nearly) allows this identity to be appreciated: "vigilate et orate ut non intretis in temptationem spiritus quidem promptus est caro autem infirma" (Matt 26:41); "vigilate et orate ut non intretis in temptationem spiritus quidem promptus caro vero infirma" (Mark 14:38).

68 For example, at points, Savile subtly aligns Tacitus with the late Elizabethan political stratagems of his friend the Earl of Essex. See Womersley, "Sir Henry Savile's Translation of Tacitus," 316–17.

69 A point emphasized by both McGrath, *In the Beginning*; and Nicolson, *God's Secretaries*.

70 Christopher Hill, *The English Bible and the Seventeenth-Century Revolution* (London: Allen Lane, 1993), 65.

71 For example, the 1662 Book of Common Prayer began to make use of this translation for its set biblical texts, further consolidating the influence of the King James Bible. See David Daniell, *The Bible in English: Its History and Influence* (New Haven, Conn.: Yale University Press, 2003), 488.

72 The best study is now Tassilo Erhardt, *Händels Messiah: Text, Musik, Theologie* (Bad Reichenhall: Comes Verlag, 2007). Erhardt shows how the libretto by Charles Jennens (1700–1773)—who also assembled the text for other works by Handel based on biblical texts, including *Saul* and *Israel in Egypt*—was heavily influenced by Richard Kidder's virulently polemical *A Demonstration of the Messias* (1726), which focused heavily on the apologetic significance of the Old Testament. Some of the biblical texts in the libretto of the *Messiah* are taken indirectly from the Great Bible through the intermediary of the *Book of Common Prayer* (1662).

73 For specific examples of its influence on English literature until the twentieth century, see Hannibal Hamlin and Norman W. Jones, eds., *The King James Bible after Four Hundred Years: Literary, Linguistic, and Cultural Influences* (New York: Cambridge University Press, 2010), 181–334. See also Robert Alter, *Pen of Iron: American Prose and the King James Bible* (Princeton, N.J.: Princeton University Press 2010).

Chapter 2: Translating Majesty

1 Throughout this essay, I have modernized the usage of i/j and u/v, but have otherwise retained original seventeenth-century spelling. I wish to thank my husband, Gary Knoppers, for his expert assistance with the Hebrew and Greek cited in this essay.

   For concise and helpful accounts of the English Revolution, see John Morrill, *The Nature of the English Revolution* (New York: Longman, 1993); Ann Hughes, *The Causes of the English Civil War*, 2nd ed. (Basingstoke: Palgrave Macmillan, 1998); and essays in N. H. Keeble, ed., *The Cambridge Companion to Writing of the English Revolution* (Cambridge: Cambridge University Press, 2001).

2 *King Charles His Speech Made upon the Scaffold at Whitehall Gate, Immediately before his Execution, on Tuesday the 30 of Jan. 1648: With a Relation of the Manner of His Going to Execution* (London, 1649), 7–8.

3 *King Charles His Speech*, 8.

4 On the Hampton Court Conference and the making of the King James Bible, see Alister McGrath, *In the Beginning: The Story of the King James Bible and How It Changed a Nation, a Language, and a Culture* (New York: Doubleday, 2001); Adam Nicolson, *God's Secretaries: The Making of the King James Bible* (New York: Harper Collins, 2003); and Gordon Campbell, *Bible: The Story of the King James Version 1611–2011* (New York: Oxford University Press, 2010). More broadly on English versions of the Bible, see David Daniell, *The Bible in English: Its History and Influence* (New Haven, Conn.: Yale University Press, 2003).

5 See David Norton, *A Textual History of the King James Bible* (New York: Cambridge University Press, 2005); and the essays in David G. Burke, *Translation That Openeth the Window: Reflections on the History and Legacy of the King James Bible* (Atlanta, Ga.: American Bible Society, 2009).

6 For Christopher Hill, *The English Bible and the Seventeenth-Century Revolution* (New York: Penguin, 1993), the English Bible, and particularly the Geneva version, was decidedly on the side of the revolutionaries who found in biblical story and metaphor authorization for social and political transformation. Hill argued that when the revolution failed, and the king returned in 1660, the Bible was likewise "dethroned."

7 On James I, see the concise account in Christopher Durston, *James I* (New York: Routledge, 1993); and on the Jacobean church, see Charles Prior, *Defining the Jacobean Church: The Politics of Religious Controversy, 1603–1625* (Cambridge: Cambridge University Press, 2005); and essays in Kenneth Fincham, ed., *The Early Stuart Church, 1603–1642* (Basingstoke: Palgrave, 1993).

8 William Barlow, *The Summe and Substance of the Conference, which, it pleased His Excellent Majestie to have with the Lords, Bishops, and other of his Clergie … in his Majesties Privy-Chamber, at Hampton Court* (London, 1604), 5.

9 James would later boast in a letter to the Earl of Northampton that "we have kept such a revell with the puritanis heir [here] these two days as was never heard the like, when I have peppered thaime as soundlie, as ye have done the papists," *Letters of King James VI and I*, ed. G. P. V. Akrigg (Berkeley: University of California Press, 1984), 221.

10 Barlow, *Summe and Substance*, 45.

11 Barlow, *Summe and Substance*, 46.

12 The first of fifteen rules for the translators instructed that "the ordinary Bible read in the Church, commonly called the Bishops' Bible, to be followed, and as little altered as the Truth of the original will permit." Reproduced in Norton, *Textual History*, 7. As other scholars have noted, and my own assessment of the term "majesty" shows, the KJV does not particularly adhere to the Bishops' Bible, despite the directions.

13 *The Translators to the Reader*, King James Bible, 1611, sig A4ᵛ, from machine-readable transcript based on *The Holy Bible, Conteyning the Old Testament, and the*

New: Newly Translated out of the Originall Tongues: & with the Former Translations Diligently Compared and Revised by His Majesties Speciall Comandement, in "The Bible in English" database, Chadwyck-Healey Literature Collections (ProQuest Information and Learning, 2011), http://collections.chadwyck.co.uk/. All references to early English Bibles are taken from this site.

14 *Translators to the Reader*, sig A6ᵛ.

15 Naomi Tadmor, *The Social Universe of the English Bible: Scripture, Society, and Culture in Early Modern England* (Cambridge: Cambridge University Press, 2010), examines the language of friends and neighbors, women and wives, slaves and servants, and princes and captains to show how variations in the Hebrew Bible were rendered in language that cohered with and undergirded social, familial, and state relationships in early modern England. Tadmor makes a compelling case for the "Englishing" of the Hebrew Bible, showing how semantic shifts and transpositions in the process of translation not only affected individual words but constructed a social universe.

16 *Translators to the Reader*, sig B2ᵛ.

17 *Oxford English Dictionary* [hereafter *OED*], s.v. "majesty," n. I 1 a and b.

18 *OED*, s.v. "majesty," n. 2.

19 As documented in "The Bible in English" database, http://collections.chadwyck .co.uk. The database is spelling-sensitive, and for the KJV, majesty is spelled "maiesty" or "maiestie."

20 The dates given are those editions available on "The Bible in English" database. The Coverdale Bible (Cov) incorporates much of the earlier Tyndale translations of the Pentateuch, Job, and the New Testament. Coverdale also had a role in the Great Bible (GB). The Thomas Matthew Bible (TM), published under that pseudonym by John Rogers, combined the Tyndale's New and (partial) Old Testament translations, with Coverdale's translations of the Old Testament and Apocrypha. The Bishops' Bible (Bish) was produced under the authority of the Church of England. The Rheims-Douai (RD) translates the Latin Vulgate. The Geneva Bible (Geneva), as one might expect from the product of Protestant exiles during the reign of the Catholic Queen Mary, offers the most radicalized marginalia. And yet the King James (KJV) does not particularly favor any one earlier translation.

21 *To the Most High and Mightie Prince, James by the grace of God King of Great Britaine, France and Ireland, Defendor of the Faith, &c*, King James Bible, sigs. A2 and A2ᵛ.

22 *To the Most High and Mightie Prince*, sig. A2ᵛ.

23 Ludwig Koehler and Walter Baumgartner, eds., *The Hebrew and Aramaic Lexicon of the Old Testament*, rev. by Walter Baumgartner and Johann Jakob Stamm, trans. and ed. under the supervision of M. E. J. Richardson, 5 vols. (Leiden: Brill, 1994–2000), 1:169a, s.v. "*gā'ôn*." Cited hereafter as *HALOT*. The KJV translates *gā'ôn* as "majesty" in Job 40:10, Isa 2:10, Isa 2:19, Isa 2:21, Isa 24:14, Ezek 7:20, and Mic 5:4.

24 *HALOT*, 1:240a, s.v. "*hādār*." The word is translated as "majesty" in KJV Ps 21:5, Ps 29:4, Ps 45:3, Ps 45:4-5, Ps 96:6, and Ps 104:1.

25   *HALOT*, 1:241a–b, s.v. "*hôd.*" Translated as "majesty" in KJV 1 Chr 29:11; 1 Chr 29: 25; Job 37:22; and Ps 145:5.

26   *HALOT*, 1:169, s.v. "*gē'ût.*" Translated as majesty in KJV Ps 93:1 and Isa 26:10.

27   *HALOT*, 1:178, s.v. "*gᵉdûlâ.*" Translated as "majesty" in KJV Esth 1:4.

28   *HALOT*, 5:1977a–b, s.v. "*rᵉbû.*" Translated as "majesty" in KJV Dan 4:36 and Dan 5:18-19.

29   *HALOT*, 5:1858, s.v. "*hădar.*" Translated as "majesty" in KJV Dan 4:30.

30   For example, an exhortation to trust in the Lord in KJV Ecclesiasticus 2:18 depicts the faithful as saying, "We wil fal into the hands of the Lord, and not into the hands of men; for as his majestie [*megalosynē*] is, so is his mercie." In reference to God's everlasting covenant with the elect, Ecclesiasticus 17:13 writes that "Their eyes saw the majestie of his glory [*megaleion dosēs*], and their eares heard his glorious voice," while a later chapter asks: "Who shall number the strength of his majestie [*megalosynēs*]?" (Ecclesiasticus 18:5a). Second Maccabees 15:13 in the KJV uses the language of majesty in a vision of the supernal prophet Jeremiah: "There appeared a man with gray haires, & exceeding glorious, who was of a wonderfull and excellent majestie" (*megaloprepestatēn einai tēn peri auton hyperoksēn*). The KJV Prayer of Manasses King of Judah 1:5 also attributes majesty to the divine: "For the Majestie of thy glory [*megalopepeia tēs doxēs sou*, literally splendor of your glory] cannot bee borne, and thine angry threatning towards sinners is importable: but thy mercifull promise is unmeasurable and unsearchable."

31   *Megalosynē* (greatness), rendered as majesty in KJV Heb 1:3, Heb 8:1, and Jude 1:25; and *megaleiotēs* (grandeur, splendor, majesty), rendered as majesty in KJV 2 Pet 1:16.

32   For a concise account of kingship in ancient Israel and the Old Testament, see Carol Meyer, "Early Israel and the Rise of the Israelite Monarchy," in *The Blackwell Companion to the Hebrew* Bible, ed. Leo G. Perdue (Oxford: Blackwell, 2005), 61–86; and Lester J. Hoppe, "The History of Israel in the Monarchic Period," in Perdue, *Blackwell Companion*, 87–101.

33   Cf. "thankes" (Cov), and "praise" (variously spelled) in GB, TM, Bish, RD, and Geneva.

34   Cf. "the glorie of a kingdom" (RD), "soch a glorious kyngdome" (Cov), and "so glorious a kingdom" (variously spelled) in GB, TM, Bish, and Geneva.

35   Cf. Ps 21:5, where *hādār* is translated as "great beautie" (RD, ch. 20), "honour" (Geneva), and "honor and great worship" (variously spelled) in Cov (ch. 20), GB, TM, and Bish. (The Psalms chapter numbering differs in Cov and RD from the other versions.)

36   Cf. Ps 29:4, where *hādār* is translated as "with honour" in Bish, "in magnificence" in RD (ch. 28), and "glorious voice" (variously spelled) in Cov (ch. 28), GB, TM, and Geneva.

37   While Bish translates *hādār* in Psalm 45:2-4 as "majestie" in both cases, Geneva renders both usages as "glory"; Cov (ch. 44) translates the word as "renowne"; TM as "worshippe and renowne"; RD (ch. 44) as "thy beautie and fayrnesse."

38 Cf. Psalm 96:5-6, where *hādār* is translated as "worship and glory" in Cov (ch. 95), GB, TM, and Geneva. RD (ch. 95) reads "Confession, and beauty in his sight: holinesse, and magnificence in his sanctification," while Bish (like the KJV) uses the term "majesty."

39 Cf. Psalm 104:1b-2, where *hādār* is translated as "majesty and honor" in TM, GB, Cov (ch. 103), and Bish, with "confession and beautie" in RD (ch. 103) and "glorie and honour" in Geneva.

40 Geneva and Bish (like the KJV) translate *hôd* in Psalm 145:5-6 as "majesty." TM reads, "As for me I will be talkynge of thy worshyp, thy glory, thy prayse, and wonderous workes"; GB reads, "I wylbe talkyng of thy worship, thy glory, thy prayse, & woderous worckes"; while RD (ch. 144) translates, "They shal speake the magnificence of the glorie of thy holines: and shal tel thy mervelous worke." Cov (ch. 144).

41 Geneva, GB, TM, Cov, and Bish (like the KJV) translate the term as "majesty," although RD reads, "In the strength of my powre, and in the glorie of my beautie" (Dan 4:26).

42 Cf. "worship" (Cov, GB), "glory" (Geneva, Bish), "dignity" (TM), and "more ample magnificence" (RD 4:33).

43 Belshazzar was not actually historically a king, but a regent (and son) of King Nabonidus. Daniel, however, presents him as the son and heir of Nebuchadnezzar.

44 The KJV confirms the usage in Geneva and Bish, although Cov uses "dignity and high estate," and TM and GB use "dignity with worship and honor" (Dan 5:18) and "high estate" (Dan 5:19). RD renders the passage "gave to Nabuchodonosor thy father kingdom and magnificence, glorie and honour" (Dan 5:18-19).

45 Rendered as "goodly array" in Cov, TM, Bish, GB, and Geneva.

46 Rendered as "shone in the clearness" in Cov, TM, GB, and Bish, and as "shoane with majestie" in Geneva.

47 Rendered as "fear of thy majesty" in Cov, TM, GB, Bish, and Geneva.

48 Rendered as "majesty" in Cov, TM, Bish, GB, Geneva, and RD.

49 See Cov, Bish, GB, Geneva, and RD. TM, however, translates the passage as "because they made therof not only costly Ieweles for their pompe and pryde, but also abhomynable ymages and Idoles."

50 See the concise account of Charles I in Michael B. Young, *Charles I* (New York: St. Martin's, 1997); and Kevin Sharpe's massive defense of the king in *The Personal Rule of Charles I* (New Haven, Conn.: Yale University Press, 1992). See also essays on the Caroline church in Fincham, ed., *Early Stuart Church*.

51 On Cromwell and the Bible, see John Morrill and Philip Baker, "Oliver Cromwell and the Sons of Zeruiah," in *The Regicides and the Execution of Charles I*, ed. Jason Peacey (Basingstoke: Palgrave, 2001), 14–35; and Blair Worden, "Oliver Cromwell and the Sin of Achan," in *History, Society and the Churches: Essays in Honour of Owen Chadwick*, ed. Dereck Beales and Geoffrey Best (Cambridge: Cambridge University Press, 1985), 125–45.

52 On the trial and execution, see essays in Peacey, *Regicides and the Execution*.
53 All quotations from *Eikon Basilike* are taken from *Eikon Basilike, with Selections from Eikonoklastes*, ed. Jim Daems and Holly Faith Nelson (Peterborough, Ont.: Broadview, 2006), and are cited parenthetically by page number. On the making of *Eikon Basilike*, see Elizabeth Skerpan Wheeler, "*Eikon Basilike* and the Rhetoric of Self-Representation," in *The Royal Image: Representations of Charles I*, ed. Thomas N. Corns (Cambridge: Cambridge University Press, 1999), 122–40.
54 On the authorship of *Eikon Basilike*, see Robert Wilcher, *The Writing of Royalism, 1628–1660* (Cambridge University Press, 2001), 287–307.
55 On Shakespearean soliloquy making the king accessible, see Paul Stevens, "Milton's Janus-faced Nationalism: Subject, Soliloquy and the Modern Nation-State," *Journal of English and Germanic Philology* 100, no. 2 (2001): 265–66. On the king as husband and father, see Joad Raymond, "Popular Representations of Charles I," in Corns, *Royal Image*, 62. Andrew Lacey demonstrates the resilience of the sacred martyr in *The Cult of King Charles the Martyr* (Woodbridge, Suffolk: Boydell, 2003).
56 *Eikon Basilike*, 70.
57 *Eikon Basilike*, 95, 77.
58 *Eikon Basilike*, 80.
59 *Eikon Basilike*, 129.
60 *Eikon Basilike*, 162–63.
61 On early readers' marks and coloring in *Eikon Basilike*, see Laura Lunger Knoppers, "Material Legacies: Family Matters in *Eikon Basilike* and *Eikonoklastes*," ch. 3 in *Politicizing Domesticity from Henrietta Maria to Milton's Eve* (Cambridge: Cambridge University Press, forthcoming 2011).
62 Because this early twentieth-century edition gives the Latin as well as the English, I am quoting Milton's prose from the *Columbia Works of John Milton*, gen. ed. Frank Patterson, 18 vols. (New York: Columbia University Press, 1931–1938). References will be cited parenthetically as *CW* with volume and page numbers.
63 An earlier view of *Paradise Lost* as turning away from politics to piety and inner faith has been challenged in recent years. On the epic poem as continuing Milton's oppositional discourse to monarchy, see Laura Lunger Knoppers, *Historicizing Milton: Spectacle, Power, and Poetry in Restoration England* (Athens: University of Georgia Press, 1994); and David Loewenstein, "The Radical Religious Politics of *Paradise Lost*," in *A Companion to Milton*, ed. Thomas N. Corns (Oxford: Blackwell, 2001), 248–62.
64 All quotations from John Milton's *Paradise Lost* are taken from *Paradise Lost*, ed. Barbara K. Lewalski (Oxford: Blackwell, 2007), and will be cited parenthetically by book and line number.

Chapter 3: The King James Bible in Britain

1 Gordon Campbell, *Bible: The Story of the King James Bible, 1611–2011* (New York: Oxford University Press, 2010), 132–38.
2 David Daniell, *The Bible in English: Its History and Influence* (New Haven, Conn.: Yale University Press, 2003), 604.

3   John Lewis, *A Complete History of the Several Translations of the Holy Bible and New Testament into English both in Manuscript and in Print*, 3rd ed. (London: W. Baynes, 1818), ch. 5, with favorable estimate by Matthew Poole at 332.

4   Matthew Pilkington, *Remarks upon Several Passages of Scripture* (1759), 114, quoted in David Norton, *A History of the English Bible as Literature* (Cambridge: Cambridge University Press, 2000), 230.

5   Anthony Purver, introduction to *A New and Literal Translation of All the Books of the Old and New Testaments* (1764), quoted in J[oseph] Estlin Carpenter, *The Bible in the Nineteenth Century* (London: Longmans, Green, 1903), 53n.

6   Edward Harwood, *A Liberal Translation of the New Testament* (1768), quoted in James Blaikie, *The English Bible & Its Story: Its Growth, its Translators & Their Associations* (London: Seeley, Service, 1928), 303.

7   *Critical Review* 63 (1787): 40, quoted in Norton, *English Bible*, 241.

8   Vicesimus Knox, *Essays, Moral and Literary* (1778), 267, quoted in Norton, *English Bible*, 243.

9   Edward Irving, *Babylon and Infidelity Foredoomed of God: A Discourse on the Prophecies of Daniel and the Apocalypse which Relate to These Latter Times, and until the Second Advent*, 2 vols. (Glasgow: Chalmers and Collins, 1826), 1, 308.

10 Linda Colley, *Britons: Forging the Nation, 1707–1837* (New Haven, Conn.: Yale University Press, 1992), ch. 1.

11 A. S. Herbert, *Historical Catalogue of Printed Editions of the English Bible, 1525–1961* (London: British and Foreign Bible Society, 1968), 346.

12 Charles Foster, *The Life of John Jebb, Bishop of Limerick*, 2 vols. (London, 1836), 2, 454, quoted in Samuel Hemphill, *A History of the Revised Version of the New Testament* (London: Elliot Stock, 1906), 21.

13 Henry Todd, *A Vindication of our Authorised Translation and Translators of the Bible* (London: F. and J. Rivington, 1819); [Richard Laurence], *Remarks upon the Critical Principles and the Practical Application of those Principles adopted by Writers who have at Various Periods recommended a New Translation of the Bible as Expedient and Necessary* (Oxford: W. Baxter, 1820).

14 Leslie Howsam, *Cheap Bibles: Nineteenth-Century Publishing and the British and Foreign Bible Society* (Cambridge: Cambridge University Press, 1991), ch. 2.

15 Roger H. Martin, *Evangelicals United: Ecumenical Stirrings in Pre-Victorian Britain, 1795–1830* (Metuchen, N.J.: Scarecrow, 1983), 92.

16 Philip Doddridge, *The Family Expositor*, 6 vols. (London: John Wilson, 1739–1756); *The Holy Bible, containing the Old and New Testaments, with Original Notes... by the Rev. Thomas Scott*, 4 vols. (London: Bellamy and Robarts, 1788–1792).

17 Campbell, *Bible*, 150.

18 British and Foreign Bible Society Minutes of General Meetings, May 1, 1805, quoted by Martin, *Evangelicals United*, 112.

19 Howsam, *Cheap Bibles*, 15.

20 John Owen, A Letter to a Country Clergyman occasioned by his Address to Lord Teignmouth (1805), 55, quoted by Martin, *Evangelicals United*, 101. Emphasis in original.

21 *Times*, September 28, 1819, 4; *Times*, December 16, 1819, 4. Both are advertisements of forthcoming books with the phrase in the title.

22 *Times* Digital Archive, 1785–1985, http://archive.timesonline.co.uk/tol/archive/. The statistics are for the form "Authorized Version"; the alternative "Authorised Version," which was less common, shows a similar increase.

23 *Times*, April 1, 1856, 13; *Times*, October 1, 1859, 14. These are book advertisements.

24 John Pye Smith, *Eclectic Review*, January 1809, 31, quoted in Samuel Newth, *Lectures on Bible Revision* (London: Hodder & Stoughton, 1881), 101.

25 C[ecil] J. Cadoux, "The Revised Version and After," in *The Bible in Its Ancient and English Versions*, ed. Henry Wheeler Robinson (Oxford: Clarendon, 1940), 236–37.

26 Thomas Curtis to the secretaries of Cambridge University Press, January 27, 1832, quoted in Howsam, *Cheap Bibles*, 111.

27 Luther A. Weigle and C. F. D. Moule, "English Versions since 1611," in *The Cambridge History of the Bible: The West from the Reformation to the Present Day*, ed. S. L. Greenslade (Cambridge: Cambridge University Press, 1963), 366.

28 John R. Beard, *A Revised English Bible the Want of the Church and the Demand of the Age* (London: E. T. Whitfield, 1857), 143.

29 Weigle and Moule, "English Versions since 1611," 370.

30 Weigle and Moule, "English Versions since 1611," 370.

31 Henry Craik, *Hints and Suggestions on the Proposed Revision of our English Bible* (London: Bagster and Sons, 1860), 8–9.

32 J. B. Lightfoot, *On a Fresh Revision of the English New Testament* (London: Macmillan, 1871), 80. This is the classic account of the revisers' case.

33 Charles Haddon Spurgeon, preface to *The English Bible: History of the Translation of the Holy Scriptures into the English Tongue with Specimens of the Old English Versions*, by Hannah C. Conant (London: Arthur Hall, Virtue, 1859), xi.

34 "Preface to the Revised Version of the Old Testament," in *The Holy Bible Two-Version Edition* (Oxford: Oxford University Press, 1899), xxiii.

35 Weigle and Moule, "English Versions since 1611," 372.

36 Lightfoot, *Fresh Revision*, 170.

37 W. F. Moulton, *The History of the English Bible*, 5th ed. (London: Charles H. Kelly, 1911), 229.

38 "Preface to the Revised Version of the Old Testament," xxvii.

39 C. J. Ellicott, "The Revision of the New Testament: Its Origins, Method and Characteristics," *Baptist Magazine*, July 1881, 306–7.

40 Joseph Agar Beet, "The Revised Version of the New Testament," *Expositor*, August 1881, 106.

41 James Stuart, "The Revised Bible," *Baptist Magazine*, July 1885, 318.

42 "The Revised English New Testament," *Church Quarterly Review*, July 1881, 538.

43 John Clifford, *General Baptist Magazine*, June 1881, 226.

44 John W. Burgon, *The Revision Revised* (London: John Murray, 1883), 225.

45 Frank Ballard, *Which Bible to Read—Revised or "Authorised"?* 2nd ed. (London: H. R. Allenson, 1898), vii; William Canton, *A History of the British and Foreign Bible Society*, 5 vols. (London: John Murray, 1904), 1:18n2.

46 Frederick Brittain and Bernard Lord Manning, *Babylon Bruis'd and Mount Moriah Mended* (Cambridge: W. Heffer & Sons, 1940), quoted in F[rederick] F. Bruce, *The English Bible: A History of Translations* (London: Lutterworth, 1961), 152.

47 John R. Green, *A Short History of the English People* (London: Macmillan, 1874), book 7, ch. 1, quoted in Hemphill, *Revised Version*, 16.

48 Matthew Arnold, *On Translating Homer* (London, 1861), quoted in Hemphill, *Revised Version*, 15.

49 Frederick W. Faber, *The Life of S. Francis of Assisi* (London, 1853), 116.

50 Charles Bradlaugh, *The Bible: What is it?* (London: Austin, 1870), 52, 350. I owe this point to Tim Larsen.

51 Canton, *British and Foreign Bible Society*, 3:61–62.

52 Hemphill, *Revised Version*, 13, 14.

53 *Life & Work*, April 1911, 119; *British Weekly*, March 30, 1911, 734; *British Weekly*, March 23, 1911, 695.

54 *British Weekly*, March 16, 1911, 685; *British Weekly*, March 30, 1911, 733.

55 *British Weekly*, April 6, 1911, 9.

56 *British Weekly*, April 6, 1911, 5.

57 *British Weekly*, March 23, 1911, 694.

58 *Life & Work*, May 1911, 132.

59 Professor Milligan, "The Romance of the English Bible," *Life & Work*, March 1911, 84–86.

60 *British Museum Bible Exhibition 1911: Guide to the Manuscripts and Printed Books exhibited in Celebration of the Tercentenary of the Authorised Version* (London: British Museum, 1911), 20.

61 William Muir, *Our Grand Old Bible* (London: Morgan and Scott, 1911), 178.

62 Peter J. Thuesen, *In Discordance with the Scriptures: American Protestant Battles over Translating the Bible* (New York: Oxford University Press, 1999), 35–37.

63 William Canton, *The Bible and the Anglo-Saxon People* (London: J. M. Dent & Sons, 1914), 264–65.

64 Henry W. Hoare, *The Evolution of the English Bible* (London: John Murray, 1901), 3.

65 *British Weekly*, April 6, 1911, 9.

66 Baikie, *English Bible*, 7.

67 Muir, *Grand Old Bible*, 179.

68 Moulton, *English Bible*, 251.

69 Cadoux, "Revised Version and After," 266.

70 Hugh Pope, *English Versions of the Bible* (St. Louis, Mo.: B. Herder, 1952), 320.

71 Ronald A. Knox, *On Englishing the Bible* (London: Burns Oates, 1949), 13–14.

72 Baikie, *English Bible*, chaps. 14–16 and 20–23.

73 *British Weekly*, March 16, 1911, 685.

74 David Daniell, *William Tyndale: A Biography* (New Haven, Conn.: Yale University Press, 1994).

75 Daniell, *Bible in English*, 619–20.

76 James G. Frazer, *Passages of the Bible Chosen for their Literary Beauty and Interest* (London: Adam and Charles Black, 1895).

77 Campbell, *Bible*, 248.

78 Campbell, *Bible*, 236.

79 *British Weekly*, March 23, 1911, 694.

80 T. S. Eliot, "Religion and Literature," in *The Faith That Illuminates*, ed. V. A. Demant (London, 1935), quoted in Campbell, *Bible*, 255.

81 C. S. Lewis, *The Literary Impact of the Authorized Version* (London: Athlone, 1950).

82 James H. Moulton, "The Old Bible and New Knowledge," in Moulton, *English Bible*, 260.

83 Herbert, *Historical Catalogue*, 447, 461.

84 F. F. Bruce, *The English Bible: A History of Translations* (London: Lutterworth Press, 1961), 168.

85 *Christian World*, August 22, 1907, 5.

86 Herbert, *Historical Catalogue*, 482.

87 J. B. Phillips, "The Problems of Making a Contemporary Translation," *Bible Translator* 16 (1965): 28, quoted in Daniell, *Bible in English*, 745.

88 Daniell, *Bible in English*, 740–41.

89 Daniell, *Bible in English*, 748.

90 Daniell, *Bible in English*, 751; Derek Wilson, *The People and the Book: The Revolutionary Impact of the English Bible, 1380–1611* (London: Barrie & Jenkins, 1976), 147.

91 John Drane, "Bible Use in the Scottish Churches," in *Prospects for Scotland: Report of the 1984 Census of the Churches*, ed. Peter Brierley and Fergus Macdonald (Bromley, Kent: MarcEurope, 1985), 26.

92 T. S. Eliot in *Sunday Telegraph*, reprinted in *The New English Bible Reviewed*, ed. Dennis Nineham (London: Epworth, 1965), 101, 96.

93 Roger Coleman, *New Light and Truth: The Making of the Revised English Bible* (Oxford: Oxford University Press, 1989), 44.

94 Rachell Trickett et al. to editor, *Times*, November 14, 1979, 13.

95 Douglas Feaver to editor, *Times*, November 19, 1979, 13.

96 *Times*, December 22, 1979, 2; *Times*, June 12, 1980, 5.

97 Thuessen, *Discordance with the Scriptures*, 4; F. F. Bruce in *Christianity Today*, reprinted in Nineham, *New English Bible Reviewed*, 20.

98 Drane, "Bible Use," 26.

99 *English Churchman*, January 19 and 26, 2007, 9. I am grateful to Robert Strivens for access to this and the following source.

100 J. P. Thackway, "Is the AV Difficult to Read? Some Interesting Statistics," *Bible League Quarterly*, January-March 1997, 281.

101 David Blunt, *Which Bible Version: Does It Really Matter?* (London: Trinitarian Bible Society, 2007), 13–14.

102 J. P. Thackway, "The Five Pillars of Scripture: Some Thoughts for Today," *Bible League Quarterly*, 33.

103 Personal observation.

104 J. P. Thackway, "The Story of Our Authorised Version 3," *Bible League Quarterly*, October-December 1997, 378.

105 Tony Blair, *A Journey* (London: Hutchinson, 2010), 76, 536, 364.

106 Personal experience.

107 *Independent*, December 22, 2010, 12.

108 Moulton, "Old Bible," 253.

109 Lewis, *Literary Impact*, 20; Knox, *Englishing the Bible*, 14.

Chapter 4: The King James Version at 300 in America

1 "Tercentenary of a Great Book," *Youth's Companion*, February 9, 1911, 74.

2 John F. Genug, "Why the Authorized Version Became an English Classic," *Biblical World* 37 (April 1911): 227.

3 "Chicago Churchmen Prepare to Celebrate Tercentenary Anniversary of the King James Bible with Massmeeting and Special Exhibits," *Chicago Daily Tribune*, March 26, 1911, B6.

4 "Christmas Broadcast 2010," Official Website of the British Monarchy, http://www.royal.gov.uk/ImagesandBroadcasts/TheQueensChristmasBroadcasts/ChristmasBroadcasts/ChristmasBroadcast2010.aspx.

5 Verlyn Klinkenborg, "The King James Bible at 400," *The New York Times*, January 8, 2011, http://www.nytimes.com/2011/01/09/opinion/09sun3.html.

6 The biblical character of American society at that time is well on display in George C. Rable, *God's Almost Chosen Peoples: A Religious History of the American Civil War* (Chapel Hill: University of North Carolina Press, 2010).

7 Margaret T. Hills, *The English Bible in America* (New York: American Bible Society, 1962), 345–54.

8 Henry Otis Dwight, *The Centennial History of the American Bible Society*, 2 vols. (New York: Macmillan, 1916), 2:576–77.

9 *The Works of Francis J. Grimké*, ed. Carter G. Woodson, 4 vols. (Washington, D.C.: Associated Publishers, 1942), 1:473–89.

10 See Christopher H. Evans, *The Kingdom Is Always but Coming: A Life of Walter Rauschenbusch* (Waco, Tex.: Baylor University Press, 2010), 175–202, 230–36.

11 Contents of the twelve pamphlets are found in the entry for *The Fundamentals* in "WorldCat.org."

12 I am not treating the number of full-length books on the history of the Bible and the KJV that were published to coincide with the tercentenary. Most of these seem to have come from Britain—like W. F. Moulton, *The History of the English Bible*, 5th ed. (London: Kelly, 1911); A. W. Pollard, *Records of the English Bible: The Documents Relating to the Translation and Publication of the Bible in English, 1525–1611* (London: Frowde, 1911); and J. O. Bevan, *Our English Bible: The History and its Development* (London: Allen, 1911).

13 For early American coverage, see "Tercentenary of the Bible: Historic Celebration Planned in All English Lands on April 23, 1911," *Washington Post*, November 25, 1910, 6; and "The Bible Tercentenary," *The New York Times*, March 5, 1911, 12.

14 That disruption provided the headline for coverage in the *New York Times*: "Suffragette Stir at Bible Jubilee," *The New York Times*, March 30, 1911, 11. I have found no American source that dismissed this protest as it was dismissed by at least some in Britain. See "Stray Thoughts," *Penny Illustrated Paper*, April 8, 1911, 482: "Had they got what they asked for these women would now be in a madhouse."

15 "Bible Anniversary in London: Premier Asquith and Ambassador Reid Speak at the Celebration," *New York Observer and Chronicle*, April 20, 1911, 496.

16 "Bible Memorial Here," *The New York Times*, April 26, 1911, 7. A full agenda of events was outlined in "Tercentenary of the Bible," *The New York Times*, April 22, 1911, 12.

17 "Honor 300 Years' Work of Bible," *Chicago Daily Tribune*, May 1, 1911, 11.

18 "Defies Atheists to Equal Bible: W. J. Bryan Challenges Agnostics at King James Tercentenary Celebration," *Chicago Daily Tribune*, May 5, 1911, 7. Earlier coverage included "Chicago Churchmen Prepare to Celebrate Tercentenary Anniversary of the King James Bible with Massmeeting and Special Exhibits," *Chicago Daily Tribune*, March 26, 1911, B6; and "Bible Event Is Postponed: Big Program for May 4," *Chicago Daily Tribune*, April 24, 1911, 6.

19 Both statements are found in "Bible Memorial Here," *The New York Times*, April 26, 1911, 7.

20 "The American Tercentenary of the English Bible," *The New York Times*, April 27, 1911, 8.

21 "Honor 300 Years' Work of Bible," *Chicago Daily Tribune*, May 1, 1911, 11. For similar views, see "The King James Bible: Apropos of the Tercentenary," *Century Magazine*, May 1911, 148–49: "The English Bible is so deeply embedded in the thought, speech, and character of the English-speaking peoples that it has a place in literature and an authority greater than that of any other book. . . . [It is the] great text-book of English faith, speech, and morals." Or John Vaughan, "The Authorized Version of the Bible," *Living Age*, April 8, 1911, 77: it is "the first great English classic—not only, as Hallam admits, is it 'the perfection of our English language' but its influence on the religious and social life of successive generations of English-speaking peoples at home, in the colonies, and in America can hardly be exaggerated." Or F. T. Tagg, *The Ter-Centenary of the Authorized Version of the English Bible, 1611–1911* (Baltimore, Md.: Methodist Book Concern, 1911), 17: it is "the noblest monument of biblical scholarship in the world."

22 Three of the longer lists are found in Vaughan, "Authorized Version," 82; Anon., "The Authorized Version of the Bible," *Living Age*, April 15, 1911, 187; and Tagg, *Ter-Centenary*, 50.

23 Genug, "English Classic," 224–25.

24 Walter R. Betteridge, "The Accuracy of the Authorized Version of the Old Testament," *Biblical World* 37 (April 1911): 262.

25 "Chicago Churchmen Prepare to Celebrate Tercentenary Anniversary of the King James Bible with Massmeeting and Special Exhibits," *Chicago Daily Tribune*, March 26, 1911, B6.

26 J. Paterson Smyth, "Three Centuries of the English Bible: Social and Literary Influence of the King James Version," *American Review of Reviews* 43 (May 1911): 571.

27 "The King James Bible and English Speech," *Macon Daily Telegraph*, April 2, 1911, 4.

28 Anon., "Authorized Version," 187.

29 Genug, "English Classic," 228.

30 John Fox, "The Influence of the English Bible on English Literature," *Princeton Theological Review* 9 (July 1911): 388.

31 Vaughan, "Authorized Version," 78.

32 Anon., "Authorized Version," 186.

33 J. M. Somerndike, "The Tercentenary of the King James Bible," *World To-day* 20 (January 1911): 87.

34 "The King James Bible and English Speech," *Macon Daily Telegraph*, April 2, 1911, 4. For a similar assertion, see Vaughan, "Authorized Version," 82: "For three centuries it has been the Bible of the English race, irrespective of sect or party, of Church or community."

35 T. O. Crouse, introduction to Tagg, *Ter-Centenary*, 4. For similar views, see Tagg, *Ter-Centenary*, 51. And "Tercentenary of a Great Book," *Youth's Companion*, February 9, 1911, 74: by enlarging "the bounds" of a "great spiritual democracy," it "preceded and fostered the growing political democracy not only among the English races, but throughout the world." Also, B. A. Greene, "The Influence of the Authorized Version on English Literature," *Biblical World* 38 (June 1911): 400, quoting Horace Greeley: "It is impossible to mentally or socially enslave a Bible-reading people."

36 Smyth, "Three Centuries of the English Bible," 571.

37 "The King James Bible: Apropos of the Tercentenary," *Century Magazine*, May 1911, 148.

38 "Selling Bibles and Reading Them," *Colorado Springs Gazette*, April 6, 1911, 4. Also, on Lincoln's use of Scripture, see "The King James Bible: Apropos of the Tercentenary," *Century Magazine*, May 1911, 148.

39 "Bible Anniversary in London," *New York Observer and Chronicle*, April 20, 1911, 496.

40 Edgar J. Goodspeed, "The New Testament of 1611, as a Translation," *Biblical World* 37 (April 2011): 271.

41 Henry Thatcher Fowlers, "The Great Modern Versions of the English Bible," *Biblical World* 37 (April 2011): 285.

42 Genug, "English Classic," 229.

43 Smyth, "Three Centuries of the English Bible," 571.

44 Betteridge, "Accuracy of the Authorized Version," 264–65.

45 "Mr. Taft on the Bible," *Morning Oregonian*, April 2, 1911, 6.

46 Quoted in Smyth, "Three Centuries of the English Bible," 575. The same quotation appears in Tagg, *Ter-Centenary*, 46; and, with variations, in many other sources.

47 E. Olive Dutcher, "The Douay Version," *Biblical World* 37 (April 1911): 243.

48 Dutcher, "Douay Version," 246.

49 J. Oscar Boyd, "The Character and Claims of the Roman Catholic English Bible," *Princeton Review* 9 (October 1911): 597.

50 Tagg, *Ter-Centenary*, 36.

51 J. K., "The Tercentenary of the Authorized Version," *Month* 117 (January–June 1911): 423.

52 "Pulpit, Press and Platform," *America*, April 29, 1911, 70–71.

53   J. M. M. Charleson, foreword to Henry G. Graham, *Where We Got the Bible: Our Debt to the Catholic Church* (Pasadena, Calif., 1911), 5.

54   Theodore Roosevelt, "The Bible and the Life of the People," in *Realizable Ideals* (1911; repr., Freeport, N.Y.: Books for Libraries, 1969), 67, 69, 73, 74.

55   Roosevelt, "Bible," 74, 78, 83, 90.

56   Wilson to Mary Allen Hulbert Peck, in *The Papers of Woodrow Wilson*, ed. Arthur S. Link, vol. 23, *1911–1912* (Princeton, N.J.: Princeton University Press, 1977), 11.

57   Wilson, "An Address in Denver on the Bible," in Link, *Papers of Woodrow Wilson*, 23:12–13.

58   Roosevelt, *Realizable Ideals*, 1–2.

59   Wilson, "An Address in Denver on the Bible," in Link, *Papers of Woodrow Wilson*, 23:13, 18, 20.

60   Details of the event are from Bryan's weekly newspaper, *Commoner*, May 12, 1911, 3; the quotations that follow are from an eleven-page pamphlet, *Hon. William J. Bryan on the Bible: The Book of Supreme Influence* (New York: American Bible Society, 1911), the text of which is almost identical to what was printed in *Commoner*.

61   For an interesting effort at responding to that challenge, to which Bryan did not reply, see the documentation in a book written by a skeptic about biblical miracles, M. M. Mangasarian, *The Bible Unveiled* (Chicago: Independent Religious Society, 1911), 28–34.

62   William Jennings Bryan, "Speech Concluding Debate on the Chicago Platform," in *The First Battle: The Story of the Campaign of 1896* (Chicago: W. B. Conkey, 1896), 206.

63   Theodore Roosevelt, *Theodore Roosevelt's Confession of Faith before the Progressive Convention, August 6, 1912* (New York: Mail and Express, 1912), 32.

64   For a full development of Wilson's covenantal thinking, see John M. Mulder, *Woodrow Wilson: The Years of Preparation* (Princeton, N.J.: Princeton University Press, 1978).

65   The judgments that follow depend particularly on Lawrence W. Levine, *Defender of the Faith: William Jennings Bryan, the Last Decade, 1915–1925* (New York: Oxford University Press, 1965); Arthur S. Link, "Woodrow Wilson and His Presbyterian Inheritance," in *The Higher Realism of Woodrow Wilson* (Nashville, Tenn.: Vanderbilt University Press, 1971); Arthur S. Link, "The Higher Realism of Woodrow Wilson," in *Higher Realism*; John Milton Cooper, *The Warrior and the Priest: Woodrow Wilson and Theodore Roosevelt* (Cambridge, Mass.: Harvard University Press, 1983); Edward J. Larson, *Summer for the Gods: The Scopes Trial and America's Continuing Debate over Science and Religion* (New York: Basic Books, 1997); Richard M. Gamble, *The War for Righteousness: Progressive Christianity, the Great War, and the Rise of the Messianic Nation* (Wilmington, Del.: ISI, 2003); Michael Kazin, *A Godly Hero: The Life of William Jennings Bryan* (New York: Knopf, 2006); Gary Scott Smith, *Faith and the Presidency: From George Washington to George W. Bush* (New York: Oxford University Press, 2006); and Joshua David Hawley, *Theodore Roosevelt: Preacher of Righteousness* (New Haven, Conn.: Yale University Press, 2008).

66 Larson, *Summer for the Gods*, 103–4.

67 Grimké to Wilson, November 20, 1912, in Woodson, *Works of Francis Grimké*, 4:129.

68 Grimké to Wilson, September 5, 1913, in Woodson, *Works of Francis Grimké*, 4:133–34.

69 John Fox to Wilson, April 3, 1916, in Link, *Papers of Woodrow Wilson*, vol. 36, *January–May 1916*, 481.

70 Wilson, "An Address in Denver on the Bible," in Link, *Papers of Woodrow Wilson*, 23:15–26; Wilson, "Remarks Celebrating the Centennial of the American Bible Society," in Link, *Papers of Woodrow Wilson*, 36:631.

71 For one version of this speech, see *William Jennings Bryan: Selections*, ed. Ray Ginger (Indianapolis: Bobbs-Merrill, 1967), 135–50.

72 For support of this contention, though not with direct consideration of the Bible, see Levine, *Defender of the Faith*; and Kazin, *Godly Hero*.

73 Crouse, introduction to Tagg, *Ter-Centenary*, 6. Tagg himself said something similar in *Ter-Centenary*, 11: "It is impossible to separate the Bible from the God which it reveals, or from His providence which it interprets, or from the plan of salvation which it unfolds."

74 Fox, "Influence of the English Bible," 397. A similar sentiment was expressed more succinctly by an Episcopal bishop during the Chicago celebrations. See "Honor 300 Years' Work of Bible," *Chicago Daily Tribune*, May 1, 1911, 11: "The Bible . . . did not create religion; it grew out of it."

75 See R. S. Sugirtharajah, "Postcolonial Notes on the King James Bible," in *The King James Bible after 400 Years: Literary, Linguistic, and Cultural Influences*, ed. Hannibal Hamlin and Norman W. Jones (New York: Cambridge University Press, 2010), 146–63.

76 Tagg, *Ter-Centenary*, 53–54.

77 Roger Casement, "The Keeper of the Seas" (August 1911), in *The Crime Against Europe: The Writings and Poetry of Roger Casement* (1915), 6.

78 A. J. Maas, "The English Protestant Version of the Bible after Three Hundred Years," *Ecclesiastical Review: A Monthly Publication for the Clergy* 45 (November 1911): 612–13, 619.

79 Maas, "English Protestant Version," 613.

80 Fox, "Influence of the English Bible," 400–401. See C. S. Lewis, *The Literary Impact of the Authorized Version* (1950; Philadelphia: Fortress, 1963).

81 Greene, "Influence of the Authorized Version," 400.

82 "Tercentenary of a Great Book," *Youth's Companion*, February 9, 1911, 74. The "not necessarily religious but obviously literary" was a common theme: see also Genug, "English Classic," 225.

83 Smyth, "Three Centuries of the English Bible," 571.

84 Frederick W. Loetshcer, "The English Bible in the Spiritual Life of the English-Speaking People," *Princeton Theological Review* 9 (July 1911): 407.

85 Tagg, *Ter-Centenary*, 47–48.

86 Dietrich Bonhoeffer, "Protestantism Without Reformation," in *No Rusty Swords: Letters, Lectures and Notes from the Collected Works of Dietrich Bonhoeffer*, ed. Edwin

H. Robertson, trans. Edwin H. Robertson and John Bowden, vol. 1, *1928–1936* (New York: Harper & Row, 1965), 105, 117–18.

Chapter 5: The King James Bible, Mission, and the Vernacular Impetus

1   The phrase "Englishing the Bible" occurs in the title of a study of the effects of the KJV on English Catholic Bible translation. The "cadences of the Authorized Version," writes Knox, were designed to be received "with the ears of childhood." Ronald A. K. Knox, *On Englishing the Bible* (London: Burns and Oates, 1949), 41.

2   Adolf Deismann, *The New Testament in the Light of Modern Research: The Haskell Lectures* (New York: Doubleday, 1929), 95, 106, 136.

3   Thomas Fuller, quoted in Donald Coggan, *The English Bible* (London: Longmans, Green, 1963), 17.

4   See John Michael Wallace-Hadrill, *The Frankish Church* (Oxford: Clarendon, 1983), 386.

5   The KJV translators noted that the Roman Catholic Church had never denied the translatability of Christianity and was not in principle opposed to Bible translation: they only required a written license for it. It was that issue that drew the objections of the translators: the Catholic Church, they felt, ought to play to the script and not interpose artificial barriers between Scripture and its natural milieu of translation. With the gold of Scripture, Christians must not be afraid to come to the touchstone of vernacular validation. In point of fact, Catholics were perhaps best fitted to translate the Bible into English. "They have learning, and they know when a thing is well, they can *manum de tabula* ('hands off the tablet,' quoting Cicero)." Erroll F. Rhodes and Liana Lupas, eds., *The Translators to the Reader: The Original Preface to the King James Version of 1611 Revisited* (New York: American Bible Society, 1997), 44.

6   Rhodes and Lupas, *Translators to the Reader*, 54.

7   G. R. Elton, *Reformation Europe: 1517–1559* (Cleveland: Meridian, 1964), 52.

8   E. R. Dodds, *Pagan and Christian in an Age of Anxiety* (New York: W.W. Norton, 1970), 121.

9   Quoted in Olga S. Opfell, *The King James Bible Translators* (Jefferson, N.C.: McFarland 1982), 13–14. Erasmus declared himself in almost identical words. See Desiderius Erasmus, *Christian Humanism and the Reformation: Selected Writings, with the "Life of Erasmus" by Beatus Rhenanus*, ed. John C. Olin (New York: Harper Torchbooks, 1965), 96f. But the case for wide access was bitterly contested. Said the Duke of Newcastle: "The Bile under every weaver's and chambermaid's arm hath done much harm. . . . For controversy is a civil war with the pen which pulls out the sword soon afterwards." Quoted in Christopher Hill, *The English Bible and the Seventeenth-Century Revolution* (London: Penguin, 1994), 47.

10   Coggan, *English Bible*, 19.

11   Quoted in F. E. Manuel, *The Religion of Isaac Newton* (Oxford: Oxford University Press, 1974), 36.

12   Quoted in F. F. Bruce, *The English Bible: A History of Translations from the Earliest English Versions to the New English Bible* (London: Lutterworth, 1970), 107.

13 Luther A. Weigle, "English Versions since 1611," in *The Cambridge History of the Bible: The West from The Reformation to the Present Day*, ed. S. L. Greenslade (Cambridge: Cambridge University Press, 1975), 3:363.

14 B. F. Westcott, *A General View of the History of the English Bible*, 3rd ed. (London: Macmillan, 1911), 121.

15 Douglas Bush, *English Literature in the Earlier Seventeenth Century: 1600–1660*, Oxford History of English Literature (Oxford: Oxford University Press, 1945; repr., 1952), 65.

16 Bush, *English Literature*, 66.

17 Rhodes and Lupas, *Translators to the Reader*, 63.

18 Donald Coggan, *English Bible*, 13.

19 Bush, *English Literature*, 72.

20 Hill, *English Bible*, 31.

21 Milton emphasized this sense of Scripture against privilege and hierarchy. "Let them chant what they will of prerogatives," he wrote in 1641, "we will tell them of Scripture; of custom, we of Scripture; of acts and statutes, still of Scripture, till . . . the mighty weakness of the Gospel throw down the weak mightiness of man's reasoning and puts an end to tyranny and superstition." Quoted in Hill, *English Bible*, 43. The contention that divine instruction was a plain tablet rather than a puzzle of arcane fragments placed by an inscrutable power beyond the reach of ordinary mortals was a central conviction of the day. John Dod and Robert Cleaver, for example, argued in the seventeenth century that the godly came mainly from the lower classes because God preferred poor, despised, industrious, and laboring people to titles, birth, or genealogy. Dod and Cleaver, *A Plaine and Familiar Exposition of the Ten Commandments*, 1662, 93ff, 274ff. Also Hill, *English Bible*, 73.

22 Qur'an 12:2; 13:38-39; 16:104-5; 20:111; 26:194-96; 39:23-24; 41:2-3, 41-44; 42:5; 43:2-4. The verse numbering follows the European Flügel version as distinguished from the Cairo version.

23 Published as J. D. Y. Peel, "For Who Hath Despised the Day of Small Things? Missionary Narratives and Historical Anthropology," *Comparative Studies in Society and History, An International Quarterly* 37, no. 3 (July 1995): 581–607.

24 Isaiah 62:1. Crowther inscribed the text in a copy of *The Church Missionary Intelligencer*, 1850.

25 James Frederick Schön and Samuel Crowther, *Journals*, 2nd ed. (London: Frank Cass, 1970), 177.

26 David Livingstone, *Missionary Researches and Travels in South Africa* (London: John Murray, 1857), 114.

27 Cited in J. F. A. Ajayi, *Christian Missions in Nigeria, 1841–1891: The Making of a New Elite* (Evanston: Northwestern University Press, 1969), 127–28.

28 Ajayi, *Christian Missions in Nigeria*, 72.

29 Ajayi, *Christian Missions in Nigeria*, 184.

30 Ajayi, *Christian Missions in Nigeria*, 224.

31 Ajayi, *Christian Missions in Nigeria*, 222.

32 Mojola Agbebi, *Inaugural Sermon*, New York, 1903, extract in J. Ayo Langley,

ed., *Ideologies of Liberation in Black Africa, 1856–1970* (London: Rex Collings, 1979), 72–77. Also S. I. J. Schereschewsky, *The Bible, Prayer Book, and Terms in our China Missions* (New York, 1888), 6–8. Stephen Neill estimates that the *Book of Common Prayer* has been translated into more than two hundred languages. Stephen Neill, *The Christian Society* (London: Nisbet, 1952), 135.

33   Modupe Oduyoye, "The Planting of Christianity in Yorubaland: 1842–1888," in *Christianity in West Africa: The Nigerian Story*, ed. Ogbu Kalu (Ibadan: Daystar, 1978), 251–52.

34   A. T. Robertson, *Grammar of New Testament Greek* (London: Hodder and Stoughton, 1915), 7.

35   Quoted in J. B. Danquah, *The Akan Doctrine of God* (London: Lutterworth, 1944), 186.

36   Andrew W. Amegatcher, "Akropong: 150 Years Old," *West Africa*, July 14, 1986, 1471–73.

37   Bengt G. Sundkler and Christopher Steed, *A History of the Church in Africa* (Cambridge: Cambridge University Press, 2000), 719.

38   Amegatcher, "Akropong," 1472.

39   Hans W. J. Debrunner, *A History of Christianity in Ghana* (Accra: Waterville, 1967), 144.

40   See, for example, Metzger, *The Bible in Translation: Ancient and English Versions* (Grand Rapids: Baker, 2001).

41   2 Cor. 5:17. Ajayi, *Christian Missions in Nigeria*, 17.

42   *The New York Tribune*, June 5, 1869. Excerpt in *Missionary Album: Portraits and Biographical Sketches of the American Protestant Missionaries to the Hawaiian Islands*, (Honolulu: Hawaiian Mission Children's Society, 1969), 17. A *New York Times* reporter went over the same ground and concluded that missionaries were the first to learn the Hawaiian language and to reduce it to writing, "translating the Bible and documenting centuries of Hawaiian culture and history." Michelle Kayal, "Churches Try to Protect Hawaii's Native Tongue," *The New York Times*, February 22, 2003, B4.

Chapter 6: Regions Luther Never Knew

1   World Christian Database (WCD), http://www.worldchristiandatabase.org/.

2   Philip Jenkins, *The Next Christendom*, 3rd ed. (New York: Oxford University Press, 2011).

3   Philip Jenkins, *The New Faces of Christianity* (New York: Oxford University Press, 2006).

4   William Cowper, "Boadicea: An Ode," in *The Complete Poetical Works of William Cowper*, ed. Humphrey Summer Milford (London: H. Frowde, 1907), 310–11.

5   Martin Luther, *Works*, ed. Jaroslav Pelikan (Saint Louis, Mo.: Concordia Publishing House, 1955–1986), 35:395–98 (emphasis added).

6   Martin Luther, *Works*, 35:395–98.

7   Luther, "Preface to the Revelation of St. John," quoted in "Luther's Treatment of the 'Disputed Books' of the New Testament," at http://www.bible-researcher .com/antilegomena.html.

8   Luther, *Works*, 35:395–98.

9   Quoted in Jenkins, *New Faces of Christianity*, 55.

10   Quoted in Jenkins, *New Faces of Christianity*, 55.

11   Samuel Ngewa, "The Place of Traditional Sacrifices," in *Africa Bible Commentary*, ed. Tokunboh Adeyemo (Grand Rapids: Zondervan, 2006), 1503.

12   Tesfaye Kassa, "Hebrews," in Adeyemo, ed. *Africa Bible Commentary*, 1489.

13   Tokunboh Adeyemo, "Jude," in Adeyemo, ed. *Africa Bible Commentary*, 1539.

14   Harold W. Turner, *Profile through Preaching* (Geneva: World Council of Churches, Commission on World Mission and Evangelism, Edinburgh House Press, 1965).

15   *The African Bible* (Nairobi, Kenya: Paulines Publications Africa, 1999), 2052.

16   Solomon Andria, "James," in Adeyemo, ed. *Africa Bible Commentary*, 1512.

17   *The African Bible*, 2052.

18   Andria, "James," in Adeyemo, ed. *Africa Bible Commentary*, 1516.

19   Jenkins, *New Faces of Christianity*, 75.

20   Jenkins, *New Faces of Christianity*, 219.

21   Jenkins, *New Faces of Christianity*, 88–89.

22   Kosuke Koyama, *Water Buffalo Theology*, 25th anniversary ed. (Maryknoll, N.Y.: Orbis, 1999), 119, quoted in Jenkins, *New Faces of Christianity*, 88.

23   Koyama, *Water Buffalo Theology*, 119, quoted in Jenkins, *New Faces of Christianity*, 88.

24   *The African Bible*, 2052.

25   Koyama, *Water Buffalo Theology*, 121, quoted in Jenkins, *New Faces of Christianity*, 88–89.

26   The Dalai Lama, "Introduction," in *Revelations*, ed. Richard Holloway (London: Canongate, 2005), 359–66. John P. Keenan, *The Wisdom of James* (New York: Newman Press, 2005).

27   Fidon R. Mwombeki, "The Book of Revelation in Africa," *Word and World* 15, no. 2 (1995), 145–90, quoted in Jenkins, *New Faces of Christianity*, 54–56.

28   Mwombeki, "The Book of Revelation in Africa," 145–90, quoted in Jenkins, *New Faces of Christianity*, 54–56.

29   Cited in Jean-Pierre Ruiz, "Biblical Interpretation," in *El Cuerpo de Cristo*, ed. Peter Casarella and Raul Gomez (New York: Crossroad, 1988), 84.

30   Elias Githuka, "Revelation," in Adeyemo, ed. *Africa Bible Commentary*, 1564.

31   Khiok-Khng Yeo, *What Has Jerusalem to Do with Beijing?* (Harrisburg, Pa.: Trinity Press International, 1998), 233–34.

32   Desmond Tutu, "Dark Days," *JTSA* 118 (2004): 27–39, at 30–31.

33   Emmanuel A. Obeng, "Use of Critical Biblical Methods," in *The Bible in African Christianity*, ed. Hannah W. Kinoti and John M. Waliggo (Nairobi, Kenya: Acton, 1997), 19.

34   Jenkins, *New Faces of Christianity*, 152–53.

35   Luther, *Works*, 35:167–69.

Chapter 8: The Word That Endureth Forever

1   Thomas Babington Macaulay, *The Miscellaneous Writings of Lord Macaulay* (London: Longmans Green, 1868), 118.

2   Gordon Campbell, *Bible: The Story of the King James Version 1611–2011* (New York: Oxford University Press, 2010), 275.

3   Cleland Boyd McAfee, *The Greatest English Classic: A Study of the King James Version of the Bible and Its Influence on Life and Literature* (New York: Harper A. Brothers, 1912), 244, 286.

4   Alister E. McGrath, *In the Beginning: The Story of the King James Bible and How It Changed a Nation, a Language, and a Culture* (New York: Doubleday, 2001), 310.

5   McAfee painted a rosy picture of the "greatest scholars" analyzing and debating previous versions in an orderly manner—working not for pay but "for the joy of working." McAfee, *Greatest English Classic*, 62–64.

6   David Norton, *A Textual History of the King James Bible* (New York: Cambridge University Press, 2005), 27; David Norton, "Imagining Translation Committees at Work: The King James and the Revised Versions," in *The Bible as Book: The Reformation*, ed. Orlaith O'Sullivan (Newcastle, Del.: Oak Knoll, 2000), 6.

7   David Daiches, *The King James Version of the English Bible: An Account of the Development and Sources of the English Bible of 1611 with Special Reference to the Hebrew Tradition* (Hamden, Conn.: Archon, 1968), 208.

8   Campbell, *Bible*, 55.

9   C. S. Lewis, "The Literary Impact of the Authorised Version," in *They Asked for a Paper: Papers and Addresses* (London: Geoffrey Bles, 1962), 44.

10 David G. Burke, introduction to *Translation That Openeth the Window: Reflections on the History and Legacy of the King James Bible*, ed. David G. Burke (Atlanta, Ga.: American Bible Society, 2009), ix, xv.

11 David Crystal, *Begat: The King James Bible and the English Language* (New York: Oxford University Press, 2010), 258.

12 McAfee, *Greatest English Classic*, 280–87; Robert Alter, *Pen of Iron: American Prose and the King James Bible* (Princeton, N.J.: Princeton University Press, 2010), 10.

13 Hannibal Hamlin and Norman Jones, eds., *The King James Bible after Four Hundred Years: Literary, Linguistic, and Cultural Influences* (New York: Cambridge University Press, 2010), 19.

14 Albert S. Cook, *The Authorised Version and Its Influence* (New York: G. P. Putnam's Sons, 1910; reprint, Folcroft, Pa.: Folcroft Library Editions, 1976), 20.

15 Gustavus Paine, *The Men Behind the King James Version* (Grand Rapids: Baker, 1977), 182.

16 Olga Opfell, *The King James Bible Translators* (Jefferson, N.C.: McFarland, 1982), 119 (emphasis in original).

17 Campbell, *Bible*, 273–74.

18 Leland Ryken, *The Legacy of the King James Bible: Celebrating 400 Years of the Most Influential English Translation* (Wheaton, Ill.: Crossway, 2011), 114.

19 David Norton, *The King James Bible: A Short History from Tyndale to Today* (New York: Cambridge University Press, 2011), 1; Macaulay, *Miscellaneous Writings*, 118.

NOTES ON THE CONTRIBUTORS

Robert Alter is Class of 1937 Professor of Hebrew and Comparative Literature at the University of California at Berkeley. Having published widely in the field of comparative European literature, he is also the author of *The Art of Biblical Narrative* (1981) and *The Art of Biblical Poetry* (1985), and his translation of Genesis, published as *Genesis: Translation and Commentary* (1997), as well as *Psalms: a Translation with Commentary* (2007) and, more recently, *The Wisdom Books: Job, Proverbs and Ecclesiastes* (2010), mark him as one of the ablest of translators of the Bible in modern times. His latest book, *Pen of Iron: American Prose and the King James Bible*, was published by Princeton University Press in 2010.

Beth Allison Barr received her Ph.D. in 2004 from the University of North Carolina at Chapel Hill and currently is an assistant professor of history at Baylor University. Focusing her research on women, religion, and sermon literature in late medieval and early modern England, she is the author of *The Pastoral Care of Women in Late Medieval England* (2008) and an editor of *The Acts of the Apostles: Four Centuries of Baptist Interpretation* (2009). She also has published articles on women and men in the late medieval confessional and gendered language in late medieval pastoral texts.

David W. Bebbington is professor of history at the University of Stirling, Scotland, and has several times served as Visiting Distinguished Professor of History at Baylor University in Waco, Texas. His publications include *Evangelicalism in Modern Britain: A History from the 1730s to the 1980s* (1989); *The Dominance of Evangelicalism: The Age of Spurgeon and Moody* (2005); and, most recently with Baylor University Press, *Baptists through the Centuries: A History of a Global People* (2010). He is preparing a study of global religious revivals in the Victorian era for Oxford University Press.

David Lyle Jeffrey is Fellow of the Royal Society of Canada and Distinguished Professor of Literature and Humanities at Baylor University. He is also Guest Professor at Peking University (Beijing). His books include *A Dictionary of Biblical Tradition in English Literature* (1992); *Chaucer and Scriptural Tradition* (1984); *People of the Book: Christian Identity and Literary Culture* (1996); *Houses of the Interpreter: Reading Scripture, Reading Culture* (2003); and a co-authored book, *The Bible and the University* (2007).

Philip Jenkins is Edwin Erle Sparks Professor of the Humanities at Penn State University, and also holds the rank of Distinguished Senior Fellow of the Institute for Studies of Religion at Baylor University. Jenkins is a well-known commentator on religion past and present: the *Economist* has called him "one of America's best scholars of religion." His books include *The Next Christendom: The Rise of Global Christianity* (2002) and *The Lost History of Christianity: The Thousand-Year Golden Age of the Church in the Middle East, Africa, and Asia—and How It Died* (2008). His most recent book is *Jesus Wars: How Four Patriarchs, Three Queens, and Two Emperors Decided What Christians Would Believe for the Next 1,500 Years* (2010).

Laura L. Knoppers is professor of English at Penn State University, where she also served as director of the Institute for the Arts and Humanities from 2001 to 2005. A specialist in seventeenth-century British literature, religion, and politics, she is the author of *Historicizing Milton: Spectacle, Power, and Poetry in Restoration England* (1994); *Constructing Cromwell: Ceremony, Portrait, and Print, 1645–1661* (2000); and *Politicizing Domesticity from Henrietta Maria to Milton's Eve* (2011). Her scholarly edition of John Milton's *Paradise Regained* and *Samson Agonistes* (2008) won the John Shawcross Award from the Milton Society of America. Her edited books include *Puritanism and Its Discontents* (2003) and *The Cambridge Companion to Early Modern Women's Writing* (2009). Knoppers is past president of the Milton Society of America and current editor of the annual *Milton Studies*.

Alister E. McGrath is professor of theology, ministry, and education at King's College, London, and director of the Center for Theology, Religion and Culture. For many years he was professor of historical theology at Oxford University. He has a long-standing interest in translation theories and hermeneutics of the Renaissance and Reformation, an issue explored in depth in his *Intellectual Origins of the European Reformation* (2003). His recent books include *In the Beginning: The Story of the King James Bible* (2001); *Christianity's Dangerous Idea: The Protestant Revolution* (2008); and the best-selling textbook *Christian Theology: An Introduction*, now in its fifth edition.

Mark Noll is the Francis A. McAnaney Professor of History at the University of Notre Dame. His recent publications include *God and Race in American Politics: A Short History* (2008); *The Civil War as a Theological Crisis* (2006); *The Rise of Evangelicalism: The Age of Edwards, Whitefield and the Wesleys* (2004); *America's God, from Jonathan Edwards to Abraham Lincoln* (2002); and *The New Shape of World Christianity* (2009). In the not too distant future he hopes to complete a book on the rise, decline, and lingering effects of America's Bible civilization.

Lamin Sanneh is the D. Willis James Professor of World Christianity at Yale Divinity School. A life member of Clare Hall, Cambridge University and an Honorary Research Professor at the School of Oriental & African Studies in the University of London, he was appointed by John Paul II to serve on the Pontifical Commission of the Historical Sciences at the Vatican and by Pope Benedict XVI to the Pontifical Commission on Religious Relations with Muslims. He is the author of more than a dozen books on Islam and Christianity, including *Encountering the West: Christianity & the Global Cultural Process: The African Dimension* (1993) and *Whose Religion Is Christianity? The Gospel Beyond the West* (2003), and is general editor of the new Oxford Studies in World Christianity.

CPSIA information can be obtained at www.ICGtesting.com
Printed in the USA
BVOW031948040213

312383BV00001B/2/P